NO RESERVE
The Limit of Absolute Power

Martín Redrado
Translated by Dan Newland

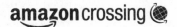

No Reserve: The Limit of Absolute Power was first published in 2010 by Editorial
Planeta as *Sin Reservas: Un límite al poder absoluto*.
Translated from Spanish by Dan Newland.
First published in English in 2011 by AmazonCrossing.

Published by AmazonCrossing
P.O. Box 400818
Las Vegas, NV 89140

ISBN-13: 9781935597230
ISBN-10: 193559723X

Table of Contents

Prologue

I have no doubt that emerging countries will play a leading role in the decades to come. The kickoff provided by China when it opened its doors to the world, in just a short time becoming a major world power; the veritable explosion of world-class new technologies that India is producing; Brazil's economic growth with social inclusion, which has garnered it the kind of worldwide recognition to permit it to host the 2016 Olympic Games, becoming the first South American country ever to do so; these are but a few examples of the leading roles that emerging countries are taking on.

Furthermore, the 2008 world crisis has placed emerging countries in a privileged position. While the United States, Europe, and Japan are still suffering the collapse of credit, industry and employment, developing nations in Asia and South America present a sound growth rate and have become attractive places in which to invest.

Be that as it may, the question that arises when one tries to gain deeper knowledge of these countries is how do their governments behave? How do those at the highest levels of power act? *No Reserve: The Limit of Absolute Power* is a book that provides insight into this little-explored question. It offers the reader the possibility to understand how decisions are made at an executive power level in emerging countries.

I directed the Central Bank of Argentina for five years and four months. During that period, I came to know firsthand how the Executive Branch, which is still in the same hands today as then, pulls the strings of power in one of the emerging countries of greatest potential in South America.

Supported by previously unpublished documents, this book reproduces the dialogs that I had with the highest authorities in my country, and provides a chronology of the crisis that was unleashed when an attempt was made to devise a new role for the international reserves of the Central Bank, on the strength of an executive decree and in conflict with the law. *No Reserve* is a first-person narrative that tells precisely what happened in key spots where decisions are made that affect the destiny of an entire society.

This story provides a look at the web of power in Argentina from an insider's point of view. In fact, I wrote these pages while I was still in office. This is why *No Reserve* offers readers something about emerging countries that cannot be found elsewhere. It demonstrates a clear example of a nation that could rank among the most important in the world, but that, when it comes to increasing its development, finds itself immersed in difficulties, due to certain attitudes taken by those who govern it.

It has only been in the past twenty-five years that emerging countries in the South American region—including Argentina—initiated the road to democracy, following decades of military coups, crimes, prohibitions, and even the disappearances of individuals. But today, in Argentina as in neighboring countries, the elections of governing officials and members of Congress are held without any major disturbances or threats.

Despite the importance of this fact, Argentina's institutions still show certain weaknesses. Currently in this country, republican checks and balances are frequently undermined by the eagerness of one power to advance on the institutional territory of another.

At the end of last year, the Central Bank, which, during my term, functioned as an institution with independence of criteria but did so while taking an active role in attending the country's current problems, became the victim of such abusive and improvised attitudes.

Readers will also find the complete story of the work that my team and I carried out during these years at the head of the Central Bank and of how, as a result of the measures taken by the institution, the country managed, from 2008 on, to steer clear of one of the worst global crises in the history of modern capitalism.

While several of the world's leading countries succumbed to bank closures, plummeting stock markets and high unemployment rates, and while, still today, others are facing tough situations, as in the cases of Greece, Ireland, Portugal, and Spain, Argentina came through the crisis practically unscathed, thanks to a series of economic measures implemented by the Central Bank under my direction.

At the beginning of this century, my country lived through one of the worst economic and social crises in its history. In 2002, however, Argentina managed to leave "intensive therapy" and take the road to a process of growth.

Argentina learned its lesson, and while in 2000 and 2001 we provided an example to the world of what should not be done, in this new era of worldwide upheaval, we have become an example to be followed. In these pages, readers can also find a description of the mechanisms that we employed in successfully facing up to this grave crisis.

Additionally in *No Reserve*, I provide an outline of my vision for Argentina in the years to come, as an example of the good fortune that could well await emerging nations, if they do what they should. I also present an agenda for sustainable growth.

In this sense, this book can be considered an opportunity to observe the strengths, weaknesses, and present scenario displayed by an emerging region that promises to play a more leading role in the years to come, within the complex framework of the world economy.

Chapter 1

The Beginning of the End

December 14, 2009, was a really nice day, with a temperature of sixty-two degrees Fahrenheit. I got up feeling great. I had spent the weekend with my family, talking about the upcoming summer vacation time. After a year that had started out so rocky as a result of the world economic crisis, all indications were that we could expect 2009 to close as calm as the waters of a garden pond.

We still hadn't figured out where we would go that summer. But it didn't matter. It was nine months before the end of my term as President of the Central Bank. I had the satisfaction of knowing I was going to conclude a period of transition for the Argentine economy (2004–2010), after the collapse produced by the default on its public debt without any big scares. During these years we had established the pillars for a monetary, foreign exchange, and financial policy for the decades to come. This was a major legacy given our history of economic instability.

Reading the news confirmed my peace of mind, although this was overshadowed by one sad note: The great academician, Paul Samuelson—the first American ever to receive the Nobel Prize for Economics (in 1970)—had died. His death took me back to my earliest days at the University of Buenos Aires, since the first book I asked for at the library was by that renowned economist.

I recalled, with a certain amount of concern, the words of my friend Alan Greenspan, former chairman of the Federal Reserve, who, just the night before, had warned on the NBC television network that the risk of U.S. inflation would rise when the worst of the world economic crisis, which had originated in 2007 on the subprime mortgage market, was over.

The words of this veteran economist—who had remained in his post for eighteen years during the terms of four American presidents (three Republicans and a Democrat)—no longer made the markets tremble, but they did continue to be the object of attention, considering his extensive background.

That Monday, like any other day, I pulled up the financial news pages of Reuters and Bloomberg to see how the markets were operating. I've always thought that it was indispensable for a central banker in Argentina to know before sunrise what's happening in the rest of the world.

On that particular Monday, I read that there was an upward trend on the Asian markets and that the markets in Europe were following suit.

It appeared I wasn't the only one who was feeling calm. A bailout plan had been announced a few hours earlier for Dubai World—the biggest publicly traded firm in that Arab emirate—which had fallen into default. This was sure to prevent some serious consequences for the world economy and scenes of panic that could have rivaled those observed when the Lehman Brothers banking operation collapsed the year before.

But all of this feeling of having the situation in hand suddenly evaporated when I turned on my cell phone and listened to a message that had been recorded on it at eight thirty. It was from Isidro Bounine, one of President Cristina Kirchner's private secretaries. I was being called to Government House to hear a confidential announcement at noon.

This message seemed strange to me, so I didn't hesitate for even an instant and called back.

"How are you? Martin Redrado speaking. Excuse me, but I never go to these meetings...Are you sure about this invitation?"

Since I had taken up my post, I had never taken part in meetings held at Government House or at the Presidential Residence in Olivos. The fact was that, as president of the Central Bank, I didn't feel I had any business showing up for any official announcements that the president or her cabinet ministers might make.

So I asked Bounine to reconfirm. Five minutes later, my cell phone rang. Once again, it was the presidential private secretary's voice:

"Yes, it's right, but you're not just invited to the meeting. The President wants to see you half an hour before the announcement, at 11:30. Remember, 11:30 in the office at Government House."

Like any other day, my driver showed up at 8:45 a.m. to pick me up at my home and drive me to the Central Bank Building in the heart of downtown Buenos Aires. Meanwhile, I used my BlackBerry to keep tabs on the day's international and local financial developments. Although there continued to be nothing on the domestic or world scene that drew my attention very much, I had already begun to feel worried deep down regarding this presidential announcement. I was getting a bad feeling about it. Something strange was going on. The fact that I had not been informed in advance and that I was to take part in a secret meeting was making me feel that the surprise would not be a pleasant one.

Seventy-two hours earlier, I had completed my last trip of the year. My friend and colleague Ángel Gurría, secretary-general of the Organization for Economic Cooperation and Development (OECD), had invited me to give a talk in Paris, the headquarters city for this organization. The group's members are the world's most highly developed countries—together with a handful of emerging nations, including Mexico and Chile—and at its meetings, common problems are discussed and domestic and international policies are identified. It is known as "the club of wealthy nations," since its members account for 70 percent of the worldwide gross product. Brazil was a serious candidate to join its ranks in the months to come.

As I had done on most of my lightning trips since I had taken up my post, I left Buenos Aires the night before, landed at Charles de Gaulle Airport fourteen hours later, had a shower at my hotel, ate lunch, gave my talk, and returned to the airport so as to be back in my country again the next day.

Fifty percent of the audience on that late-autumn day in Paris had been made up of European business leaders, interested in knowing how Latin America had managed to come through the global crisis so unscathed.

Ángel Gurría—a former debt negotiator and former Treasury minister and foreign minister of Mexico—compared our region with Asia, while I focused my talk on local strengths. The title of my December 11 presentation was *Argentina Has Withstood the Crisis: The Role of the Central Bank of Argentina*

I have always liked to prepare my presentations in a very personal way, adding in key contributions from my valuable team of collaborators. Some of them had been with me since I had returned to Argentina from the United States in 1991, others since my time as Trade Representative (2002–2004), and still others were Central Bank staffers. All of them were very important, both when it came to debating ideas and when it came time to instrument fundamental measures.

At the glamorous palace that houses the OECD, I stressed that growing demand for agricultural raw materials would uphold prices in the medium term, that interest rates would only rise in the long term, but within a more liquid and unstable credit market, and that I was predicting that Argentina's trading partners would grow more than the rest of the world, which would open the way for a good level of recovery following the drop in economic activity in 2009.

Faced with such a select audience, I couldn't resist the temptation to explain the four pillars with which to come to terms with domestic and international financial instability: a consistent monetary policy, a countercyclical policy designed to permit one to sidestep critical scenarios, a managed floating foreign exchange rate, and regulatory and supervisory measures aimed at protecting the savings of Argentine citizens.

The sequence had consisted, I explained, of first ensuring exchange rate stability, then making adjustments to strengthen demand for local currency, and, finally, introducing liquidity into the market in order to consolidate the economic upturn. Both Ángel Gurría and Europe's main businesspeople were in agreement in their praise of the Argentine Bank's role as a retaining wall that held back the world tide and permitted the country to overcome a crisis of such proportions.

While I was waiting for my plane to leave Terminal E of the airport at 11:15 p.m., I felt especially comforted by the comments I had received, because they recognized the results that we had achieved at a monetary and financial level. They particularly underlined the role of the Central Bank for having prevented Argentina from once again falling into one of its now traditional systemic breakups.

Once I settled into my seat on the plane and relaxed, I thought, "What a quiet year's end we're going to have!" This was no little relief, after a constantly dizzying twelve months that had begun with Lehman's fall and had deepened with the renationalization of our pension system and the subsequent elimination of private pension fund management firms (AFJPs) in November of 2008.

Those financial shakeups were swiftly reflected in pressures brought to bear for a sharp devaluation of the peso against the dollar—pressures which, at the Central Bank, we rejected out of hand, giving rise to major policy discussions within the government.

Later, there were fears of the possibility that Argentina might once again default on debt payments due to the weakening of fiscal revenues. But then we got through a major due date on August 3 (the Boden 12 bond) and things began to settle down.

On the weekend of December 12 and 13, I had the feeling that it was now smooth sailing, that the worst of the crisis was over even if I still had certain challenges to face over the course of the nine months left in my term, in order to continue to perfect monetary policy instruments: raising the levels of banking and credit penetration—in other words, creating more raw materials so as to be able to lend more—and, parallel to this, finding the right road by which to bring back voluntary capital markets.

Just like on any other Monday, I called a meeting of Bank officials, so as to be able to follow the development of the markets and, especially, in order to analyze the week's supply and demand for dollars.

There was nothing to make me foresee a storm on that front. At 11:20 a.m., I left the building at Reconquista 266, got into my car, and headed for the national executive offices at the so-called Pink House. Despite the fact that I only had a short distance to travel, I turned on the radio to see if the media were anticipating anything regarding that suspicious noon meeting.

There was speculation about an announcement, but without going into any great detail. Nothing upset the administration more than leaks, to such an extent that it had been known to give greater priority to silence than to the technical consistency of some of the measures announced.

In point of fact, most of the midmorning radio shows were focusing on the jamming of the communications system on board the presidential helicopter the Friday before, in which the chief of staff had received some serious threats against her life. It was a serious incident that everyone was repudiating.

The enigma continued. At the Pink House, I got out of the car and walked across the esplanade on the side of the building facing Rivadavia Street. After climbing the double-wide marble staircase next to the presidential elevator (built in 1910, during the presidency of Roque Sáenz Peña, using carved cedar adorned with three beveled crystal mirrors forming the national seal), I continued until I reached one of the two waiting rooms adjoining the President's office.

The atmosphere seemed quite calm in the area. There were several officials and guests walking around—perhaps with my same level of uncertainty about what was going on—and then they headed for the *Salón de la Mujer* (Women's Hall), where the meeting was to take place.

In the minutes that I was there waiting, after greeting several government officials, I was able to observe the great effort that had gone into sprucing up the image of the first floor of Government House. The President had ordered the rugs removed and the original floor left bare, which not only underscored the abundant natural light in that place, but also the great importance the President lent to aesthetics.

The refurbishing had continued in her office, which I entered at 11:35. The fabric on the walls was cream colored, contrasting with the sky blue of the upholstery on the presidential chair, which now replaced the former fabric that had been red. The wooden armchairs that had originally been purchased by President Julio Argentino Roca (1880–1886 and 1898–1904) were retrieved from the basement of Government House, where they had languished unused, to be re-upholstered in natural-colored leather, and new lighting had been added to the ceiling. Portraits of the country's patriots, such as José de San Martín, Manuel Belgrano, Manuel Dorrego, and Mariano Moreno, had also been recovered and hung.

The only thing that hadn't been changed while she was away on a trip to India was the gold-adorned presidential desk, where— contrary to the custom of former presidents Eduardo Duhalde and Néstor Kirchner—she received her guests. For meetings, those two presidents had always preferred the long wooden table in the middle of the room, even when they were getting together with a single guest.

The routine meetings that I had with the President were slated every fifteen days, unless the economic situation obliged us to see each other more often. The dynamics of these conversations always led us to discuss both the local and international situation.

I recalled, in particular, a get-together we had had in October, when she was in an especially good mood and showed me the remodeling that had been carried out in the wing of the Pink House that faces onto Plaza de Mayo, the city's main square, overlooked by the balcony often used in the past by Eva Perón and that had now been converted into a room in which to receive ambassadors. At the time, several of the President's assistants who spoke to me expressed their surprise at this unusual gesture of deference.

Two months later, the climate was completely different. I walked in, passing the three armchairs—two single ones and a double one—located to the right of the entrance and strode the fifteen steps to her desk. She was accompanied on her left by Economy Minister Amado Boudou, and on her right by Legal Secretary Carlos Zannini. The presence of Boudou and Zannini quickly whisked away any doubts I might have had about the nature of the meeting: "It's bad news," I thought. "They want to do something with the reserves."

Despite all of this, the charade was kept up. The President received me with that smile she characteristically wears when she is about to try to sell you some argument that's a hard one to buy. I took a seat and, without beating around the bush, bluntly asked, "What kind of maneuver are you planning?"

The other two looked at Cristina, who was holding in her hands a decree that was to become as talked about as the famous Resolution 125 [a tax increase that sparked farming protests against the administration]. She was smiling broadly. Her attitude and the first words out of her mouth demonstrated to me that her intention was to persuade me at all costs.

I had always held the President and her husband, the former president, at a prudential distance, although this had never kept us from talking over important issues. In that split second, I recalled an incident in 2005 when journalist Horacio Verbitsky (as told to me by an executive from the daily *Página 12*) had asked Néstor Kirchner, "How can you have Redrado as president of the Central Bank?" Kirchner had responded: "For the simple reason that he knows what he's doing. And none of our own people has the economic and financial know-how that Redrado does. So if you've got some other candidate, bring him on."

Four years later, this respectful relationship had been broken. On that Monday, December 14, President Cristina Kirchner was showing me copies of the decree with an attitude of congeniality, but also of reluctance. She would quickly show me a page, read a paragraph from it, then leave the page on her desk, as if to safeguard it. Then she repeated the process with each of the other pages. Her intention was obviously to hide the controversial nature of the decree from me.

"The concept of this initiative," said the President, "is that we can't be at the mercy of the comings and goings of the international markets. We want, we need, to put out signs of certainty."

My reply was immediate:

"There is no sign of uncertainty with regard to Argentina's willingness and capacity to pay. That is clear following the payment of the $2.5 billion corresponding to the maturity date of the Boden 12 bond in August, a payment which was made without new monetary printing."

The country's international rating—which measures the differential for emerging market dollar bonds over the yield for U.S. bonds—was at 733 basis points on December 14, compared with the 880 points recorded the day after that major payment in August. Although it would fall in the days following the presidential announcement, this was due entirely to a general improvement in emerging markets as a whole and not to any effect of the launching of this controversial measure which created a fund grabbing the reserves of the Bank.

This fund was to be created by taking "surplus and freely available" reserves totaling US$6.569 billion administrated by the Central Bank and handing them over to the National Treasury so that they could be used to pay debts.

The opening lines of the decree, surprisingly enough, justified this fund, which was destined to raise the fiscal deficit, by saying that "Argentina is about to begin the year that commemorates the bicentennial of its struggle for independence," as if such an epic definition could take away from the gravity of this issue.

I quickly scanned a few paragraphs of the copy of the decree and was nonplussed. I addressed her first, and then our two other interlocutors:

"There's a major risk here. Have you thought about the embargoes placed on reserves by the bondholders? They didn't come in on the 2005 debt restructuring, and they have a very active legal strategy in the courts in the United States and, to a lesser degree, in Europe."

Zannini swaggeringly responded, "There's no problem with the embargoes, because we're going to give a T-bill to the Central Bank…"

"But the government is determining that they (the reserves) will be used for purposes other than the monetary or financial regulation purposes that the Central Bank has," I retorted. That is not permitted by law. How was it possible that I had to clarify such an obvious technical point?

The so-called "vulture funds," which bought nonperforming debt at a very low price and then started to litigate very aggressively in order to be paid 100 percent of the face value of the bonds, had managed to present an "alter ego" theory, by which the Central Bank was, in reality, the same as the government. And therefore, these bondholders could attach the Bank's funds in order to satisfy their claim. This rash decision made it appear that they were right.

"But haven't you sought advice from the law firm of Cleary, Gottlieb, Steen & Hamilton, who represents you in the United States?" I asked.

Zannini and Boudou exchanged glances, but nobody responded, because no one had thought to talk to the attorneys that defended the state abroad.

When we fell into discussion of that point, I decided to advance against the predominantly confusing idea surrounding surplus reserves, warning them that one had to be careful with the definition of that term.

It was only at that moment that Boudou's presence in the meeting really struck me. He was nodding agreement at everything I said. He was probably the minister with the lowest technical level of any I had ever known, but he had a capacity for media communication.

He said, "This is something we've been giving some thought to, and I think it's pretty on target. The thing is, transferring those assets to the Treasury is going to improve our earnings."

According to his line of reasoning, the reserves provided a yield of only 0.5 percent. According to mine, the earnings on those assets were considerably greater, because one had to take into account the yield provided by the rise in the value of the currencies that formed part of those reserves.

"Let's see now," I said, rounding out my point, "is the aim to lower financing costs, or to spend what we don't have?"

The President, who until then had remained silent, responded, "No, no, no." (Cristina likes to repeat certain monosyllables for emphasis). "We've got to lower the financing costs," she said, full of conviction.

"But then again," Boudou added, letting slip what wasn't being said, "we may just use a little of it…if financing is short…"

Their explanations were pretty vague and deliberately ambiguous. When I saw that in the discussion of details we weren't going to get anywhere in reaching an agreement, I insisted: "It's important for us to show, like any *normal* country, that we have a financing program, that we've figured out how much money we have to come up with to pay debts due, and, later, issue bonds on the voluntary market."

Believe it or not, this hadn't been done since the term of Miguel Peirano as economy minister, toward the end of Néstor Kirchner's administration. During that administration, on November 14, 2007, a total of US$574 million was obtained on the Bonar X (a ten-year bond, e.g., 2017 maturity date) at 10.5 percent per annum, thanks to the intervention of then Finance Secretary Sergio Chodos. Ironically enough, it was to be Chodos who, two years later, as a board member of the Central Bank, would be in charge of designing the controversial Fund with Boudou.

A few days after that bond was launched in the private sector, Argentina fell once again into a direct sale of debt with Venezuela, a government that claimed to be "a friend" to Argentina, but that charged the same interest rates as the market it so disdainfully decried, and added insult to injury with the total lack of transparency inherent in these operations.

But my arguments with regard to the financial market were left floating in the air, and my feeling of pessimism redoubled as the meeting petered out. There was no natural flow to the debate, and neither side managed to convince the other.

Suddenly, as if to provide relief from the suffocating atmosphere, the President exclaimed, "Do you know what the number on the fund decree is? Two thousand ten! It's going to be our lucky number!"

I'm not big on luck, so I made a last-ditch effort. "Look, why not create a guarantee fund for debt payment and put it in the Central Bank Balance Sheet, earmarked for specific use, so it won't generate an inflationary effect, because it won't imply new money printing?"

"Well..." she hesitated, "Keep on studying it and keep me posted."

These last words by the President left me anything but satisfied. She immediately asked us to go to the *Salón de la Mujer* for the announcement of the plan. I was left perplexed. The President stood up, thus tacitly adjourning the meeting.

"I'd like to keep talking about this," I said to try to persuade them to put off what already seemed inevitable.

But the President went off to fix her makeup. Then Zannini went off to the ceremony. When Boudou stood up, however, I stopped him.

"Are you the beast that came up with this?" I asked.

"Martín," he said, "it was a lot worse before…"

With that, Boudou followed Zannini out the door. I didn't know what to do. On the one hand, I was anxious to go back to my office to think this through and try to resolve the delicate situation. On the other, I knew I should go to the public meeting the President had called. In the end, my sense of duty and commitment won out. The big room was full of invited guests. I sat next to the door in a chair with casters on it. My head was buzzing with ideas that came to no conclusions.

Withdrawn from the staging of this event, I sat there thinking, searching for a rational solution to this idea that would surely cause the greatest institutional crisis since the administration's clash with farming.

By the time the ceremony was over, all of the pieces were falling into place in my mind. Despite having all of the discussions of our meeting milling around in my head, I was able to see things in their proper dimension. What had happened that day was that the whole concept of "being *normal*"—like any other country that finances the due dates for its debts by resorting to voluntary credit—had been tossed out the window. We appeared to have come close to that concept of Argentina's reality at the Annual

General Meeting of the International Monetary Fund (IMF), held in Istanbul in October 2009. There, a critical path had been discussed with IMF officials and private investors, which consisted of the possibility of auditing the much-questioned figures being put out by the Argentine National Institute of Statistics and Census (INDEC) and, especially, of the economy in general. Also discussed was the Paris Club, holders of bonds that were still in default and, finally, the possibility of Argentina's returning to the open capital markets.

But this path was obviously too restricting for the political powers. Given their financing needs, they had decided not to respect any limits whatsoever and to grab the funds that were in the Central Bank.

Their reasoning was, "We've used the cash from the Social Security System (ANSES) and from the National Bank (*Banco de la Nación Argentina*). Now, in the two years we've got left, we'll finance our increased spending, not with voluntary funding, but with Central Bank financing." That meant higher inflation.

Despite the gravity of the situation, I figured I should keep an open mind. Although my intuition told me that something had broken, I also told myself that there were possibilities for mending it, that we could reach the end of our term. Eight months lay ahead. I should defend my ideas while seeking solutions, even if not the best ones possible. I once again applied my system of evolutionary thought, which would allow me to move ahead over rough road, or, in other words, I would seek solutions, even if not the ones I would have preferred, but ever defending my principles.

Even so, for both technical and political reasons, it wasn't going to be easy to take a step backward, since already, in a single act, two errors had been made. The first was to have drafted a

Decree of Need and Urgency (DNU) at a time when Congress was in recess, thus failing to permit lawmakers to participate in the decision, as established by law. The second was nothing more and nothing less than going against what I consider to be the role of the Central Bank: to be neither a branch office of the Economy Ministry, as happened in the 1980s, nor an "autistic" agency (a Bank withdrawn into itself and closed to society), as happened in the 1990s, when no monetary plan existed and we had an expansive fiscal policy, fixed exchange rate, and growing debt, a combination that ended up exploding. Argentina's Central Bank should be, then, an agency that exercised control by opposing whoever spent money (e.g., the National Treasury) in order to ensure the savings, stability, and tranquility of the Argentine people as a whole.

In the days to follow, some officials childishly sought to "ideologize" the concept of the Central Bank's autonomy, without explaining why it is important to maintain that organization's discretionary independence, since its job is to safeguard the country's monetary and financial security. What this means in practice is that the Bank must make use of the instruments at its disposal and apply strictly professional criteria in doing so, but with an all-encompassing vision of how the economy as a whole works.

I got back to my office at 1:35 p.m. Outside, the first clouds appeared on the horizon, with a high of eighty-four degrees. I immediately called a meeting of the Bank's economists and lawyers to tell them about the new decree. And I concluded by saying, "This decree is a fact. We're going to study it and analyze the legal ins and outs, and the ones that have to do with reserve management."

In the room with me were María del Carmen Urquiza (legal studies and briefs manager), Hernán Lacunza (general manager),

Pedro Rabasa (assistant manager for economics and finance), Juan Carlos Barbosa (reserve administration manager), Juan Basco (assistant general manager for operations), and Julio Siri (operations manager).

Some of them showed surprise when they heard me say, "Start analyzing this issue without any kind of preconceived notion." I said the same thing to some of the members of the board. Simultaneously—I didn't want to waste any time—I asked the people in the legal department to get in touch with our attorneys in New York, so as to analyze the implications of such a decision.

The intention wasn't to block the decree, but to seek alternatives that were rational, to bring to the table some well-grounded debate within the board of directors, and to comply with the objective of returning to voluntary markets, thus preventing foreign reserves from being grabbed. The afternoon passed without anything major happening. I kept to myself, studying the economic scope of this measure and the repercussions that its announcement might generate in the rest of society.

The next day, the executive decree, DNU 22010/09, was published in the *Official Bulletin* and contained the following resolutions:

- **Article 1:** This replaced Article Six of the Convertibility Law (referring to assets included in reserves, their nonattachable nature, and the definition of the monetary base) with another article, which added that "freely available reserves shall be applied to the payment of obligations contracted with international financing agencies and to the payment of services on the public debts of the National State." What this meant, in essence, was that the Central Bank had to clean up the messes (pay the debts) generated by the Economy Ministry.

- **Article 2:** This created the Bicentennial Fund for the cancellation of services on debt, falling due in 2010, under the administration of the Economy Ministry, which would regulate the fund.

- **Article 3:** The fund would total US$6.569 billion, corresponding to debts falling due with multilateral agencies for a total of US$2.187 billion and debts coming due with private holders totaling US$4.382 billion, and which the Central Bank would transfer to the National Treasury from freely available reserves. In exchange, the monetary authority would be presented with a ten-year nontransferrable Treasury bill in dollars.

- **Article 4:** The corresponding Permanent National Congressional Committee would be "made aware" of this.

- **Article 5:** Signatures on the executive order included those of President Cristina Fernández de Kirchner; Cabinet Chief Aníbal Fernández; Interior Minister Florencio Randazzo; Foreign Minister Jorge Taiana; Defense Minister Nilda Garré; Economy Minister Amado Boudou; Industry and Tourism Minister Débora Giorgi; Agriculture Minister Julián Domínguez; Planning and Public Works Minister Julio De Vido; Justice Minister Julio Alak; Labor, Employment, and Social Security Minister Carlos Tomada; Social Development Minister Alicia Kirchner; Education Minister Alberto Sileoni; Science, Technology, and Productive Innovation Minister Limo Barañao; and Health Minister Juan Manzur.

Nobody had been left out of the decree. But neither public opinion nor the political sector seemed to be aware of the gravity of this issue. Most people were probably busy closing out the year and nobody was paying attention. At the time, the only ones who seemed to be concerned were my team and I.

It had been a year of adversity, but an incipient recovery had begun to emerge. And, logically enough, political and business leaders alike were in a very relaxed mood, thinking about their summer vacations. We, on the other hand, were tuned in to a different channel.

When we began to analyze the technical details, our qualms multiplied. The decree stipulated that the reserves could be used "for payment of debt" in general, meaning in either domestic or foreign currency. In this way, emphasis was being removed from the importance of maintaining a neutral monetary effect, or, in other words, of not issuing pesos over and above the needs of the economy and, therefore, of not generating inflationary monetary pressures, which was contrary to what happened with payment of the IMF.

In the monetary program that we presented to Congress each year, we estimated the quantity of pesos people would need over the course of the following twelve months. The possibility of US$6.569 billion being monetized in pesos could end up signifying printing of 25 billion pesos more—nearly a 25 percent increase in the amount of local currency in circulation *in a single year* (!), with the subsequent inflationary impact that this would represent.

So, we decided to propose another alternative to the President: the structuring of a guarantee fund that would permit the lowering of the interest rate for the issuance of bonds. A similar plan had been developed by the Economy Ministry's finance division. But that wasn't the message put out by Minister Boudou, who maintained that the entire US$6.569 billion would be spent in 2010, or the message from Vice-Minister Roberto Feletti, who held that the reserves should be used "for development" purposes, meaning for current spending, financing public works and other programs.

At any rate, the need was emerging for these changes to be brought to the table for congressional discussion leading to a new law. And the problem was not just the US$6.569 billion in question, but the fact that total surplus reserves came to nearly US$18 billion, which meant that printing of money could actually climb to 80 billion pesos, over and above the 100 billion already in the pockets of Argentina's population.

Clearly, the message that came through was that there was no limit on monetary expansion and that the Central Bank would be the financer of public spending without any restriction whatsoever.

Despite the verbal crossfire, the fact was that there was an objective improvement in the economy at year's end.

We were coming, obviously, from an annual drop of 3 percent in the GDP, which had touched bottom in the third quarter and, by the fourth, was showing signs of recovery, compared with the last quarter of 2008, which had been very negative indeed due to the impact of the global crisis and the lack of confidence spawned locally by the compulsive elimination of the private pension management firms (AFJPs).

In any case, there was an improvement sustained by better external conditions—both financial and commercial—and a certain amount of improvement, too, in short-term investment, marked by a recovery in inventories.

Added to the certainty that the worst of the world crisis was over was the fact that, for the first time in decades, foreign exchange movements had not been abrupt, despite the fact that many analysts and some businesspeople had been convinced to the contrary.

Furthermore, there was a feeling that "the seven-year itch" might develop into a new, terminal, economic crisis, following the horrific experience of 2002, which reflected a disorderly retreat from one-to-one peso/dollar convertibility and the immersion of more than half of the population into poverty.

There was no lack of arguments to make people think that 2009 would end up being a relapse year, since, over the past four decades, crises had been repeated every six or seven years in the country: the 1975 *Rodrigazo*, the 1982 explosion of the so-called *crawling peg exchange rate* and default, the hyperinflation crisis of 1989, the 1995 Tequila crisis, and the 2001–2002 end of one-to-one exchange convertibility and the biggest default in the history of sovereign debt.

But the jinx had been broken: There was no monetary, financial, or devaluation meltdown, and the conditions were thus ripe for a 4 percent minimum and 6 percent maximum growth rate in 2010, if Argentina could achieve access to voluntary financing. The difference between these two figures was no minor consideration in terms of formal job creation and reductions in poverty and indigence. That's why we were insisting so strongly on the need to gain access to international credit.

It wasn't a question of ideology, but one of practicality.

Since 2003, the country had recorded average annual economic growth of 8 percent, thanks to a high rate of idle capacity, sharp improvement in profitability levels for several key sectors of the economy as an effect of the devaluation, and a major increase in fiscal savings.

Nevertheless, these conditions, which created the illusion that we could, in the long run, "live on our own," were running out. It was of fundamental importance that we reestablish confidence so as to attract investors. It was true that the rate of investment had grown significantly with respect to the economy's total production level as of 2003. But the world crisis had brought stagnation, and no major projects were appearing that could be capable of ensuring genuine job expansion or of quelling inflationary pressure, which, as everybody knows, exerts its greatest impact on the most vulnerable segments of society.

Another major element in those last months of 2009 was the halt that had been put to capital flight, which had been one of the most important conditioning factors for the economy since the government's 2007 intervention in the national statistics bureau, INDEC, at a time when the country's risk rating was 170 basis points—lower even than that of Brazil, an economy that the financial markets saw as "the star of South America."

Capital flight, it is worth noting, refers to the formation of assets in foreign currency, which many times never even leaves Argentina. This phenomenon reached a ceiling of US$3.5 billion for October of 2008, and then leveled off at between US$1 billion and US$1.5 billion a month. In 2008, capital flight nearly tripled the level recorded the year before and was 23 percent higher than the monumental US$18.7 billion recorded in the second half of 2001 and for the same period in 2002. In 2009, this same trend continued, reaching US$11.195 billion in the first half of the year and hitting a peak just before legislative elections in June.

After those elections, however, capital flight began to decline until, in October, the balance was positive, with earnings of US$54 million for the quarter. But the debate over the use of reserves and the independence of the Central Bank reversed this situation, and in January of 2010, capital flight of US$1 billion was recorded.

A stable end to 2009. A good outlook for the 2010–2011 agricultural harvest. Argentina's prospects were good, even though some dark clouds were appearing on the horizon: on the fiscal front and, in parallel, on the political front.

The fiscal outlook was weak at the end of 2009, with an increase in annual primary spending recorded at 35 percent. While part of this increased spending was justified, as a means of absorbing the impact of the world crisis, there were two aspects of it that bore consideration: For one thing, a system of public service subsidies was being maintained that benefited the middle and upper segments of society and, for another, the tax structure remained highly dependent on the economic cycle.

As a result, the government would be able to achieve only a primary budget surplus thanks to funds that had formerly been managed by private pension administrators (AFJPs) and thanks also to special drawing rights transferred by the IMF on a one-time basis to all of its shareholders, as a means of mitigating the world crisis, which kept the state from recording a deficit of about 8.17 billion pesos.

Tax collection grew by 13.2 percent, coming in under the inflation rate estimated by a number of indices, and by 8 percent if one subtracts moneys previously paid into the pension system, and thus barely outdistancing the 7.7 percent increase in consumer prices reported by INDEC. Both figures were well below the 22 percent tax collection increase projected in the 2009 budget. So it was that the so-called savings (which were no such thing) ended up coming to 17.277 billion pesos, or 47 percent lower than for the year before. Furthermore, the extraordinary funds from the IMF and the pension system failed to hide the financial deficit, following debt payments of 7.731 billion pesos.

Without access to voluntary credit, and considering the low level of investment and heavy spending pressure, it was a foregone conclusion that inflation would heat up. Several reliable indices placed price increases at 13 percent for 2009.

So, at the end of December, we presented a monetary program that took into account a rise in the demand for money in the economy, but that placed strict limits on it, so as not to validate price increase pressures. Since the hyperinflation suffered at the end of the 1980s and the beginning of the 1990s, people had been left with the feeling that there could only be inflation if there were a surplus supply of money.

With no coordination of measures, the Central Bank was acting as a last bastion of rationality, seeking to ensure that the economy didn't fall into a process financed by currency issue and, therefore, by inflation, especially not when greater wage pressure was foreseeable as a result of rising prices.

At times, the government's decision making appeared highly fragmented. Each member of the administration tended to his or her own space, especially those responsible for the country's economic decisions, and this was aggravated by an extreme sensation of passivity. Furthermore, in such questions of public policy, the President wasn't as comfortable as she was when it came to international, legislative, or legal affairs.

We at the Central Bank had consistently pushed for coordination of macroeconomic policies. Indeed, there had been a fleeting attempt to achieve this at the end of 2008, when then-Cabinet Chief Sergio Massa formed a crisis committee made up of then-Economy Minister Carlos Fernández, Finance Secretary Hernán Lorenzino, and the Central Bank management. But the suspicion that this move bred in the political camp ended up squelching the initiative when it was barely a week old.

The debt-repurchasing program that was being studied in that group ended up being instrumented in such a timid way that it fell apart in a show of total lack of conviction—having been implemented using very small amounts that convinced no one of its intention. And this is what ultimately led to the "grab" for reserves.

Despite not having set a clear course, Argentina could have clear sailing and reach safe port in 2011 as long as there were no new disruptions. It might not be "the star" of South America, but it could "wriggle by," as my children might say. While it was capable of earning an A-plus on the exam, it would squeak by with a C-minus. But what possible explanation could there be for squandering such an opportunity?

Chapter 2

Why Do Emerging Countries Keep Reserves

From the end of 2009 on, our society was practically forced to become familiar with a concept that was absolutely alien to its everyday life: that of Central Bank reserves.

The reserve concept can be compared to that of auto or homeowner's insurance. Nobody likes having to pay the premium every month just in case of some eventual accident, theft, hailstorm, or other contingency. But when one of these disasters actually befalls us, we are grateful that we had coverage. Sure, it would be a lot better if we had the security of knowing that if disaster were to strike, "someone" would come along and repair the damage for us, so that we wouldn't have to make the effort to pay the premium every month. But that is clearly no more than wishful thinking.

The same is true of the reserves, which consist of the foreign currencies any central bank possesses as backing for the bills and coins in circulation, bank deposits, and other liabilities. In short, these reserves are what back up the savings of all of the citizens. The reserves are made up of convertible currencies (dollars, euros, pounds sterling, yen), gold, and SDRs (Special Drawing Rights)—a foreign exchange resource created by the International Monetary Fund (IMF) for countries that pay debts they have among themselves or with the IMF. SDRs can also work the other way around: The IMF can transfer these to countries upon granting them a loan, or, as happened in 2009 as a result of the world financial crisis, the IMF can transfer a proportion to a country in the form of extended capital.

The Central Bank maintains its reserves as working capital, available for immediate use whenever it should be required. This has especially been the case for Argentina in the last few years, with the Central Bank directing a foreign exchange policy designed to prevent abrupt leaps in the peso/dollar rate, thus putting behind us our past karma of mega-devaluations. Additionally, reserves are invested in securities or bonds with a high credit rating, so as to permit the Bank to obtain earnings on these holdings. This has been the case since the Central Bank's founding, on May 31, 1935. The main aim of this new institution, as expressed in Article 3 of its charter, was "the concentration of sufficient reserves destined to moderate the consequences of fluctuations in exports and foreign investment capital or currency, credit, and commercial activities." Despite successive changes as a result of the crises suffered in its seventy-five-year history, the Central Bank's charter had always honored this concept with regard to utilization of its reserves.

In early March 2008, I had a conversation with President Cristina Kirchner prior to the summit of economy ministers and central bank governors of the G-20 countries in the outskirts of London, in which I began to explain to her how the reserves served as a protective shield against the ins and outs of the international crisis that had begun as of August 2007. In developing the scenarios for the rest of 2008, I projected deterioration of the situation due to the "hole" in the capital standing of several American and European banking institutions as a result of their having granted loans that were uncollectable.

Right then, she interrupted me: "Maybe a portion of the reserves could be invested here in Argentina."

"But I've already clarified this point to Nestor Kirchner about this issue on at least three occasions," I said.

"Well, you were talking to a former president!" she exclaimed categorically. "*I'm* the President now!"

"That's true," I said. "Allow me to share my view with you: It is best, as we've been demonstrating, not to alter the destination of the reserves. After the financial crisis exploded, the reserves permitted us to provide our citizens with exchange rate predictability."

I was surprised that she returned to this issue, which I thought had been laid to rest. Later, I would understand the reasons behind her insistence.

On March 11, 2008, a change was announced in export taxes for primary agricultural exports, going from a fixed withholding to a floating coefficient system. Resolution 125, drafted by then-Economy Minister Martín Lousteau, fell on farmers right in the midst of their soybean and corn harvests. It was a bad technical measure imposed as a means of facing some fiscal problems that the government was suffering at the time. I'll refer to this issue in detail in the next chapter.

Unlike her husband (the former president), this President preferred to analyze ideas in writing. So I wrote her a three-page brief, in which I summarized the importance of having a self-insurance policy in the form of reserve backing and the advantage that this could yield, not only for the population in general, but also for the economic stability of the country as a whole. In order to keep this report out of the hands of intermediaries—although her administration was only three months old, there were already troubled waters resulting from its conflict with farming—I had my secretary "hand deliver" it to her secretary.

In the memo, entitled "A Shield that Protects Us," I started off by emphasizing the virtues of being able to count on these reserves, especially in a world that was so thoroughly suffering the effects of a crisis in the United States that was that country's worst since the Great Depression that began in 1929.

There, I listed the key points that are illustrative in understanding the conflict that was unleashed at the end of 2009 with regard to the Central Bank reserves:

"For the first time in decades, Argentina is now in condition to face a major international crisis with solvency and without setbacks. The United States is going through a crisis in the heart of its banking system; the credit market remains literally closed and the effects on the mainstream economy and assets are making themselves felt. The European economy, for its part, is going through a situation that is no less worthy of concern, since the soundness of its banking system is also under scrutiny, and this presages scares ahead, even if with some delay. Without a doubt, this situation is going to affect world economic growth, and the emerging world along with it. Within this circle of countries, the particular situation of each of them, together with their level of exposure to the different risks involved, will determine the degree of impact that their citizens will receive."

Up to that point, I explained the fundamental context, so as to permit an understanding of the consequences of a domestic policy decision. However, in our country, the governing class in general, and analysts in particular, tend to look only inward at what's happening within our borders.

This summary was aimed at underscoring the fact that, with the world's wealthiest nations on the brink of a recession, there was still no way to have a clear view of the magnitude of the negative impact that this crisis might generate for emerging countries from both a commercial and financial standpoint. Since 2003, these nations had been enjoying exceptional price conditions for raw materials, a low interest rate, and prudent macroeconomic policies that, almost without exception, were favoring economic growth, regardless of the pace set by each individual government or the heritage that each country carried on its back.

"Within this context, the US$50 billion in foreign reserves that the Central Bank has accumulated in its vaults are not just some curious statistic, or some fortuitous result, but, rather, are the fruit of a deliberate policy of reserve accumulation for prudential aims. This reserve fund not only constitutes the best antidote with which to immunize our economy against the external comings and goings of a rarefied international context, but also to maintain two such fundamental public assets as monetary stability and financial stability."

With this paragraph, I felt I was making clear the "macro" objectives of the reserves, but it was advisable to bring this message "down to earth," so as to give the President eventual arguments, above and beyond discussion of the economy.

This was why, after asking, "What does this mean to the common citizen? How does it benefit him or her," I sought to provide a conclusive answer:

"It is my belief that the reserve accumulation strategy has three distinctive features: It is useful (this has been proven in light of recent international financial turbulence); it is healthy (it has sound fundamentals that outweigh its eventual cost); and it is consistent (since it is coherent with our economic history and with the times in which our economy is developing). This provision permits us to get through the pendulum swings of the global economy without surprises and, at the same time, to move ahead with a monetary policy that guarantees a balanced monetary market, providing for sound conditions and for the confidence of the citizenry."

Later, I went on to talk about its main feature: its usefulness.

"It is undeniable that a high level of foreign reserves better prepares us for an external financial crisis like the one that was recently unleashed. The robust nature of this monetary scheme clearly proved itself in the face of the first symptoms, in the four-month period from July to October of 2007, when capital flight was similar to that suffered during the 'Tequila Effect' of 1995. This could easily have turned into a run on currency, heightening exacerbated inflation pressures that would end up affecting the level of economic activity and, with it, job stability among our citizens. But these risks did not materialize. The administration used these reserves, with ample backing, to intervene on the markets, permitting us to deactivate speculative movements that brought pressure to bear on the exchange rate and on interest rates."

In this paragraph, I wanted to put out a conclusive message: In Argentina, contrary to other countries, no excessive exchange flotation is tolerated, as seen in the minimal movements in the dollar/peso rate. If it fluctuates a couple of cents upward or downward, a large part of society start fearing that there could be a sharp devaluation, or that the government might peg the value of the dollar, with the negative effects that this stagnation could generate in the competitiveness of our producers abroad.

After a few considerations about the importance of having left behind the fragility of the past, I focused on the idea of stability, which is so dear to a country that has suffered recurrent crises.

"Foreign reserves back money in circulation. Their accumulation allows for an aggressive policy of monetary absorption that balances supply with the course of evolution of the demand for money. Even though the managed floating exchange system does not

require it, international reserves provide backing to the pesos that people demand, thus guaranteeing the equilibrium of the monetary market."

It was also necessary to underscore the positive effect of these reserves on another fundamental tool of the economy: credit.

"The reserves are not sufficient to cover all of the liquidity required by depositors in the financial system, but they do, additionally, make possible a continuous rise in credit available to businesses and families. Being able to count on an ample supply of foreign reserves provides depositors with confidence, facilitating the availability of resources to finance productive projects. The experiences of the third quarter of 2007 provide an important lesson: Financial stability was guaranteed without sacrificing the growth rate of credit."

Having explained the importance of reserves to both savings and credit, I concluded that, although the accumulation of reserves had been debated by certain sectors since their inception, "this has constituted one of the central tenets of macroeconomic policy." I insisted that domestic tranquility might well become "one of the best legacies that we can bequeath to the future."

It wasn't a matter, as would be repeated some time later, of placing the reserves on "an altar," but of understanding their relevance and (why not?) of explaining that the President could differentiate herself from her predecessors by not leaving the same trail of nefarious episodes behind her, like the megadevaluations of 1982 or 1989, or the repeated confiscation of our citizens' deposits.

I felt sure that I had fully covered the entire battery of arguments to defend this strategy within the Executive Branch of Government.

But I still had to ratify this before the private sector, skeptical, as they always were, of politicians' capacity to understand the importance of "insurance" or "shields," and accustomed to twisting the arm of whatever administration was in office every time there was a run against the peso.

In this sense, I put out a very explicit message at a charity banquet organized in August of 2007, at the Sheraton Hotel in the Retiro district of Buenos Aires, by the charismatic U.S. Ambassador to Argentina, Earl Anthony Wayne. I was seated at the same table with him—formerly in charge of economic affairs at the State Department—and Woods Staton, holder of the McDonald's fast-food franchise for the entire region. On my left was Mario Vicens, the former Treasury secretary during de De la Rua Administration (1999–2001) and president of the Argentine Banking Association (ABA). Vicens represented foreign banks with branches in Argentina.

Eloquent yet discreet, Mario tossed out a challenge with regard to the wiggle room we had at the Central Bank for making use of reserves in the face of a strong attack from speculators:

"The market knows you've got the foreign currency. But it doesn't know if they'll let you use it."

Without letting my smile fade, I opted to answer him in English, so that the rest of the diners at the table could understand what I was saying. I said, "Wait and see, and you will see."

The U.S. subprime crisis was in its first stage. Going back to the metaphor used in chapter 1, we had taken out our insurance policy, but we still didn't know how sound our insurance company would be if called upon to respond to a claim.

In other words, faced with Vicens's doubts—like those of any other business leader—the response was to show that we could sell off as much as the people might demand, guided, of course, by certain precepts of economic history: When there's a financial crisis, besides transmitting security, you have to hand over the pesos or foreign currency gradually so as to reduce the level of nervousness, especially in the wake of the 2001 freeze on deposits that was still very much present in the minds of society. While the bank tellers were not supposed to rush to attend the people that lined up at their branches, customers did, indeed, have to be able to see that the cash was available.

I sought to explain that this was probably the first time that we had ever broken a historical cycle of continuous crises by showing players on the market that they weren't going to overrun us. This was, indubitably, what reserves were good for.

The very abrupt changes seen in the Argentine economy during the twentieth century conspired against a credible defense of stability. Why would anyone believe that this time it was going to be possible to avoid a shock, when such a great part of our history demonstrated just the opposite?

While my response was neither complete nor conclusive, it was essential to an understanding of the root of the change: Reserves had been demonstrating their role as an agent in the reduction of volatility since 2003, a period in which, although much was made of the importance of the fiscal surplus—as of the 4 percent of the gross domestic product achieved in 2004—these savings began to dwindle, first slowly, and then at a swift clip, until they disappeared entirely in 2009.

Within the framework of historical volatility, reserves too had seen sharp rises and falls. Between 1948 and 1972, they had reached a floor of US$97 million in 1958 and a peak of US$760 million in 1968. During that period, which was characterized by a closed, strongly isolated economy, reserves fell by a 1.7 percent annual average.

As of 1973, this changed, and there began to be a positive trend that averaged an annual 5.4 percent until 2004, in harmony with what was happening in the rest of Latin America.

During this period (1973–2004), there are some points that are worth highlighting: i.e., the so-called *tablita* [a crawling peg of the exchange rate system] created by Economy Minister José A. Martínez de Hoz and applied by the military dictatorship as of 1978, which caused the exchange rate to lag, turning the performance of foreign reserves (as happened in the 1990s with convertibility) highly cyclical, driven, above all, by capital flow. In 1981, a program of "controlled" devaluations fell apart and was followed by a disorderly period of economic adjustment, with reserves standing at a third of the level achieved in 1979.

In the 1980s, that "shooting star" known as the Austral Stabilization Plan (1985) didn't manage to achieve a substantive change in capital inflow, nor did it create a major rise in reserve levels, which remained under US$5 billion until they hit a new low of just US$1.13 billion during a spate of hyperinflation from April through June 1989.

A second period of hyperinflation, from January through March of 1990, did little to change this critical reserve situation, which was a mirror reflection of the country's poor macroeconomic performance. The managed floating exchange rate policy applied later on that year permitted greater stability and a rise in reserves to approximately US$5 billion at the start of the Convertibility era in April 1991.

The dazzling image that this plan achieved in its initial period permitted the attraction of strong capital flows, and foreign reserves rose at a dizzying pace between 1991 and 1993, but this came to a halt in 1994, when the [Tequila] crisis broke in Mexico, with our reserves falling to US$14.5 billion in December of that year and to US$8.6 billion by March of 1995. Later, they were on an upward trend, regaining ground to once again reach US$14.55 billion in December of 1995, but with the help of a package from the International Monetary Fund. From then on, reserve levels continued to rise, peaking at US$26.2 billion in 1999, thanks to bond issues on the capital markets. However, by this time, a domestic recession had already begun due to a lagging exchange rate and the combined effects of crises in Asia (1997), Russia (1998), and Brazil (1999). The year 2001 was characterized by the unending flight of deposits and by the Central Bank's being powerless to act as the lender of last resort due to the tenets of the convertibility system, which, by this time, had ended up holding the country hostage. And the agony was only prolonged a few months more thanks to a "shield" of loans granted by the IMF, the World Bank, the Inter-American Development Bank, and the government of Spain. During that time, the administration sought to imbue its economic policy with a great deal of creativity but all without any connection to reality, which was marking the formal end of the "one-to-one" exchange era.

The first part of 2002 was characterized by the need to stabilize expectations, particularly with regard to the exchange rate, after the dollar skyrocketed from 1.40 pesos at the beginning of Eduardo Duhalde's administration (January) to 4.00 pesos by the end of March. Nevertheless, even though they were at a low level then, the country's reserves of US$6.8 billion, recorded in July of that critical year, kept predictions that were gloomier still of an even greater devaluation (or worse still, of hyperinflation) from coming true.

From then on, the reserve trend was upward and came accompanied by another positive signal: a surplus in both foreign trade and the current account (with there being a greater influx than flight of foreign currency). This was driven by fiscal savings, contrary to what had happened in the Convertibility era, when the country failed to take advantage of world "confidence" in order to build a sound basis for the domestic economy.

Although the influx of capital was the main source of reserves under Convertibility, nobody bothered to question the monetization of this income, presuming that it was due to a genuine demand for money. But once the fixed exchange rate was abandoned, it became necessary to have an absorption policy to soak up the excess liquidity from our purchases of dollars so as to avoid inflationary pressure. There are three ways to accumulate these assets:

1. Through the difference generated between export revenues and imports of goods and services.
2. Through the difference between incoming funds from foreign loans and moneys paid out in the form of principal and interest on such loans.
3. Through the difference between foreign investments and the demand for savings in foreign currency, a phenomenon known as "capital flight."

Meanwhile, there are also ways to sterilize the pesos left over: placement in short- and medium-term Central Bank notes (Lebac and Nobac); cancellation of debts contracted by banks during the 2001–2002 financial crisis (rediscounts); liability swaps (banks give the Central Bank their excess cash and, in exchange, receive a return on that money); and, to a lesser degree, the sale of government securities.

Like the reserves, all of these mechanisms have a "countercyclical" effect, since they moderate the expansion or retraction on the demand for money. To a certain extent, they act as a major breakwater against a gigantic wave, but a barrier with sufficient porosity so as to keep the coastline from ever being left high and dry.

While this focus has been brought into question because of the effect it has on the institution's balance sheet, the yield that these investments provide has, in all these years, permitted the Bank to show a surplus, rather than the deficit that local orthodox pundits predicted.

Time and again, it has been suggested that the accumulation of reserves is not the best "insurance" against a crisis. Surely not, and that's why it is referred to as "the second best." So then, what would the best solution of all be?

* * *

In mid-October of 2008, six of us Latin American central bankers held a private meeting as the world economic crisis was brewing. The venue chosen for the get-together was the Hyatt Hotel in Santiago, Chile. In the middle of the hotel's lobby, there is a grand atrium that permits one to look up at all twenty of the building's impressive floors, to which access is gained by means of elevators that rise on the outside of the structure, offering a view of the elegant Las Condes neighborhood.

The meeting was held on a Sunday, in order to maintain strict reserve. It was convened by the four of us central bankers from the region who most actively took part in the meetings of the BIS (Bank of International Settlements), headquartered in Basel—a sort of "central bank of central banks," namely, Guillermo Ortíz of Mexico, Henrique Meirelles of Brazil, José De Gregorio of Chile, and yours truly. We also decided to invite José Uribe of Colombia and Julio Velarde Flores of Peru.

At nine in the morning, we entered a fairly sober room that contrasted with the grandness of the hotel. We sat at an oval table.

The first to speak was Meirelles, and with certain regret, regarding the causes of the sharp devaluation that the *real* was suffering at the time against the dollar. Many Brazilian exporters had foreseen a constant appreciation of the exchange rate and had sold export futures contracts based on the calculation that the value of the *real* versus the dollar would go from 1.80 to 1.20. But when Lehman Brothers crashed, capital began to stampede in panic from the region and, instead of appreciating, the *real*'s rate against the dollar went to 2.00, thus throwing off the situation of those who had speculated in favor of an appreciation.

Faced with this scenario of foreign currency flight, the Central Bank of Brazil had to step in and cover these positions, thus generating a thunderous drop in the *real*. But when our Brazilian colleague's story reached its most dramatic pitch, he said something that brought relief to all of us:

"How fortunate that we've accumulated reserves, because we're going to be able to use them over the next few months to mitigate the leaps in the exchange rate."

Ortíz sketched a similar outlook with regard to the Mexican financial sector and admitted, somewhat angrily, that the financial managers who had set up these foreign exchange futures hadn't had the slightest idea what they were all about, but were really pleased while the money was coming in because the exchange differences with the dollar allowed them to cash some very succulent checks every month. That is, until the crisis in the world's top-ranked economy smacked them all in the face.

For me, the satisfaction was double, since both men had been staunch defenders of nonintervention in their foreign exchange markets. Brazil's reserves totaled about US$200 billion and Mexico's about US$86 billion. Meirelles sold at least US$20 billion and Ortíz about US$10 billion to defend their respective currencies.

Over the next six hours, each of us made his presentation. At three o'clock, we enjoyed a luncheon together before returning to our respective countries. For the first time ever, six central bankers had sealed a relationship based on trust, respect, and personal regard, an unprecedented occurrence in a region in which it had always been every country for itself, and at the expense of its neighbors and partners.

To my mind, of the international meetings I had attended over the course of that five-year period, this one had been, without a doubt, the one that had most influenced my decision making, because it imbued me with the confidence of knowing that the main countries of the region were all on the same track. And the best that could have happened was that this meeting never was leaked to the communications media, thus generating a high level of openness and trust among all of us.

So it was that I returned to Buenos Aires convinced that I had to defend our exchange rate without permitting sharp changes in it—as were being pushed by several private-sector leaders and certain government officials who believed that this would somehow magically allow them to recover competitiveness. At the same time, I was convinced of the need to improve fiscal accounts, which had deteriorated significantly.

All of us central bankers in the region realized that since we didn't have the strong currencies, like the dollar or the euro, which acted as a safeguard in the rest of the world, our foreign reserves were the best shield we could have.

With the end of World War II, the Bretton Woods Agreement, which promoted economic order in the second half of the twentieth century, gave birth to the International Monetary Fund. At first, this organization focused on promoting sustainable worldwide foreign exchange policies. Decades later, it would spearhead bailout packages for developing and impoverished nations, escorted by the World Bank and, later on, by regional development banks—in our case, the Inter-American Development Bank. (IDB).

Nevertheless, the adjustment schemes provided by the IMF in connection with its loans—which were practically identical for Asia and Latin America as of the mid-1970s—ended up being lethal beyond any collateral benefits. Stability and financial investments were achieved, but the price paid was a major economic imbalance and, moreover, a very high social cost in terms of unemployment and poverty.

So it was that, at the end of the 1990s, there began to be widespread rejection of these proposals, which came together in what was known as the "Washington Consensus," which promoted unrestricted economic liberalization. These prescriptions, promoted by financial institutions, came to be seen as the only possible road to achieving growth. But they later demonstrated their defects when they sought to adapt to the specific realities of each country in Latin America.

The Southeast Asian crisis in 1997 brought the first manifest rejection of the IMF. In countries like Malaysia, the IMF's name ended up being cursed, and the institution's officials were not permitted to enter that nation for more than a decade.

The Washington-based institution began setting ever-expanding conditions on the loans it granted, when the money for these loans belonged, in reality, to the very countries that were members of the fund. An excessively narrow view of reality ended up isolating the IMF from its best clients and condemned it to irrelevance before the world financial crisis. While Eastern Europe would suffer the effects of a fixed exchange rate, Latin America and Asia differentiated themselves from the rest, thanks to their ceaseless accumulation of foreign reserves.

The idea, then, of being able to count on an "ultimate international lender" to resort to when everything else crumbled and fell ended up being a mirage. Countries ask for help and, in return, receive demands for economic contraction, which, in the end, only serve to feed the flames of their crises. It was for this reason that sovereign funds also began to emerge, based on fiscal resources or public companies, like those of Abu Dhabi, Kuwait, Singapore, Norway, China, and, nearer to home, Chile.

Argentina, on the other hand, had consistently missed the opportunity to maintain its surplus. When, in 2005, the possibility of creating an anticyclical fund with resources from the federal Treasury had been touted, then-Economy Minister Roberto Lavagna, who had, in fact, been the father of this concept, opposed its institutionalization because he was afraid that political officials in the government might end up misspending these funds.

In retrospect, a fund like that might have served as a fiscal equivalent to the accumulation of foreign reserves, so as to permit increased public spending or a reduction in taxes in 2008, when the economy's growth stagnated—everywhere except in the much-questioned figures put out by INDEC [the statistics bureau].

It is possible that, with such resources, the administration might have had a greater measure of flexibility with regard to export taxes, without having to generate such a high level of tension and, later, direct confrontation with farmers. But, this said, it is also true, as Mr. Lavagna indicated, that there is a tendency within Argentina's tax structure toward overspending, with little concept of the correlation between spending and collection.

And so it was that the "grab" that Lavagna foresaw finally happened—first with the money of future pensioners and later with the Central Bank's reserves.

Although these might appear to be separate issues, reserves and the fiscal surplus travel hand in hand along the same path. And both affect the greater or lesser soundness of a country's growth.

In my international presentations over the course of 2009, I emphasized, on a number of occasions, the concept of deviation as applied to Argentina's growth over the past thirty years—or, in other words, how much the economy had grown, on average, and how much it had "strayed" from that line.

Argentina's deviation has been double with respect to Latin America and triple compared to Southeast Asia. It was out of this that there emerged the idea that the reserves weren't there just to be watched over, but to be utilized at critical times as a means of avoiding these deviations, which took such a high toll in terms of jobs and poverty.

This was where temporary progress was achieved in the relationship with the Kirchners. But more than as a means of mitigating crisis, they saw reserve accumulation as a process that would permit subsequent use of these resources for other purposes, such as financing the deficit, which was precisely what ended up happening at the beginning of 2010.

The reserve accumulation policy has proven effective in a number of different foreign exchange systems, although the fact is that the world is moving, in general, toward more flexible than fixed systems, like that which Argentina had in the previous decade. Convertibility generated relief from an inflationary context and a false sense that a peso was worth a dollar. But several years later, this led to a crisis, like that which takes place every time the exchange rate is fixed or caused to lag behind.

In a managed floating exchange system, the reserves were a key factor in preventing market operators from being able to guess where the peso would remain set against the dollar. The concept was to ensure that there were no abrupt fluctuations. But it was also important for exchange rate market operators not to second-guess us on the exchange rate if our movements were too overly predictable.

That's why it is dangerous to set objectives for the nominal exchange rate, or, in other words, to say "the dollar should now be at such-and-such a peso value." Every time there has been an attempt to rigorously defend this idea, the country has ended up losing out.

Similarly, there are other concepts related to reserves that were far too cavalierly bandied about during the crisis caused by the Bicentennial Fund and that are worthwhile analyzing in detail.

One of these is the concept of "freely available reserves," as included in Executive Decree No. 2010/09, which opened the way to the use of foreign reserves to pay private creditors and which was first declared null and void by Justice and later repealed by the government itself when it was faced with the impossibility of making it stick legally.

The Convertibility Law provided that reserves could not total less than the monetary base (money in circulation plus the deposits of banking institutions in the Central Bank), even though the monetary authority maintained greater backing to cover other monetary liabilities.

Be that as it may, all of this backing was insufficient to stem the flow in 2001, when there was a mass withdrawal of deposits to convert these funds into dollars, which fled the system. As of Federal Law 25,561 of January 6, 2002, which declared a public emergency and reformed the foreign exchange system, this restriction was lifted, so that the Central Bank could make use of monetary regulation instruments within a floating currency framework.

In December of 2005, Decree No. 1599/05—which allowed full payment of Argentina's debt with the IMF and was later debated and ratified in Congress, becoming Federal Law No. 26,076—introduced the concept of "freely available reserves," defined as the difference between foreign reserves and the monetary base. At the time, it was provided that the IMF payment should not signify an increase in domestic currency issue. Furthermore, this legislation is drafted in such a way as to imply that "freely available reserves" shall be used only on a onetime basis.

This is, however, a less than practical definition if it fails to take the Central Bank's debts into account. And thus the idea, according to the administration, that, at the end of 2009, there were "excess" reserves totaling about US$16 billion, was questionable, to say the least.

On December 15, when Decree No. 2010 was published, Argentina's foreign reserves stood at US$47.717 billion. But that amount was reduced to US$39.778 billion if the minimum cash balance required to back foreign currency deposits (dollars mostly) was discounted. Since, at the time, the Central Bank's liabilities totaled 173.835 billion pesos, the fact was that no surplus actually existed. On the contrary, there was a shortfall of US$5.785 billion if you subtracted minimum reserves and Bank debts.

Therefore, although the administration kept constantly insisting that using "a part" of the allegedly surplus reserves wouldn't place the stability of savings at risk, the truth was that the numbers belied this.

Even if they were going to use only the US$6.569 billion provided for in Decree 2010, the foreign reserve backing on the monetary base would drop from a ratio of 151 percent to just 73 percent. It's easy to imagine what would happen, then, if the administration were to take possession of the entire "reserve surplus" totaling US$16 billion.

At a slightly more sophisticated level of discussion to determine whether the Central Bank actually has excess reserves, you have to employ the tools recommended in academia with regard to what the optimum level of reserves is, at which a certain level of tranquility can be maintained when a major run on deposits occurs.

When the economy is a small and open one like Argentina's, at both a trade and financial level, it proves difficult indeed to determine precisely what this optimum level might be, even in the face of the solid growth rate experienced from January 2003, when reserves totaled US$8.25 billion, until March of 2008, when they reached US$50 billion, prior to the start of the administration's clash with farmers. In 2004, they rose to US$19.646 billion; in 2005, to US$26.7 billion; in 2006, despite payment of the IMF, from US$9 billion, to US$32.3 billion; in 2007, to US$46.151 billion; in 2008 (following major capital flight), to US$46.739 billion; and in 2009, they stood at about US$48.1 billion.

It was precisely this that was one of my arguments in that meeting I had with the President, Zannini, and Boudou on December 14, 2009: namely, that in practice, no surplus of reserves existed, and that, for Argentina, the optimum level of reserves corresponded to the potential demand for dollars on the part of depositors. If we take a look at the total pesos held by the population (including money in circulation, current accounts, savings accounts, and fixed-term deposits), the country's foreign reserves cover 66 percent of the total.

Nobody is going to exchange that entire flow of money into dollars at the same time. But in a worst-case scenario, one would do well to take this reference into account so as to know how to act in the face of a mass run against the peso.

* * *

On September 1, 2009, at the Monetary and Banking Meetings organized each year by the Central Bank, an unexpected discussion ensued between Olivier Blanchard, director of economic research at the International Monetary Fund (IMF), and me regarding reserve accumulation as a strategy for preventing the consequences of economic crises. Olivier is a great economist whom I had gotten to know at several different international meetings. He is the economic mind behind IMF Managing Director Dominique Strauss Kahn.

Blanchard maintained that this strategy was "insufficient," as were currency swap agreements signed among central banks, in seeking to ensure liquidity when a global crisis was having an extremely serious impact on international financial flows.

We had insured ourselves, through innovative agreements with Brazil and China, with a fund of US$12 billion in reserves for the country. And although this prestigious economist was seeking to defend the flexible credit lines the IMF was offering as the best alternative to higher reserves and those swaps, the fact was that the IMF program had been accepted by only three countries (Mexico, Colombia, and Poland)!

I once again defended the "self-insurance" strategy, bearing in mind the nonexistence of a last-resort international lender that could be considered sufficient, flexible, and properly capitalized. Curiously enough, three months later, the Argentine Executive Branch used the same line of argument as the IMF—after so maligning that institution ever since 2003—in defending its pretended use of reserves to pay debt.

Blanchard's aim wasn't as much to criticize the accumulation of reserves as it was to promote his own "product" with the promise of making it more attractive. In a private conversation that he and I had following those highly beneficial meetings, I explained to him that in order for the IMF's flexible credit line to be able to replace the idea of reserve accumulation, it would have to undergo substantial changes.

Nevertheless, this discussion left me with a concept that I proposed to my G-20 peers a few days later in London: that the IMF should offer swaps to central banks the way the Federal Reserve had done with several countries. This would permit these institutions to avoid loss of assets while, at the same time, circumventing the concept of nefarious demands being brought to bear by the multilateral organization whenever it agrees on a program.

As a follow-up, I drafted a proposal to launch liquidity insurance on a worldwide level, but with the focus on emerging markets. Before an audience of major officials of multilateral organizations and the world's highly developed nations at the G-20 meeting held in London by mid-September 2009, this is what I proposed:

"Do you want us to stop accumulating reserves? Then offer us insurance that is onerous and on which the premium that we pay corresponds to the level of risk the countries pose."

Asia supported me on this—even that Asian giant, China, which had been the leader in reserve accumulation in recent decades. The mistrustful response of the wealthy nations, for their part, was that if the emerging countries were to stop accumulating reserves, then there would be room to give thought to that kind of insurance.

It was right in the midst of this arduous international discussion in which we were embroiled that, back in Buenos Aires, two or three government officials decided that Argentina should go, yet another time, against the grain of the rest of the world.

Chapter 3

My Arrival

Thursday, September 16, 2004, was formally my last day as Argentina's Secretary of Trade. I was in Madrid, taking part in a seminar hosted by the Spanish newspaper *ABC* that was being staged in the Hotel Intercontinental on magnificent Avenida La Castellana. After I gave my talk, I was invited to lunch along with other speakers. Among these was Popular Party leader Mariano Rajoy, who sat on my right. I found him to be a conceptually sound man who had not yet been able to digest his defeat by José Luis Rodríguez Zapatero. In the afternoon, I met with Spanish Trade Secretary Pedro Mejía to explore trade opportunities between our two countries. At 11:45 p.m., I boarded an Iberia flight back to Argentina.

I settled into my seat and read the first thirty pages of Sun Tzu's *The Art of War*, required reading for anyone interested in strategy. Then I put the book away in a carry-on bag. I needed to rest. I closed my eyes, thought about my children and my wife, and fell fast asleep. Drugged with sleep, I suddenly heard the echoing of a voice, which turned gradually into a clearer, more real sound. I half-opened my eyes. It was the flight attendant who was talking to me. I looked at her without understanding what she was saying. Then she repeated the sentence: "Sorry to wake you," she said timidly, "but the President wants to talk to you."

"Tell him we can talk tomorrow," I said, half asleep and thinking she meant the president of Iberia, calling to apologize for the problems with my reservation in Madrid. I paid no more attention to her and went to sleep.

A quarter of an hour later, I again heard the echo, and then the voice. It was the same flight attendant. This time her attitude was firmer, tenser.

"We have this telex that arrived from…"

She handed me the piece of paper she was holding. I had to rub my eyes before I could read it. Finally, I opened my eyes up wide and read: "President Kirchner wants to contact you. Please call him at the following number…"

I was groggy. I looked at my watch. It was 4:15 in the morning. We had been in the air for about four hours. We would be just past the Canary Islands, near the coast of Africa.

I finally managed to connect by means of one of those on-board satellite phones. At the other end, I heard the voice of the cabinet chief:

"Hi, Martín, Alberto Fernández here. How are you? What're you up to?"

"I'm on a flight back from Spain. Do you have any idea what time it is?" I asked.

"Sorry, but it's urgent." And, with that, he got right to the point. "I'm putting the President on. He wants to talk to you."

Without preliminaries, President Kirchner said:

"I'm calling you because Alfonso's term is up on September 24. I'm offering you the Central Bank presidency."

I was surprised, incredulous. Was I dreaming? I managed to blurt out two words and a suggestion, "OK, OK, let's talk about it tomorrow."

It was only then that the nickel dropped: "But, why isn't Prat Gay's mandate being renewed?" I asked.

"If you want, we can talk about that tomorrow, when you get back…"

At that point, I realized I was awake and decided to dig deeper with another question: What would happen to my team that had been with me since 2002, first with Carlos Ruckauf under the administration of Eduardo Duhalde, and then, from the beginning of the Kirchner administration, with Rafael Bielsa?

The President's response was short and blunt: "No problem. If you want, we can also talk about who your successor will be," he quipped with characteristic sarcasm.

It seems like a "must" for politicians to be quick on their feet and to always be able to come back with some ironic response.

The call ended. The rest we would talk about in person.

I was fortunately able to put what lay ahead out of my mind and go back to sleep until the plane landed at Ezeiza International.

Back in mid-August, Alfonso Prat Gay had phoned me to tell me that he had suggested to the chief economist for Banco Bilbao Vizcaya that he should invite me to speak at a seminar that *ABC* was staging in Spain. The topic: relations between Mercosur, South America trade bloc formed by Brazil, Argentina, Uruguay and Paraguay, and the European Union.

He asked me if I planned to be in Europe on that date. Coincidentally, I was planning a trip because European Trade Commissioner Pascal Lamy was ending his term in office and would be replaced by Britain's Peter Mandelson.

Since negotiations were fairly advanced for opening up European Union markets to producers from Mercosur and vice versa, I had organized a luncheon with Mandelson, who had served as both trade and industry minister under Tony Blair's government, and also as head of relations with Northern Ireland, where he had handled the Good Friday Peace Agreement.

I felt satisfaction over the advances made in the ambitious negotiations between the European Union and Mercosur. Argentina stood to gain access, particularly in the agro-business segment, to greater export levels than it was used to. We continued, meanwhile, to run into problems in textiles, we hadn't defined our guidelines in the automotive industry, and we were still at odds with Brazil over the level of liberalization we were willing to negotiate in services, especially in shipping.

Beyond these differences, my personal relationship with Lamy was a highly fluent one. And with the changing of the guard in that post, I figured that it was essential to establish the same kind of relationship with his successor.

So when Prat Gay called me about going to the Madrid seminar, I told him that I could go following my trip to London and Frankfurt, for a presentation by auto parts makers at the Automechanika trade fair, a key event for promoting increased sales for that industry.

The stopover in London was important. Mandelson and I had lunch at the Argentine Embassy in London, located in the vicinity of Grosvenor Square, on the Monday before I was offered the Central Bank job. Our country's mission in Britain was headed up by an excellent diplomat, Federico Mirré. We talked about the problems hindering multilateral trade negotiations in the so-called Doha Round of World Trade Organization (WTO) talks, devoted to the liberalization of the goods and services trade.

It was a cordial meeting, even though Mandelson wasn't up to speed on the details of negotiations, since it would still be another sixty days before he took up his post. So our talks centered on the main issues we both saw as forming part of the negotiations. The meeting achieved its aims for both of us, since we were able to exchange views on everything from the world economy to English literature.

At that moment, I had no idea that my next stop in Frankfurt would be my last mission as trade negotiator for Argentina, a job I had done for nearly three years and in which I had maintained strong interaction with the mainstream economic sectors and with the rest of the country's economists—ties which I would later continue to pursue as head of the Central Bank.

As Trade Representative, conversations with the private sector were developed through formal committees—like the ones forged in *Fundación Export.Ar*, a foreign trade foundation directed by a member of my team, Marcelo Elizondo, and with the participation of major players. At the Central Bank, on the other hand, these encounters were off the record in order to find out the real opinions of opinion makers. This did not mean, however, that decisions were made jointly. My criterion as the public authority always took precedence over any private interest. But I had always been characterized by my willingness to listen to a variety of opinions within the framework of the decision-making process. The discussions had always pivoted around the concept of how to interact more to the rest of the world. At the Central Bank, meanwhile, the main issue was how to achieve monetary and exchange stability while expanding credit in local currency.

On Friday, September 17, my plane landed at 7:50 a.m. I stopped by my house in Belgrano, had a quick shower, and sped off to Government House.

I was greeted by the cabinet chief, whom I had known for ten years. The first thing I asked him was what had happened with Prat Gay.

"Actually, until noon yesterday," Fernández said, "the files on Alfonso and Pedro (Lacoste, the Central Bank's vice president) were all set to be sent to the Senate. Tomorrow, Néstor [Kirchner] will be traveling to the U.N. General Assembly meeting. But yesterday, Alfonso [Prat Gay] asked for a meeting at 6 p.m. to talk about the debt restructuring process."

Alfonso Prat Gay had assumed the presidency of the Central Bank in December of 2002, the same year in which Roque Maccarone, Mario Blejer, and Aldo Pignanelli had been in that spot.

He had worked for J.P.Morgan Bank. In 2001, he was on the verge of taking a post on the Central Bank's Board of Directors, with a nod of approval from then-Economy Minister Domingo Cavallo, but at the last minute, his file wasn't presented because of some problem to do with earnings abroad on his tax reporting. He took up the presidency to finish the term of Pedro Pou, which had begun in September of 1999.

When he was about to begin his own six-year term, Alfonso voiced dissent with the handling of debt restructuring being implemented by Economy Minister Roberto Lavagna.

Alberto Fernández told me that he had tried to convince Prat Gay not to take up this question with President Kirchner so close to his file's being sent to the Senate, but the attempt had not been successful.

"I recommended that he rather not speak," said Fernández, "but he insisted that he couldn't take responsibility with regard to this issue from here on. At the meeting, he was highly critical of the job Lavagna was doing, and he told Kirchner that the [debt] reconstruction that Argentina was carrying out was going to meet with a really poor reception on the markets, and that he had other ideas on the subject."

There was a constant temptation on the part of Central Bank presidents to co-direct foreign debt negotiation along with the economy ministers, even though, in the end result of such encounters, the ministers came out on top, because it was under the responsibility of the Treasury.

Some months before he left the Central Bank, Prat Gay had stated in a public debate in the United States that "Argentina missed the opportunity to negotiate the debt when it was on its knees," meaning in 2002 or 2003, before strong economic recovery began, back when it could have obtained more advantageous conditions from the creditors that had been affected by the default declared at the end of 2001. Truth be told, it would have been highly unlikely that anybody would have wanted to negotiate with the transition government of the Duhalde administration.

Therefore, when I took up the presidency of the Central Bank, I adopted a response that I would repeat throughout my term. When the press asked me about issues that was not specifically related to the Bank, I would say: "I only take care of my own square meter." And this attitude also implied a point of reciprocity: Let everyone else stay out of my natural space.

Nevertheless, in Prat Gay's case, the situation was even more complicated. Fernández told me that Kirchner had been blunt with the economist, saying, "Look, Alfonso, the debt restructuring strategy isn't Lavagna's, it's mine. We'll keep on talking tomorrow, but it looks to me like this is an issue that you're going to have to take as one of national government policy."

According to the cabinet chief, Kirchner then closed the door to his office, turned to Fernández, and said, "Let's start looking for alternatives."

Prat Gay, on the other hand, told people in his circle that Kirchner had said they would "keep talking tomorrow," referring to Friday the seventeenth.

Fernández related another version to me as well: that Prat Gay had a fluent relationship with Bill Rhodes, Vice Chairman of Citigroup, which, for several decades, had been the visible head of Argentina's group of foreign creditors. The link between these two men fostered feelings of distrust in the President. Despite this, I don't believe that Alfonso ever acted contrary to the interests of the country. Later, Fernández repeated the offer he had made me, so I asked him what the administration's vision was for the Central Bank. His response was laconic: "Look it over, make a diagnosis, and if you want to make significant changes, let us know. I've known you for ten years. We trust you."

Alberto Fernández stood up and we walked into the President's adjoining office. Curiously enough, Kirchner received me at his desk, despite the fact that it was more usual for him to hold meetings at the conference table in his office. Although I had never seen him frequently, we spoke informally.

"Martín, congratulations!" he said. "You'll do a great job."

"Do you have any concerns you'd like to pass on to me, Mr. President?" I asked.

"No, keep on doing what Alfonso did and keep a closer eye on the banks. We lack supervisory capacity there," he said, then added, "You take care of your end of things, and every fifteen days, come see me and give me your view of the economy. I want to hear from you."

My immediate concern was to know how much field of action I had to work in.

"As you know," I said, "I've been forming a team of economists for the past ten years. What's the possibility of my naming a member of the board?

Kirchner tried to put on a nice face when he answered.

"The board is complete, but you have total freedom to put your team in managerial posts. No problem with that," he said with a smile.

I immediately returned to one of the commitments Kirchner had made when I talked to him from aboard the plane: namely, who would succeed me as the trade secretary. I proposed a three-man short list that included the man who, in the end, took my place: Alfredo Chiaradía, an economist with a vast diplomatic background who had previously been my undersecretary of Foreign Trade. I had later pushed for his appointment as our ambassador at the World Trade Organization headquarters in Geneva.

From Government House, I went to the Foreign Ministry by car to talk to Foreign Minister Rafael Bielsa. We had a fruitful chat since we enjoyed a very good personal and professional relationship. One of the things we talked about was who my successor would be as that ministry's secretary of economic relations. I told him that I proposed Alfredo Chiaradía, and who was to end up being Kirchner's pick a week later.

At 12:30 p.m., I was in Lavagna's office, and he told me that within the framework of precarious peace that he maintained with Kirchner and Fernández, they had reached an agreement that I was the man for the Central Bank job. Evidently, while they were trying to locate me, the name of former governor Javier González Fraga came up, as did that of Banco Nación President Felisa Miceli, who was to be named minister fourteen months later.

Lavagna was amiable yet blunt, as always. "Martín," he said, "there's nothing urgent at the Central Bank. There are no burning issues that you have to deal with right now. Sit down, analyze it, and we'll plan on getting together to talk weekly."

As minister, Lavagna had previously had to deal with attempts by former Central Bank presidents Mario Blejer and Aldo Pignanelli to seek a quick opening of the so-called *corralito* and *corralón*—two measures imposed to restrict withdrawal of deposits in the 2001–2002 crisis —and, later, to push for a swift agreement with the IMF and the holders of Argentine bonds.

When the shockwave of the first quarter of 2002 had been overcome following devaluation of the peso and implementation of the controversial asymmetrical "pesofication" measure, the economy began to stabilize. Lavagna wanted to handle the timing for the country's restructuring. He knew that understandably anxious domestic and foreign creditors alike would be expecting the government to normalize the situation.

I didn't need to hear anything more. I knew the minister. When I was Trade Secretary, he was ambassador to the European Union and to the World Trade Organization. When Jorge Remes Lenicov resigned as economy minister at the end of 2002 over failure to reach an agreement with the IMF and the rejection by Congress of his plan to issue a compulsory bond for savings depositors in the midst of the 2002 crisis, several names came into play. Among these, there were two who were very different from one another: Lavagna, and Guillermo Calvo, then chief analyst for the Inter-American Development Bank (IDB) and a respected academician who had reached international renown by vociferously predicting the "Tequila Effect" crisis that started in Mexico at the end of 1994. Also very close to being designated was Alieto Guadagni, a former energy secretary from the Duhalde camp, but he was, in the end, rejected by a number of the governing Justicialist Party's governors.

Carlos Ruckauf, who was then the minister of foreign affairs, asked me whom I thought was the best-suited candidate to direct the political policy at the time. I didn't hesitate to answer. "No doubt about it!" I said. "Lavagna is an excellent choice. Calvo is a great academic economist, but he'll flip over the ministry within forty-eight hours because he doesn't have the experience in handling practical issues or the political savvy that are both so necessary under circumstances like these. Lavagna has the experience and the capability."

On April 26, 2002, Duhalde appointed Lavagna. The next day, Lavagna called me to get together with him. On Sunday the twenty-eighth at 11:30 a.m., I visited him on the fifth floor of the *Palacio de Hacienda*, where the economy minister has his private office.

I'm usually fairly perceptive about the places where I go, and on walking through the corridors of that austere building at *the Street* Hipólito Yrigoyen 250, I realized that Lavagna was alone. No staff were there to accompany him, except for his new assistant, Leonardo Constantino, the same one who had gone to meet the minister on the ladder of the Air France jet that carried him from Brussels to Buenos Aires, with a stopover in Paris.

Without beating around the bush, Lavagna asked me to become the Secretary of Finance, which came to me as an absolute surprise. Just a short time before, on April 15, I had sealed an automotive trade agreement with Mexico that would permit us to increase our new car sales by fifty thousand with no trade barriers. At the time, demand from Brazil had collapsed, and many firms in the sector were thinking about pulling out of Argentina to take their production precisely to that South American giant. But we managed to open this new window and had the opportunity to work on the basis of a quota system and get into the markets without paying tariffs, in both Mexico and Chile.

The Secretary of Trade post had turned out to be a key experience in my professional life. Accustomed to working in the financial sector, here I had an opportunity, for the first time, to rub shoulders with all of the productive sectors. From one day to another, I had to analyze the auto industry, steel, aluminum, soybean production, plastics, and sugar among others. That's why, when he made the offer, I said, "Look, Roberto, the truth is that I'm really focused on what I'm doing. And I think it has a lot in common with your own vision of the economy. Let me be a sort of trade secretary that works with strong coordination between the Foreign Ministry and the Economy Ministry."

He quickly accepted the idea, because he has a long history of his own with the real sectors of the economy. A week later, Ruckauf and Lavagna, who got along really well with one another, held a press conference at the Foreign Ministry in which they announced that I was to be a secretary coordinating with both ministries.

From that point on, we held numerous private meetings regarding multilateral trade negotiations in the World Trade Organization and about all of the other issues to be included under my responsibility. We always had a very cordial relationship, even when there were differences of opinion. And too, there was always mutual respect between my collaborators at both the Foreign Ministry and the Central Bank and me.

At the Economy Ministry, Lavagna's team included Sebastián Katz (undersecretary of economic strategy and policy), Guillermo Nielsen (who eventually became finance secretary), Sebastián Palla (undersecretary of finance), and Leonardo Madcur, Lavagna's legal secretary—perhaps the one with the most difficult personality, but a man whose views were sound. At my end, I was accompanied by three members of the *Fundación Capital* think-tank: Hernán Lacunza, Carlos Pérez, and Pedro Rabasa.

It was a relationship without shocks or surprises. Each of us knew where he stood. And we worked together to reach an agreement on the main problems—the necessary coordination of fiscal and monetary policy.

I was highly used to dealing with financial issues—both in my career in the private sector (as an analyst at Salomon Brothers, managing director of Security Pacific Bank in the United States, creator of *Fundación Capital*, and *InvertirOnline.com*, as well as in a variety of consulting jobs) and in the public sector (as chairman of the Securities and Exchange Commission). But going from the Trade Secretaty to the Central Bank ended up being a major change in outlook and pace.

The most noteworthy thing about heading up the Central Bank is the fact that you are being constantly examined. At my previous job, one had more to produce results, even with the tight, ambitious work plan we had set out for ourselves that included trade negotiations on several fronts at once, and knowing full well that the economic recovery at home had to be backed by an open-ing onto the foreign markets for our products.

At the Central Bank, the evolution of the foreign exchange rate is subject to daily scrutiny by the public at large, which is constantly evaluating the Bank's actions. Then, too, there is the job of setting the country's prime interest rate. As our basic task in this regard, we decided to create a daily rate to complement the bonds issued by the institution (the Lebac and the Nobac) as a guideline for the actions of the financial system. We also had to create a new set of banking regulations that would expand credit. This involved a very broad and demanding scope that ranged from controlling the purchase and sale of foreign currency to the expansion of provisions on money laundering, and included daily assessment of the situation of every bank in Argentina.

Despite Lavagna's attempt to reassure me by telling me that I wouldn't face any urgent issues at the beginning of my term, there was, indeed, an urgent need to deal with all of the problems that had remained unsolved since the break from Convertibility and the asymmetrical "pesofication" that had followed.

When I arrived at Reconquista 266 Street on September 24, my morning was spent in phone conversations with my colleagues worldwide. I spoke with David Dodge in Canada, Guillermo Ortíz in Mexico, Henrique Meirelles in Brazil, Vittorio Corbo in Chile, Jean Claude Trichet at the European Central Bank, and the

Federal Reserve's legendary Alan Greenspan in the United States. When I received the call from this last veteran central banker, I was surprised to hear him say, "Welcome to the club." Over the course of time, I would find out that we central bankers indeed formed a kind of club, which met every two months in Basel (Switzerland). That afternoon, I gave a talk in the Central Bank's magnificent Bosch Hall, where I set down guidelines before an audience made up of the Bank's staff and the entire board: Miguel Ángel Pesce, the Bank's vice president-designate; members-designate Waldo Farías, Zenón Biagosch, and Arnaldo Bocco; Second Vice President Ricardo Branda; CPI Jorge Levy, the bank's superintendent of finance and exchange institutions; members Félix Camarasa, Arturo O'Connell, and Eduardo Cafaro; and syndics Marcelo Griffi and Luis Lamberti.

"I am assuming this post following the term of Alfonso Prat Gay, whose advances in monetary normalization are well known," I said. "But as all of you are aware, knowing me as you do, my aim is to build on what has been accomplished and to develop new challenges. I aspire to being able to hand over to the next president, on September 23, 2010, having complied with the following objectives:

"First, to recover monetary stability and provide sustainable foreign exchange and financial predictability.

"Second, to shore up financial institutions, particularly as regards their capital standing, as a means of restoring public trust, which is the core value of the system as the natural repository of our people's savings.

"Third, to promote greater banking development, which has traditionally been anemic in our country, and to do so, fundamentally, through the strongest, most trustworthy institutions, with the diversification of financial instruments to indeed return confidence to the public.

"Fourth, to consolidate and establish a prime rate for the local market, like other developing and developed countries have. This can serve to provide predictability, and has the capacity to generate market signals to orient savings toward investments.

"Finally, I have proposed, as the great challenge for this board of directors, the generation of credit in pesos, so that all of those who have dreams in Argentina can have the capacity to develop them."

Later, I underlined the spirit of consensus that had guided my professional life and on my obsession with work, but I noted that this was combined with an informal style that, in some cases, would generate great satisfaction, and in others, collisions.

I concluded by telling the staff that I highly valued their performance since 2002, in the midst of a constant emergency situation. As a career staffer would aptly put it in a conversation with me some time later, at the depth of the crisis, "we kept the house from falling."

We were putting out the fire and rebuilding the pillars of that house, the roof of which had blown off and which needed for its foundations to be shored up. It had made it through the crisis, but we still hadn't raised the pillars that could maintain a long-term policy.

The first challenge was to establish the basis of our monetary policy, we needed to decide if we were going to continue with the commitment to announce each year the expected growth of the amount of money in circulation, as had been done since 2002. This was a concrete goal in terms of establishing that issuance of pesos should correspond to the actual demand for money. Since we were beginning our term in the last quarter of the year, the decision was to continue to implement an annual target for the monetary base, but with a greater grasp on the relationship between the monetary aggregate, which the Central Bank monitored, and the demand for pesos.

Without stopping to take a breath, we analyzed the situation and made changes in the internal structure of the Bank, with the aim of making it more dynamic. We separated the economy and finance division from economic research. We turned research over to Hernán Lacunza, who had headed up the respected *Centro de Economía Internacional* (CEI) at the Foreign Ministry and had worked with me since 1997 at *Fundación Capital*. The aim was to conduct a deep-reaching study of monetary aggregates and to determine what people's demand for pesos might be. I also appointed a general manager—a post that had remained vacant for a long time. My choice in this case was Carlos Pérez, one of the best analysts in the country today.

Another urgent issue was the situation of savings depositors in the banks. My debut—clearly, a tough one—came at the beginning of October at a luncheon in Washington with Bank of Spain Governor Jaime Caruana and his second–in–command, José Viñals, parallel to the Annual Meeting of the IMF and World Bank. Spanish banks constituted a major presence on the local market. Both men showed concern regarding whether there might be some possibility of normalizing the situation following the 2001–2002 "tidal wave."

Indeed, in a talk that he gave at that meeting, Francisco González of Banco Bilbao Vizcaya had praised Brazil and Mexico while heaping harsh criticism on Argentina for the handling of its financial crisis, as well as for not having solved burning issues that were generating great concern among the people due to uncertainty about the future of their savings.

When I took up my post, a tense, strained situation prevailed. And there was, furthermore, considerable litigation surrounding these issues. This was why one of the most urgent priorities was that of reestablishing confidence. Granted, the chaos that had predominated in foreign exchange was over, thanks to rising reserves, which had begun under my predecessor, but the banking sector remained devastated. There were still deposits that hadn't been returned and compensatory bonds that the banking institutions needed. The corresponding audits, in order to be able to make delivery of the bonds pertaining to the asymmetrical "pesofication" of 2002, had not yet been carried out.

Eighteen months later, however, in June of 2006, Caruana finished his mandate at the Bank of Spain and invited me to Madrid for another luncheon. There, he told me, "Well, Martín, I have the satisfaction of knowing that we've cleared our accounts, that we've cleaned up all of the pending issues that we had between us."

My greatest concern was recovering public trust, because people weren't going back to depositing their savings in these banking institutions.

The urgency also lay in analyzing the monetary situation to see if an inflation targeting regime could be adapted. This had met with strong resistance, particularly because of the possibility of ending up adhering to a rigid proposal in a country with weak institutions, in the broadest sense of the term. We arrived at the conclusion that two instruments were available to us in working along these lines: the interest rate—which functioned only marginally due to the scarcity of credit versus total production—and the exchange rate.

One of the mistakes committed in Argentina's economic policy over the course of the past thirty years had been to make excessive use of a lagging exchange rate as a means of stabilizing the financial situation and controlling inflation. Therefore, from the outset, we believed that it was of fundamental importance—in a view that we shared with Lavagna—to coordinate fiscal, wage, revenue, and monetary policies in such a way as to maintain a low and sustainable inflation rate.

So, it was impossible to handle a plan based on inflation targets from the offices of the Central Bank, simply because we didn't have the necessary tods to achieve it. Proposing it would have been illusory and arbitrary. We were facing great irregularity in the credit system, which was still paralyzed.

This was why we made the decision, at the beginning of 2005, to establish a risk management monetary policy on the monetary front, in which we would each year lay out a central scenario in terms of the development of the main monetary and financial variables, with corrective measures as well in case something went off track.

Along these lines, we decided to generate confidence among depositors by getting credit up and running—since it was clearly stalled, especially in pesos. Taking these parameters into account, we established 2004 to 2010 as a period of transition for Argentina's economic history, with the aim of normalizing the performance of the different monetary, exchange, and financial variables. Therefore, a prime objective was to prevent the cyclical crises that had led us to experience megadevaluations, confiscation of deposits, or hyperinflation.

In 2005, we analyzed which monetary aggregate was the one that was most related to the demand for pesos. In this case, our research division made a substantial contribution to our decision-making process.

After studying several historical periods and cross-referencing a large quantity of data, we developed a report that showed that, from 1975 to 2004, the greatest correlative factor between the demand for pesos and the monetary aggregate was M2, or, in other words, money in circulation plus current accounts and savings accounts. That's why we started gravitating toward that indicator as a frame of reference and as a more concrete goal.

Parallel to this, we created a major opening to dialogue with industry and with my fellow economists. It was always my belief that the Central Bank was a venue for our profession. So every other Thursday at 3:30 p.m., our research department would select and meet with an economist from a broad ideological spectrum. For five years, all sorts of analysts visited the Central Bank, with no distinction as to which camp they belonged to, and presented papers on the current situation or on monetary policy.

There was also an open dialogue with the financial sector, as well as with the real economy. I made use of lunchtime, with meals served in the room adjoining my office, to talk one-to-one with industrialists, merchants, and agricultural producers. As I was all day long concentrating on financial variables, I spent the noon hour following up on "real" economic variables. It was of decisive importance to me that these meetings not be made public, so that each person who came to lunch could feel comfortable and say what was on his or her mind.

Most of the regulations for use in increasing credit emerged from listening to the productive sectors. I knew that credit development wasn't the product of arbitrary criteria, but of stable rules and, of course, of the regulatory contribution of our institution.

At a management level, we had a team with experience and, based on that, we made a major change in the organization chart, so as to generate a less feudal structure. When I first arrived at the Central Bank, there were four large assistant general management departments, which I proceeded to reorganize into eleven assistant managements, so as to create a more horizontal organization. Because of the kind of personality I have, I like to be able to talk as much to the staffer who is doing the spreadsheet on monetary variables as to the assistant manager in charge of that section. And on several occasions, middle managers got upset about this attitude of mine. But this kind of open dialogue generated a much stronger esprit de corps than had existed previously. It ended up being one of the best bureaucratic structures I had ever worked with in the public sector.

My other mission was to tear down the fences that had been built between the different areas of the Bank, like the one that stood between the division that drafted the institution's regulations and the division that supervised financial institutions. They argued over issues and never seemed to reach an agreement. The idea of skirting responsibility is a common trait in the public sector. The trick, then, was to make it understood that if there was a mistake, everybody was accountable for it, not just a specific sector. I never tired of saying: "Here, this or that civil servant won't get a free pass, [and] if the work is done right, it's the merit of the entire institution." These structural changes and changes in how we worked generated really strong team spirit that permitted staff to meet the challenges that we set out for ourselves in terms of monetary, exchange rate, and financial policies.

Without a doubt, the policy centerpiece consisted of getting the supply of pesos to converge with demand. The second key concept was that of creating "anticyclical insurance" by accumulating reserves. The third was to provide predictability in our foreign exchange policy by setting up a managed floating regime. Finally, we needed to coordinate with the Economy Ministry, a major job when it came to inflation—a problem that I will refer to in chapter 10.

Contrary to the cordial relationship I had always had with former presidents Carlos Menem, when I was the Chairman of the Securities and Exchange Commission, and Eduardo Duhalde, when I was at the Trade Representative, the one with Kirchner was always respectful but distant.

In point of fact, the day Kirchner took office, I was in charge of coordinating meetings with the leaders who came from abroad to attend the inauguration, held on May 25, 2003. I recall that by noon, Kirchner was tired of receiving fellow presidents in meetings that Rafael Bielsa and I attended: "OK, so when do we get down to work on local issues?" he exclaimed impatiently.

To put his mind at ease, we told him that it would be just the one day that he would be occupied receiving foreign delegations and that, generally speaking, other presidents had taken advantage of their inaugurations, not merely to feel supported by their own citizens, but also to cultivate personal relationships and forge a consensus beyond the borders of the country.

So it was that, a few days prior to the inauguration, based on an idea that I transmitted to Alberto Fernández, the chief of staff, I found myself in charge of handling a major challenge: setting up contact with President George W. Bush. While this was usual for the majority of presidents worldwide, the new administration appeared to have other priorities.

In order to ensure that the call between the two presidents was productive, I prepared an agenda with some main issues on it and then went to the apartment that Kirchner used when he was in Buenos Aires, located in the posh Recoleta neighborhood at the corner of Montevideo and Arenales. I got there at 9:15 a.m. We talked for ten minutes.

A little before ten o'clock in Buenos Aires, nine in Washington, the call was made, and the two presidents focused on matters of mutual interest, such as the war on terrorism and money laundering. The relationship between them was amiable, even cordial. Or it was, that is, until the sharp clash between them at the Fourth Americas Summit held in 2005 in the seaside resort city of Mar del Plata, which Bush attended and where Kirchner gave a nod to "counter-Summit" picketers and other social organizations that were highly critical of the United States. He also harshly rejected the Free Trade Agreement (FTAA) that Washington was promoting.

During that time, my relationship with Kirchner was almost always through Bielsa, who, for his part, was on good terms with Lavagna. That's why there were always good relations between the foreign and economy ministries.

The other major contact that I had with Kirchner was during the China visit that the President made in the last week of June 2004, with nearly three hundred businesspeople. The primary purpose of that trip was to establish strategic relation with the Asian giant and, within that year, increase annual export levels from US$2.5 billion to US$3 billion, with a key outlook in mind: product diversification, with a strong focus on soybeans oil, so as to also open up that market to such products as software, leather goods, meats, dairy products, cheese, and food products.

The trip ended up being highly productive, and bilateral contacts were intensified. But later, a serious error was made when it was leaked from Government House that China would be contributing US$20 billion to payment of a major part of the our foreign debt. The leak upset the Chinese authorities and, of course, that deal never came through.

In every mission in which I was involved, I worked jointly with others to identify both public and private interests and launch them worldwide. While working in foreign trade, I developed a program based on the four D's: **D**ouble exports;

Deconcentrate destinations; Diversify the economic sectors that export; and Distribute the benefits of these sales throughout the entire production chain. The slogan on the basis of which we worked was "country by country, product by product," and it was a program that had sparked noteworthy enthusiasm in the private sector.

The economic context helped: The economy was in a process of frank recovery. And following a brutal institutional crisis in which the country had four presidents in less than a week, President Duhalde's transition government helped lay the groundwork for Kirchner to be able to recover a presidential leadership position.

With this combination of economic improvement and solid policy, 2004 ended up being the soundest year in fiscal terms since the country's return to democracy (1983): The surplus was 4.2 percent for the federal government, with provincial governments contributing 0.8 additional percentage points, rounding out to a magnificent 5 percent, in an economy that was generating jobs and where social indicators were improving, but without inflation's taxing the most vulnerable sectors of society.

For the first time, a president was underscoring the fiscal surplus as one of the prime concepts of his economic policy. I was really optimistic. I was enthused, because this went to the root of a central trait of the country's economic policy over the past thirty years. If I were asked to explain why it had gone so badly for us in recent decades, there could be only one answer: We always lived beyond our means. "It is the history of overspending and overindebtedness," as I frequently explained to foreign officials.

The conditions were rife for Argentina to reverse the error that kept it from entering a virtuous circle, so at the end of that first year between 2004 and 2005, as president of the Central Bank, I was looking to this possibility with enthusiasm and hope.

But the good vibes didn't last long. At the end of the following year, the turn of events had begun to change my enthusiasm into skepticism and, later, into disappointment.

Chapter 4

Chronicle of a Death Foretold: Relations with the IMF

The last conversation I had with Roberto Lavagna while he was still economy minister came after legislative elections held in October of 2005, in which, after his first two years in office spent reconstructing presidential power, Néstor Kirchner consolidated his political backing.

In presidential elections held on April 27, 2003, Kirchner, won only 22 percent of the votes, with Carlos Menem (Alliance Front for Loyalty–UCD) eking out a win over him with 24.3 percent. Trailing these two candidates were Ricardo López Murphy (an economist of Radical Party extraction who was running on a ticket backed by a center-rightist coalition), Adolfo Rodríguez Saá (Justicialist Party) and Elisa Carrió (backed by a center-leftist coalition), each of whom took about 14 percent of the votes. Leopoldo Moreau, the candidate for the traditional Radical Civic Union, took sixth place with just 2.3 percent of the votes in that party's worst election in history.

But the elections had to go to a second round and, sure that he would lose by a broad margin to Kirchner in a runoff, Menem decided to drop out of the race, and Kirchner was elected president. From that time on, Kirchner seemed to have the feeling that his victory did not entirely belong to him. In point of fact, he had won, among other reasons, because of his ratification of Lavagna as economy minister and of Daniel Scioli as his running mate.

Because of this prior feeling of uncertainty, when Kirchner managed to win backing in the 2005 legislative elections—to a large extent because of what had been done in terms of economic policy over the course of the last two years—he suddenly felt strong enough to get rid of Lavagna.

Unaware of these undercurrents, I met with the minister at the beginning of November to start discussing which currency we would use to finance Argentina in the long term. Considering the price rises registered since 2002, I was pretty dubious about continuing to issue debt indexed to inflation.

The second alternative was to continue with dollar-denominated issues, but seek to limit them so as not to cause, as happened in the nineties, a major loss of currency mismatch—since most of the government revenues are in pesos while its payments must be made in foreign currency. The third option, of course, was to put out nominal peso issues, which would require stable conditions. At that point, no such conditions had been achieved.

Nevertheless, an important step had been taken: the debt swap, implemented to break the country out of default, and which had an acceptance ratio of 76 percent, with a reduction of US$67 billion in the country's liabilities. This brought a sharp reduction in Argentina's debt-to-GDP ratio and an improved profile for government debts due. But within a short time, the juggling of figures published by the statistics bureau, INDEC, would be more than enough to blur these achievements from memory.

The swap was, without a doubt, the best deal Argentina ever made with its creditors, even though it left too many casualties in its wake. A shortage of personal contact and proper explanations, and an excess of confrontation with the different players in the financial system, were to blame for this. Argentina pioneered in this field by offering a bond issue whose performance was linked directly to the country's performance. In other words, the more the country grew, the more creditors stood to receive. This concept was highly attractive since it transformed bondholders into the country's "partners." This was true to such an extent that other countries later started employing this concept. But investors ended up not lending the value to this bond that it deserved, and this was precisely because of a lack of direct and frank dialogue. Had there been better lines of communication and an attitude that better justified the issue, adherence to the swap would surely have been more successful. This would especially have been true in Italy, where retail bondholders proved most reticent to accepting this proposal.

Unfortunately, my conversations with Lavagna regarding long-term financing still weren't panning out. Since we didn't have a clearly defined instrument with which to generate long-term credit, the possibility of achieving increased domestic financing was severely limited.

We didn't have a low enough inflation rate for an extended period of time to provide loans in nominal peso amounts. Additionally, the government refused to seek some type of adjustment variable, like, say, Chile's incentive units (*unidades de fomento*), so as to avoid reheating index-linked speculation.

I began to talk with the economy minister about inflation in March 2005. The aim was to determine whether it was a logical outgrowth of relative price adjustments following the sharp devaluation of the peso in 2002, especially in the service sector, or whether it marked the start of an inflationary process sparked by the fact that the economy was reaching the limit of its capacity utilization. If this was the case, we needed to implement long-term mechanisms to increase investment and output.

In summary, we ended up spending a year and three months working intensively together. Although Lavagna began showing signs after the October legislative elections that his days at the Economy Ministry were numbered, I never thought that this would happen so quickly. Be that as it may, his unease was clear. In private meetings, he constantly expressed his irritation and criticized the President. All the same, he didn't appear to take this as a determining factor in his staying on.

At the end of November, however, a concrete signal came in a conference that Lavagna gave at the Argentine Construction Chamber, when he referred to "crony capitalism" and the cartel taking shape in public works. He was clearly pointing a finger at Federal Planning Minister Julio de Vido, a close Kirchner lieutenant. He followed up this performance with a presentation at the annual IDEA Colloquium, staged in Mar del Plata on Friday, November 25, during which he heaped criticism onto government policies.

Rumors were rife that weekend, but I figured there would be several chapters to what was basically a battle of egos to see who would hold the title of "father of the recovery." It is still my belief that, in terms of his ideas and of his economic project as such, the conditions warranted Lavagna's staying on as economy minister until the end of Kirchner's term.

I recall that, on Monday, November 28, when I received confirmation of his resignation, I was in a regular meeting of Central Bank managers and assistant managers that we held weekly. It was eleven thirty in the morning. Cabinet Chief Alberto Fernández had announced a press conference. After detailing a series of other less spectacular changes in the cabinet, he announced that the President had decided to replace Lavagna with Felisa Miceli, the President of the State National Bank (Banco Nacion). I received this news on a piece of paper that the Bank's press chief, Norma Nethe, handed me.

I was surprised, and immediately called Lavagna, with whom I had a cordial conversation. The last thing he said to me as Argentina's economy minister was, "Now, we need to support Felisa."

I expressed my willingness to do just that. There are a number of considerations that I could make about what happened afterward. But no matter whether one is for or against the ministers who came after Lavagna, one fact is irrefutable: Once he was pushed out of office, there was a clear decision to gut the Economy Ministry institutionally by stripping it of every noted, well-educated staff member of sound background who worked there. This was a preview of what would happen some months later at the statistics bureau (INDEC), later still at the tax bureau (AFIP), and, finally, at the Central Bank, once I had left.

At this point, no one questioned the fact that Kirchner wanted to act as his own economy minister. The logical question was whether, perhaps, he wouldn't need technically qualified professionals to help him demonstrate the kind of good economic management his administration had achieved up to the end of 2005, since this had provided the President with very good political dividends.

We were in the midst of that transition—Miceli hadn't even had the chance to warm up her seat yet—when payment of the International Monetary Fund (IMF) debt came up at the beginning of 2006.

Four months before, in mid-August 2005, Kirchner summoned me to one of our customary monthly meetings to discuss the economic situation. When he received me, he was accompanied by Alberto Fernández, the Chief of Staff. Contrary to what would happen later with Cristina, who always trusted her memory and then later requested detailed memos of everything that had transpired in the meetings, Kirchner wrote down all of the key concepts in a spiral notebook.

Kirchner was interested in every number to do with the domestic economy and in certain comments that I made to him about the international situation, particularly, how we saw the development of the major currencies and how the Central Bank was investing its portfolio. There wasn't anything very unusual about this conversation. But then, when we were about finished, he surprised me by saying, "Start thinking about how to pay the IMF, because I have serious doubts about Roberto's reaching an agreement with them."

* * *

At the end of 2000, Argentina had received the much-heralded "shield" package. This was IMF financing for US$14 billion that included funds from the World Bank and IDB, as well as a private-sector commitment to refinance government debt. But any illusion that this salvage deal might prevent a crisis proved fleeting, to say the least. The Alliance coalition government failed to even meet the first budget commitment set for the beginning of 2001. Then came a series of chaotic shakeups in the Economy Ministry, first headed by Ricardo López Murphy with his laboratory plan (which lasted two weeks), and then by Domingo Cavallo, who managed, at first, to convince the IMF that an expanded version of his former Convertibility Plan would serve as a life buoy to keep the economy afloat and prevent devaluation and default. Based on Cavallo's charisma and on the fact that nobody in the G7 or in the IMF wanted to be the one responsible for the death of Convertibility in Argentina, they renewed cash deliveries until, in November, the IMF realized that the imminent collapse of that monetary plan, in effect since April of 1991, was inevitable.

Then came a period of political chaos and, in 2002, the country's frustrated attempts to garner renewed support and fresh credit from the IMF—which every day came up with yet another demand. The institution's clear intention was to impose a "moral punishment" on Argentina for not having met its commitments.

In January 2003, when it became clear that Duhalde's administration had become a lame duck, Lavagna managed to sign a short-term, eight-month, transition agreement, to last, at least, until the new administration could take office. Lavagna had the skills to understand that there was no way that the country would be able to obtain new loans. So he limited his request to the refinancing of Argentina's debt with multilateral institutions for a total of US$6.87 billion, with the aim of bolstering the country's meager reserves.

All the same, doubts about the feasibility of reaching an agreement lingered until the very end of negotiations. This came as no surprise, considering that, for the first time in IMF history, its staff recommended that the institution not approve refinancing of Argentina's debt.

The one IMF official that was most visibly playing the role of "bad cop" was the institution's deputy managing director, Anne Krueger. Krueger had gone as far as proposing the establishment of a "bankruptcy court" for sovereign debt, but this concept was even rejected by the U.S. government. When the "miniagreement" negotiated by Lavagna expired, new and tougher negotiations began, with the aim of reaching a more traditional accord for the refinancing of US$21 billion over a three-year period. This agreement was finally reached on September 21, 2003, at the annual general meeting of the IMF, staged in the dazzling city of Dubai, United Arab Emirates. There, too, the administration launched a tough offer to renegotiate the debt with bondholders while in a state of default, proposing a 75 percent debt reduction.

However, there proved to be cracks in the relationship. There were too many hurdles to get over in order to reach a consensus regarding economic measures of any kind, to such an extent that, from this point on, the government began to move ever further away from the IMF.

In March 2004, the situation turned complicated, and Argentina ended up technically in default with the IMF for twenty-four hours due to the fact that both parties had taken recalcitrant positions. This time, Lavagna and Prat Gay agreed to advance Central Bank revenues with which to buy reserves and thus be able to cover the respective debt due. The payment, of course, had to be made in compliance with limits imposed by the Bank's charter.

When I took part in the IMF and World Bank general meeting in October of 2004, Lavagna was focusing entirely on negotiating with bondholders. During those days spent in Washington, he and all of the members of his team kept a low profile in developing the final terms of the offer to be made, while having to report every detail of their progress to Kirchner, back in Buenos Aires. For my part, I was starting to weave a network of connections with other Central Bank presidents. At noon on the first day, just hours after my plane landed, I talked to Alan Greenspan. Following that meeting were conversations with Meirelles, Corbo, Ortíz, Caruana, Malcom Knight of the Bank of International Settlements, Jean Claude Trichet of the European Central Bank, and Mervin King of the United Kingdom.

Like most missions to the IMF, this was a brief one. We arrived on Friday and left on Sunday. When we left the Watergate Hotel—for Dulles Airport and the return trip to Buenos Aires— Lavagna took advantage of the opportunity to talk to me about our future relationship with the IMF. Except for our driver, we were alone.

"Look," he said, "we're already using reserves to make payments to the IMF but with no monetary printing, thus with no impact on inflation, we may use more in the future to pay them. This relationship isn't going well."

We exchanged views of the meetings we had each had, and he made it clear to me that there was no longer any space for another IMF program: The staff's hard-line stance came in addition to a lack of willingness on the part of Spain's Rodrigo de Rato (the institution's new managing director) to narrow the gap between their position and ours. Rato had made a very good gesture toward Argentina in 2000, when, as finance minister, under the government of José María Aznar, he got Spain to provide our country with US$1 billion in fresh funding. But he later felt hurt when Argentina declared itself in default and included that bilateral loan—the only one provided directly by a foreign government—among the payments that were stopped. Be that as it may, Rato was not nearly as much of a hard-liner as he was reported to be and had a better attitude than his predecessor, Horst Köhler. Despite this fact, a running debate developed. Kirchner constantly refuted Rato's opinions regarding the measures Argentina should be taking, with this generating successive and endless discussions.

The IMF cast doubt on Argentina's fiscal capacity. With regard to its exchange rate policy, it questioned whether or not the peso should be allowed to appreciate. But in technical discussions, Rato showed himself to be someone who was open to dialogue, contrary to the case of the intransigent IMF staff, who did much to complicate negotiations.

So it was that Argentina began, little by little, paying its debts due with the IMF and other multilateral institutions. It did so using both reserves and temporary advances from the Central Bank to the Treasury. The economy minister was determined, if an agreement could not be reached, to cancel the country's debt as the payments came due, applying a combination of dollars purchased by the Treasury and, if necessary, reserves.

When Kirchner called me in to talk about canceling the debt with the IMF completely, I got together with our internal auditor, Marcelo Griffi, who had worked on reforming the Bank's charter following the devaluation at the beginning of 2002, and started to look for alternatives. When he began to analyze a few ideas, he remembered that, despite changes that had permitted the implementation of a floating exchange rate, the Convertibility Law had never been repealed. So in September, Marcelo produced the first draft defining the concept of freely available reserves produced over and above the monetary base.

We discussed this idea at great length. And although I was not thoroughly convinced, since it made use of a concept emerging from the Convertibility System, he finally persuaded me that this was a better route to take than amending Article 20 of the Central Bank charter. This was an article that set the limits for transfers to the Treasury, which, if they were to become lax, could lead to constant pressure to expand financing provided to the government. In order to avoid this problem, Griffi drafted a memorandum stating that the reserves could only be used to pay the IMF with no printing of pesos. In other words, reserves could only be used for a onetime payment, even if the decree talked about paying all multilateral institutions. Clearly, we weren't planning on paying off the principal owed to the World Bank and Inter-American Development Bank, because the whole point was simply to get the IMF off of our back, not to cancel loans received from those other institutions.

We also added another fundamental idea: that the payment should have a neutral monetary effect. The aim, in other words, was for it not to prompt monetary printing, thus guaranteeing— contrary to the 2010 Bicentennial Fund—that it would be a payment that would not be repeated. And opinion leaders also perceived it in this way.

The other great difference was that the IMF debt was incorporated into the Central Bank's balance sheet, which was rigorously controlled by both internal and external auditors, the federal auditor and the Bank for International Settlements, headquartered in Basel, which monitors reserve quality and liquidity. In this way, the impact of Central Bank capital would also be neutral, since it would lower the Bank's assets and liabilities in the same proportion, thus leaving its solvency intact.

At any rate, although we had the draft ready to go, we didn't broach the subject again with Kirchner. Then, in October, he asked me if I had any news on the issue. I told him that I had some ideas filed, but he never mentioned it to me again.

Toward the end of the year, something unexpected happened. It was something nobody in the market predicted would take place. On Tuesday, December 13, at five in the afternoon, while I was in my office keeping track of the Latin American and New York markets, a redline showed up on the pages of Reuters and on Bloomberg. When news agencies have a hot news item, they first put out a brief teaser to get the jump on the competition, and then they later develop the story in detail.

Both screens were highlighting announcement of Brazil's payment of US$15.5 billion to the IMF that wasn't due until 2007, thus generating a savings of US$900 million in interest payments. Russia had made a similar decision in February, paying about US$3.3 billion that it owed.

Brazilian Central Bank Governor, Meirelles, explained the measure in a communiqué.

"Pre-payment of the IMF marks an historic moment for this country," he said, "and reflects a significant improvement in macroeconomic fundamentals, as an outgrowth of the government's economic policy."

The announcement drew almost immediate and highly favorable praise from Rato, who said, "This decision reflects the increasing strength of Brazil's external position and further reflects the excellent policy track record that its authorities are accumulating and that has provided a basis for confidence on the markets and for sustained improvement in the country's macroeconomic performance."

Financial agents underscored the fact that, for Brazil, this move constituted yet another step in its search for the investment grade rating that international risk agencies might award and with which a country could attract international investment. The enthusiasm was particularly explainable within the context of the tough rhetoric heard in preelectoral speeches by Brazil's president, Luiz Inácio "Lula" da Silva, in which he would shout, "Out with the IMF!" Later, however, he developed solid and consistent fiscal and monetary policies.

Rato suggested that countries like Argentina might do well to take advantage of good worldwide economic times to carry out the kind of reforms Brazil had instituted, making specific reference to "prudent fiscal and monetary policies."

From that point on, I remained at work, taking care of routine affairs, waiting for the call I expected from the President at any moment. When it finally came, all he said was, "Come." I left for Government House with the reform of Article 6 of the Convertibility Law in hand.

Kirchner explained that it was important for us to adhere to the positive effect that Brazil had generated, so that we wouldn't be questioned and in order to be on track with the good reaction of the market. If Brazil was paying everything off, we couldn't afford to do any less.

First we talked alone for a while. Then, Legal Secretary Carlos Zannini joined in. The President asked us to start working on implementing the reform.

The Central Bank's team of attorneys was already standing by, and María del Carmen Urquiza had been brought into the project. By the next night, we had the draft ready, and I immediately took it to the president, who asked if the operation was ready to be carried out. I ran a check on how each of the payments should be handled, we evaluated the risk of embargoes, and, on Thursday, we said that we were good to go.

Meanwhile, Felisa Miceli and Alberto Fernández were forced to cut short their trip to Spain, where they had gone in search of closer ties with that country, Argentina's main ally in Europe. The economy minister called me from the Madrid-Barajas Airport before their plane took off. She sounded nervous.

"I hope you're preparing everything, because Néstor (Kirchner) just told me that he's going ahead with it," she said.

"Relax," I said. "We've been working on this matter for some time now."

On Thursday, at six in the afternoon, Kirchner convened an audience of over seven hundred people in the *Salón Blanco* (White Room) at Government House. Within a climate of euphoria, and in a hall filled to the brim with government officials and businesspeople, the President announced payment to the IMF of US$9.81 billion, a little under 9 percent of Argentina's foreign debt, for a savings of US$842 million, and using nearly 36 percent of the country's reserves. According to the president, cancellation of the debt would serve to "gain degrees of freedom in domestic decision making." He said that it would also allow Argentina to avoid being obliged to heed the demands of the IMF for the refinancing of the country's debt. He also underscored the point about the "neutral monetary effect" in regard to which I had been so insistent.

In fact, the executive decree indicated that Federal Law No. 23,928 was being modified "with the aim of establishing that reserves in excess of backing for 100 percent of the monetary base may be utilized to pay off obligations with international financial institutions, as long as such operations have a neutral monetary effect."

Rato also reacted immediately, although much more cautiously than he had in the case of Brazil. His official statement expressed his satisfaction with the measure, but he stressed that "important challenges" lay ahead for Argentina.

"The government has made this decision," Rato stated, "in accordance with its rights as a regular member of the IMF, and reflects its confidence that its external situation is sufficiently strong to guarantee an advanced payment."

Héctor Torres, Argentina's delegate to that institution, managed, after several tries, to convince Rato that he should praise the announcement, so as to soften the idea of a clash between the IMF and Argentina. We then managed to put out a communiqué that was between neutral and positive in tone, while underscoring the move as a return to normality, following the successful restructuring of our debt with bondholders. The domestic side assumed a different perspective: It signified regaining economic policy independence.

It was for this reason that, in his speech, Kirchner seized the opportunity to recall that over the past two years, "we had to pay

US$6.484 billion without their lending us anything at all, while just two months before the fall of De la Rúa's government, they handed over US$3 billion."

Parallel to this, from Mexico, U.S. Treasury Secretary John Snow welcomed the announcement, calling it "a gesture of good faith" on Argentina's part. This idea would be repeated again and again in negotiations with creditors, because everyone believed that Argentina had turned its back on the world when it announced its default, whereas these payments tended to demonstrate the opposite.

The markets reacted well, but without euphoria. Contrary to what had happened with Brazil, the risk rating agencies showed no willingness to improve the grade on Argentina's sovereign debt, which remained quite high at US$124.3 billion.

Later, it was necessary to carry out intensive technical work with the Economy Ministry. This task was coordinated by Finance Secretary Alfredo McLaughlin. Meanwhile, the decree, No. 1599/05, was sent to Congress to be debated and ratified by both houses. It received final approval in the wee hours of December 22, with a Senate vote of 43 to 19 in a session that lasted less than three hours and which was marked by something new: the first DNU (the Spanish initials for Decree of Urgent Need) that Kirchner submitted to Congress for discussion. Before the year was out, the Central Bank board had ratified it and the Ministry of Economy and the Bank began the administrative process to implement it.

The transfer was made on January 3, in a true feat of financial engineering and precision, since it was necessary to make sixteen different transfers to central banks in order to avoid embargoes by investment funds that had taken the country to court over the default. Each of those banks, in turn, canceled Argentina's debt with the IMF.

In order to make sure the payment was pulled off without a hitch, I went down to operations and personally supervised each of the transfers. We held our breath throughout. You could've heard a pin drop. We were all making sure the written confirmations came back for all of the transfers, because we knew all too well the risks of a slipup. The operation took three endless hours. We started transferring the money at ten o'clock. By one in the afternoon, receipt confirmations for all of the transfers had arrived. All of us who had been involved embraced each other.

Kirchner, meanwhile, was at his own home in Río Gallegos, Santa Cruz Province, the southern tip of the country. Shortly after the operation was completed, I called the President and explained the details. In my more than five years of work, this was the only time that he expressed explicit satisfaction.

"Martín," he exclaimed, "the handling of this operation was impeccable!"

* * *

Although I'm aware that many people later questioned this measure, all it really did was comply with Rato's mandate, which was to try to recover all of the loans the IMF had made toward the end of the 1990s. I believe, at any rate, that it was in our mutual interests.

On the domestic front, Argentina's economic policy made it impossible for us to reach any kind of agreement with the IMF. Internationally, the institution had lost a great deal of its weight, since it was no longer the global lender of last resort, had few programs to offer, and was moving toward a role as an international supervisory body, with little credit or extreme control over the policies of each country. Nor was it prepared for the crisis that was brewing in the epicenter of the capitalist world, which would break in mid-2007.

* * *

While we were busy investing so much energy in the IMF, we had also embarked on our 2006 monetary program, the first integrated program that we developed following my first year at the head of the Central Bank. On December 29, I presented this program in Congress, warning that Argentina would have to live with "a temporarily higher inflation rate than might be consistent with a long-term balance" and added that it would take "a coordinated fiscal, wage, and competition policy" in order to keep this from being a self-perpetuating phenomenon. This was a message that I would repeat again and again until I stepped down four years later.

Together with the Economy Ministry, we had predicted price rises ranging from 8 percent to 11 percent for the year, following a hefty rise of 12 percent in 2005. By that time we were observing that the fiscal soundness that had been so prevalent up to 2004 was now starting to grow lax.

We therefore decided to keep a closer eye on the development of prices by modifying the quantitative guideline used to measure compliance with the plan. Instead of using the monetary base, we decided to apply another monetary aggregate that could better track means of payment—namely, M2 (cash in the hands of the public plus sight and savings deposits). The measure was well received in the professional community.

Faced with the outlook for broad economic expansion in 2006—with growth projected at 6.2 percent for the year—we defined a monetary policy to be executed as "moderately restrictive," so as to keep the growth of monetary aggregates under control and to permit gentle rises in interest rates. The aim here was to foster savings without discouraging investment or causing an influx of speculative capital. We were also under the effect of the devaluation passing through to prices—particularly in services, which had fallen behind when compared with exportable goods—combined with "imported inflation" resulting from increased prices for the raw materials that the country imported, especially oil.

So it was that we put behind us a year of far-reaching changes: There was no longer a strong economy minister in charge, and we had shrugged off the burden of the IMF. The next question was whether we would be in any condition to take advantage of this condition in order to implement an integrated and responsible economic program. The answer to that question wasn't long in coming.

Chapter 5

Inflation

Two main criticisms have been raised during my administration. One has to do with my alleged complicity in the data put out by the national statistics and census bureau, INDEC. The other one, which is an even more serious, regards my supposed indifference to the sharp rise in prices seen over the last few years.

Both of these assumptions are absolutely erroneous. It is only necessary to analyze the actions I took and my public presentations, and to recall the controversy in which other government officials—particularly Commerce Secretary Guillermo Moreno—and I engaged in order to clarify this issue. And anyone studying the monetary policy that we developed over that five-year period would surely reach the proper conclusion. In effect, I consider inflation to be one of the most serious problems Argentina has had to face since it broke from the Convertibility System.

In order to understand the situation, you have to be aware of the overall context. Countries always seek a balance between the expansion of consumption and investment levels as a means of achieving sustainable growth, without the negative impact of inflation exerted on the most unprotected segments of the population.

That's why, in 2005, Lavagna and I were extremely concerned over a two-digit rise in the consumer price index. The next year marked a turning point: The administration went from improvisation to desperation in seeking a solution to the problem.

With scant knowledge of the transformation that had taken place in the Argentine economy in recent decades, an old price agreement mechanism of the past was dusted off, timidly in the latter part of Lavagna's term as economy minister, but unabashedly later, under his successor.

While it was true that these arrangements were a way to gain time in which to look for deeper-reaching solutions, they were not an end in themselves. As explained by two economists, Roberto Frenkel and Mario Damill, in their work entitled "Macroeconomic Policies in the Recent Development of the Argentine Economy" (CEDES, 2009):

"Following minimal levels achieved in 2003, which were under an annual 4 percent, inflation in 2004, as measured by the Consumer Price Index, doubled, and it doubled again in 2005, surpassing 12 percent. In 2006, the government managed to rein in the rise by taking certain isolated measures affecting specific markets, mainly dairy and meat products. By the end of 2006, the annual CPI inflation rate had been reduced to 10 percent. But prices for nonregulated goods that weren't subject to the agreement had risen at an annual rate of 13 percent."

With public service rates frozen and price accords in effect, inflation was contained, but the dynamic of price hikes could not be halted:

"Added to private spending demand pressures and the impact of rises in international prices (which were not entirely neutralized by fuel and energy price regulation and sectorial agreements) came an expansive twist in the 2005 fiscal policy that was accentuated in 2007. Persistent inflation pressure failed to

prompt the authorities to set up an overall stabilization program."

Nevertheless, the major economic figures remained positive, with growth of 8.5 percent in 2006, in the fourth straight year of recovery, preceded by an 8.8 percent rise in 2003, 9 percent in 2004, and 9.2 percent in 2005.

Investment, which had played a major role in the times just after the devaluation, lost footing against private sector consumption, as witnessed by a reduction in capital goods imports. Key sectors, like farming and construction—of fundamental importance in job creation—grew less than in previous years. Natural resources led the ranking for sectorial growth, ahead of industry and services.

When the agreements reached by Economy Minister Miceli failed to provide the expected results because firms found ways to sidestep controls and raise prices, the government's answer was to double—or, better said, quadruple—its bets.

An official of the ilk of Guillermo Moreno, who had shown himself to be pretty complacent toward companies as Secretary of Communications, became commerce secretary in April of 2006. He quickly showed not only that his ideas were behind by four decades, but also that he was bent on meeting his own objectives without any sort of limitation or containment. Worse still, in Kirchner's eyes, Moreno was always the most efficient official in the economy team, because he never balked at anything he was told to do.

Despite the fact that INDEC, organically speaking, belonged to the Economy Ministry, Miceli and her economic policy secretary, Oscar Tangelson (and their respective successors), effectively allowed Moreno to have that agency report to him. Moreno had two goals: to make the topic of inflation disappear from the front pages of the newspapers, and to have the inflation rate be in line with the new economic "model" by diminishing the importance of the prices of goods and services consumed by the middle and upper classes.

While this was a subject that might well have been debatable, the fact was that Moreno never had any intention of discussing it to any serious extent with anybody. In fact, he never even bothered to make public the changes made in the methodology for arriving at the "new" statistics, the variations in which ended up being distorted for every product on the list that INDEC measured.

On January 31, 2007, Clyde Trabucchi was removed as national director of statistics, as was Consumer Price Index Director Graciela Bevacqua, after both refused to accept pressure from Moreno. Beatriz Paglieri was appointed to handle retail price research. The reaction in government bonds pegged to inflation—which represented 42 percent of the public debt, for a total of US$54.349 billion—was immediate, as their price tumbled and Argentina's country risk rate rose in reaction. And so, a new phenomenon reared its head in the Argentine economy: capital flight.

On February 7, Argentina's spread over Treasury bonds rose to 204 basis points, something which hadn't happened in a little over a month. From the moment of Bevacqua's removal on January 30 until February 7, the risk perception rose by 10.3 percent.

Be that as it may, Moreno's argument seemed convincing enough to Kirchner, since, with his intervention, Argentina would save "billions of dollars" by paying less to its creditors who were holding bonds adjusted for inflation. In point of fact, while for every artificial drop of one point in measured inflation the Treasury saved about US$ 334 million in debt payments, for every point that Argentina's spread rose, the cost of its debt went up by about US$360 million. The short-term benefit undoubtedly appeared every time the government had to make payment on one of these bond issues. But the pernicious effect of this, which wasn't so readily clear, was that the country was held at bay by the private debt markets.

Nevertheless, this isolation didn't prevent a rise in the cost of credit, which rose to an interest rate of 15 percent per year in placements "negotiated" with the government of Venezuelan leader Hugo Chávez. This was a similar rate to the one charged in the much-questioned "megaswap" carried out by Economy Minister Domingo Cavallo in 2001.

The first piece of data on which doubt was cast came out on February 5: According to INDEC, prices had risen by 1.1 percent in January, when a rise of 2.1 percent had been expected. Within a few hours there were reports that only a minimum rise had been calculated in prepaid medical plans—a 2 percent increase on the co-payment system, rather than the 20 percent that installments paid by users had actually risen. A sharp rise in the price of lettuce had been left out, and so too had the fact that in tourism the prices considered were those resulting from price agreements reached by the tourism secretariat with only certain hotels and transport companies.

Paradoxically, the very workers that the government claimed to be defending were the most harmed by the real rises in food costs not included in price agreements, and by the lack of a reliable standard by which to measure the true purchasing power of their wages.

July saw the removal of most of the technical staff: this time, the ones in charge of carrying out the Permanent Home Survey (known by its Spanish initials as the EPH). This indicator measured the levels of poverty, indigence, and unemployment in the country. In this case, the index was made inaccessible for two years, with the excuse that it was "being modernized." Moreno's claim that this bit of finagling was done as a means of warding off "speculators" made no sense: Clearly, the government was even willing to underestimate the country's social problems in order not to have to face the inflation phenomenon.

Miceli, meanwhile, had to resign as economy minister in the midst of a scandal over a bag full of money found in the bathroom of her office and which she was unable to explain. She was replaced by Miguel Peirano. Alberto Fernández promised Peirano that he could get INDEC back on track and that Moreno would be sidelined. But, in the end, despite his close links to certain members of Kirchner's camp, the minister decided to resign, convinced, as he was, that nothing was going to change with Cristina as President. Peirano was a man who was well focused on the country's economic problems and with whom I worked well during the annual meeting of the IMF in October of 2007. It turned out to be a mission that was mutually complementary and in which the working climate was cordial.

I knew Peirano's successor, Martín Lousteau, because he was president of the Bank of Buenos Aires Province (Banco Provincia). The relationship between the presidents of the Central Bank and of that institution was never an easy one, due to the structural problems that the provincial bank presented. Even so, we got along well at a professional level.

At age thirty-seven, Lousteau was among those who had the highest expectations surrounding Cristina's government compared with her husband's administration, holding out hopes that it would make "a quality leap on an institutional level." This was what he told me just before he took office as economy minister, over drinks in a downtown bar one evening when other people were making their way home from work.

Like the other economy ministers since 2006, Lousteau had to feign a good relationship with Moreno, in hopes that the internal balance of power might tip in his favor. On one occasion, he explained to the President that it was simply no longer admissible to distort price indices, while she looked at him in dismay, apparently with no idea what he was talking about.

The minister's error was one that only time can cure: the sin of being young. His mandate ended when he was dumped for being responsible for the controversial Resolution 125, which led to an incomprehensible clash between the administration and farmers. His silent successor, Carlos Fernández, made no attempt to change anything, and Alberto Fernández, who followed him, was to leave that post without advancing toward his goal of improving INDEC.

In the second quarter of 2008, manipulation of economic indicators extended to those reflecting domestic production, such as industrial activity figures, and national accounts, in a systematic overestimation of activity levels.

But fiscal and financial complications made it necessary for the administration to reconsider this issue. That was why, when Amado Boudou took over the Economy Ministry in July of 2009, a certain hopeful expectation emerged among analysts: While it was true that he had been charged with the task of renationalizing the pension system, as minister he promised to develop a "road map" that would include seeking to improve confidence in INDEC while normalizing the situation of that part of Argentina's debt that was still in default.

The statistics at INDEC generated two negative factors, on top of the price hikes that weren't being recorded: The earlier-mentioned country risk index—which in February had stood at 170 basis points, and was even lower than Brazil's—would triple within two years, and capital flight, which began in February, would heat up significantly by April, when people realized that the statistics that were being manipulated weren't just for certain products, but for the index as a whole. Damill and Frenkel provide a clear relationship between these phenomena:

> *"The emergence of capital flight coincides with the subprime crisis (August 2007). This phenomenon probably had an influence on capital flight, but in weighing the factors leading to capital flight, the most significant initial effects of the subprime crisis were not negative, on the contrary, they took the form of a sharp increase in commodity prices. Fluctuations in capital flows as of 2007and throughout 2008 are correlative (…) The start of capital flight is associated with the manipulation of statistics and the outflow increased during the* (government's) *conflict with the agricultural sector in the second quarter of the year, rising once again in October following announcement of the nationalization of the AFJPs* (pension fund)."

Beyond this academic analysis lies the fact that we were clearly the only ones in the public sector who expressed our differences with INDEC, by means of the public reports that the Bank put out.

Meanwhile, inside the institution, we were figuring out what to do in order not to lose our sense of direction with regard to the inflation and production data. By this time, calculation of the level of economic activity had also been manipulated. Paradoxically, along with this maneuver, payments to creditors holding bonds emerging from the 2005 debt restructuring that were linked to growth began to rise.

So it was that, among other measures, we decided to measure price variations using the Implicit Price Index (IPI) instead of the much-questioned CPI.

The fundamental difference between the two consists of the fact that, while the IPI takes all prices for goods and services produced within a given period into account, the CPI only considers those for items included in the so-called "family basket" and which are preselected for the Permanent Home Survey. Clearly, this last index theoretically provided a more appropriate measurement of wage development, but the "contamination" of it produced the opposite effect.

The media didn't catch on to our change of methodology until eighteen months after we introduced it. One example was an article by Ismael Bermúdez in the Sunday supplement of the mass circulation daily *Clarín*, on January 25, 2009, stating that "the Central Bank doesn't use the CPI anymore…"

"In its quarterly inflation reports, in which the national and international economy is reviewed, the Central Bank has introduced a new twist: in order to track the evolution of the purchasing power of wages, or the real wage level, it no longer relates or deflates workers' pay with the Consumer Price Index. Now, it compares nominal wages with the IPI, which is also developed by INDEC for GDP calculations (…) So it is that, in its latest reports, the Central Bank maintains that the rate at which real wages rise slowed during 2008, following a sustained increase in buying power in the years before. The difference between the two official indicators has become noteworthy precisely since January of 2007; while the CPI showed an increase between 2007 and 2008 of 16.3 percent, with real wages thus rising 29 percent, the IPI marked a cumulative 6.6 percent increase for the two years."

Then the daily *El Cronista* took up the issue again on January 31, 2009, with a more eye-catching headline: "Moreno and Redrado at Odds Over How to Measure Inflation."

That article reported alleged angry statements by Moreno in reference to the Central Bank. It was the tone Moreno liked to transmit: rage and shouting as a means of imposing his arguments, although those accustomed to dealing with him learned, after a few months, not to lend much importance to his off-the-wall reactions.

But beyond these discussions, the fact was that we at the Central Bank didn't have any choice but to track inflation ourselves, in order to be able to carry forth a proper monetary program. In order to comply with this objective, in our report, we also included a number of private sector measurements.

Although it was not our job to denounce distortions, in each of our reports, we underscored our differences with the controversial statistics bureau.

As president of the Central Bank, I wasn't called upon to speak often. But when I had to, I didn't miss the chance to point to the problem of statistical credibility. Nor did I fail to express my concern over inflation. I did so, in fact, in presenting our monetary program to Congress and in government, private, national, and international meetings. In effect, on September 13, 2007, at a meeting staged in London by *Euromoney* magazine, I said, "The Central Bank is deeply concerned about the current level of inflation in Argentina. There is no reason to be complacent about it. We need to have a better coordination and convergence among fiscal, wage, and monetary policies, and in competition as well, in order to be able to make progress in this issue."

It was the same message that was coming from other quarters. But I sought to give it greater emphasis, because we needed to start coordinating policies, as I had been asking the administration to do, if we were to rein in inflation, especially considering the rise in public spending in the run-up to presidential elections slated for October 2007.

At that same London meeting, I added, "The consolidated primary balance surplus reached an exceptional level of 5 percent in 2004, only to drop to a current level of 2 percent. From this point on, it will be of essential importance to increase the primary surplus, in order for growth to be sustainable...The need to preserve and increase these surpluses is a priority, since we are still going through a transition period that is typical of postcrisis stages."

* * *

The combination of scant fiscal prudence, confusion surrounding statistics, and the international crisis was seriously undermining the country's financial stability. And although we had enough reserves to elude a sharp devaluation, there was brisk capital flight, and this was to continue up to the last quarter of 2009.

In public, the administration sought to minimize my statements. But privately, Federal Planning Minister Julio de Vido called me to pass me a message: Kirchner was "upset" about this issue, bearing in mind that it was only a matter of weeks until elections. My only intention was to underscore the problem from a technical point of view and focus on solving it, not to end up in the middle electoral agenda. So I decided to moderate the effect of my words by clarifying that "all central bank presidents everywhere in the world are worried about inflation." It was a way to say the same thing, but in such a way that there could be no doubt about my intentions.

But to the powerful planning minister, I responded that we couldn't keep skirting this issue. "If you want," I said, "when I get back to Buenos Aires we can talk about what I think about the need for a change in policy in this regard."

When I got back to Buenos Aires, I met with the President. My words came out of their own accord and unchecked. "Néstor," I said, "what I said in London is my vision. Time's running out for what Moreno's doing. It might have been a bridge to something, but now it's reaching a limit."

All Kirchner managed to say was, "We're going to keep talking about this issue."

* * *

Fifteen days later, Kirchner gave me a sign. He had decided that I should have a meeting alone with Moreno in order to clear up doubts. The first thing I asked Moreno was to provide the supposed changes in the CPI methodology. Among other things, according to my analysis, whenever a product rose by over 15 percent in a month, he removed it from the sample.

My second meeting with Moreno took place at the end of November 2007, with the participation of teams from the Central Bank and from INDEC, but I was unable to be present for the entire meeting because I was tracking pressure on the dollar. Moreno brought Ana María Edwin and Beatriz Paglieri with him and talked more about politics than about methodology. Every time he was asked for substantive data, he would change the subject. I would tell them, "Bring papers to analyze," but they provided nothing in writing.

Our last personal conversation was in January of 2008. We talked about the role of interest rates in the economy. In that very particular way he has of talking, Moreno said, "Don't you realize that you're the owner of the money and that you've got to give rediscounts so that the banks can go back to lending funds at really low interest rates?"

"And don't you realize," I responded, "that the money belongs to the people, that deposits are the raw material of the financial system, and that what you have to look at is the demand for money? If I generate a greater supply, that will mean more inflation, or that people will buy dollars, not that there will be more loans."

* * *

It was obvious that we were never going to understand each other. We talked, but we were speaking two different languages. The tone during that conversation was harsh. I ended by saying, "Guillermo, you go to Kirchner with your thesis and I'll go to him with mine. That's how we'll define it: Either you take over the Central Bank or I'm going to keep on doing what I'm doing!"

The meeting that Kirchner was going to arrange so that the three of us could keep on discussing the issue never took place. The President's decision was to keep a price policy in Moreno's hands, with the rest of the branches of the fragmented economic policy, along with us, providing the necessary response to the monetary, financial, and foreign exchange policy: in other words, risk management. In effect, we had to seek to consolidate the demand for pesos and, if things got off track, make use of every instrument available to prevent imbalances.

Even Eduardo Curia, a heterodox economist with close ties to Moreno, agreed with me that the trade secretary had adopted an almost mystical attitude, believing that he had some divine mission on Earth to evangelize all of us who didn't profess his same "religion," and whenever he realized that this was going to be impossible, the conversation would end up in confrontation.

The following dialog is from an interview with the business daily *Ámbito Financiero*, published on February 18, 2010, in the midst of the controversy over the use of Central Bank reserves to pay off government debt. The interviewee is Carlos Rodríguez, PhD, from University of Chicago, a respected economist in the world academic community.

Q: As an economist, how do you feel about the autarky of the Central Bank?
A: It was so hard to achieve that, to abandon it like this, just so as to be able to divvy up the money, is really a pity. We're going back to politics as a way of making a living.
Q: Could inflation end up being a problem again in 2010?
A: With Redrado, there wasn't any inflationary pressure from the monetary side. They haven't resorted to the printing of presos yet as a means of covering the deficit. [But] there are two years left of this administration...

Despite having a substantially different take from mine on economic policy, the words of this monetarist academic appear to be more than legitimate to validate my viewpoint: the Central Bank was not responsible for the inflationary process that unfolded as of the end of Convertibility and, particularly, during my administration.

So what did we do, what could we have done, and what didn't we do?

There are numerous points that must be considered in evaluating our role in this sensitive matter, but they can all basically be boiled down to the following: the relationship between objectives and available instruments for the Central Bank's policy; the need to structure an anticrisis plan; the situation that our economy went through following the 2001–2002 default and the international context before and after the greatest world crisis in recent decades; and the overall actions taken in Argentina's economic policy.

In accordance with the autonomy provided to it by law, the Central Bank is the institution that sets the country's monetary and financial policies. Its primary mission is to preserve the value of the country's currency. In addition, it pursues the goal of safeguarding the proper functioning of the financial system.

First off, the relationship between these two goals and the instruments available in order to comply with them must be brought into focus. The exclusive monetary policy role in the struggle against inflation may be evident in highly developed economies, where the transmission channels (especially credit) are sufficiently broad as to have a direct impact on aggregate demand. In these cases, any variation in the amount of money has a swift and direct impact—via banking intermediation (savings and credit) and the capital market—on the spending decisions of companies and families alike.

In these affluent countries, interest rates play a central role in moderating fluctuations in consumption and investment, practically making the monetary policy a substitute for fiscal policy in terms of its short-term ability to have an impact on people's pocketbooks.

The same is true of a few emerging economies which have highly developed banking systems and capital markets of relatively larger size. This is the case, among our neighbors, of Brazil and Chile.

But the situation is different for Argentina, where, following the 2001–2002 crisis, the monetary policy channels are just now being reconstructed. Credit provided to businesses and families in Argentina represents only 12 percent of domestic production, compared with an average of 35 percent in the rest of Latin America and over 100 percent in highly developed countries. Furthermore, consumer credit reacts weakly to interest rate movements.

In other words, the way that the Central Bank communicates with the people, with the real economy, is through credit. But 88 percent of the economy is outside of the credit system, handling its transactions in cash, not because of any regulatory issues, but because of the recurrent history of breakups through which the country has had to suffer.

Additionally, given the structure of the assets and liabilities in the financial system, any sharp movement in the interest rate generates a negative impact on loan quality. Here, we can't permit ourselves the luxury of taking "shortcuts" or of doing anything arbitrary. Rather, we need to patiently and persistently reconstruct the power of the credit channel as a tool of monetary policy.

The case is similar for the exchange rate as a channel for the transmission of monetary policy. A managed exchange rate system provides an anchor to stability, since it attenuates excessive exchange fluctuations, providing predictability. This is, in my judgment, the only outline possible for our country at this point in time. It would be a mistake to try to adapt the exchange policy to passing trends. This approach doesn't provide free "exchange insurance" to investors (since there is no commitment to hold the exchange rate to any certain level), but it does indeed seek to prevent excessive volatility in the nominal exchange rate, taking into account the pernicious effects of high volatility on price stability.

Are we prepared in Argentina for an exchange rate that fluctuates by 30 or 40 percent in a few days, as has happened in neighboring countries?

Exchange rate swings of this kind would sap the demand for money and risk, triggering the kind of spiraling devaluation-inflation cycle that we have experienced so many times in the past. It is precisely our history of excessive macroeconomic changes that has led to the common practice among us of keeping a close eye on the development of the dollar against the peso. Argentines are always alert to what's happening with the greenback. I recall once, after a tense day for foreign exchange at the beginning of the sub-prime crisis in 2007, I decided to take a taxi home that night. I walked the few blocks to the corner of *Avenida* Corrientes and Reconquista in order to catch one. When I got into the cab, I had a typical conversation with the driver about soccer, a bit of politics, and, of course, how the economy was going. Because the dollar's value had risen by two cents that day, the driver concluded that "this is going to end up badly."

He hadn't recognized me and I didn't identify myself, but I tried to persuade him that the conditions weren't right for any sort of abrupt change in the exchange rate, due to the great quantity of reserves that the Central Bank possessed right then.

But before I could finish my explanation, the taxi driver interrupted me and said, "Sorry, but I've been through this story several times before. When things start getting screwed up, I buy dollars."

This classic statement, which appeals to common sense, seemed more realistic to me than some of the technical discussions I'd had with others in the Central Bank. Argentines— especially those over thirty-five, who have been through a few crises—think right away of dollars, without caring whether having those bills hidden away means that they are gaining or losing compared with other savings or investment alternatives.

Any kind of exchange rate movement has the power to scare the common citizen and precipitate instability, as happened on March 3, 2009, when broad-ranging worldwide repercussions of the global crisis caused the dollar to quote three cents higher, triggering the highest volumes of dollar purchases in history— even higher than in the 2001–2002 crisis.

Our neighbors never had long years of a fixed exchange rate, like the decade of exchange rigidity under Argentina's Convertibility System. Nor had they suffered a crisis of the magnitude and intensity that we did, including the simultaneous breakdown of the institutional system and a major devaluation, as well as the destruction of the financial system and a default on the national debt. It is important, then, to avoid oversimplified comparisons of the situations of different nations, since this can lead to the formulation of erroneous recommendations, like when we talk about the "inflation goals" applied by the countries in the region that garner the highest praise from the markets.

Learning to live with greater exchange fluctuations is a long-term process in which Argentina has achieved major progress in recent years. In 2009, we witnessed how the peso depreciated along with other currencies against the dollar within the framework of a managed float, but without there being any traumatic effect on macroeconomic stability, thanks to the countercyclical policies that the Central Bank had implemented.

To the extent that families and companies alike continue to shake off their fear of a more ample float, there will be a greater margin in which to operate using this tool more assiduously, whenever doing so seems advisable. In order for this to happen, in addition to stability and continuity of policy, it has been of fundamental importance that we have shown ourselves to be capable of facing all of the shocks that have come our way since mid-2007.

All of this is true for both excessive appreciation and depreciation of the local currency.

In 2005 and 2006, we received a lot of criticism over the lack of appreciation in the nominal exchange rate. The crisis that followed demonstrated that we had been right not to let the peso be revalued during that period and in having built up anticrisis insurance. Had we allowed that to happen, it would later have generated an inverse movement of the same or even greater magnitude, and the exchange rate would have risen at least fifty percent higher. In that case, we would have had to make use of too great a quantity of reserves in order to push it back down, so as to avoid reheating inflation.

Unfortunately, Argentina has had more than ample experience in the use of the exchange rate as an anti-inflation tool—particularly with the crawling peg system (little table) introduced by Economy Minister José Alfredo Martínez de Hoz in the 1970s and in the Convertibility era (1990s). The criterion that we implemented was applied analysis of the general equilibrium, so as not to have the Bank become either the cash cage where the economy minister wanted to withdraw money, as happened in the 1980s, or the kind of "autistic" organization that it became in the 1990s.

It was for this reason that, in 2005, if I had stood before Congress and presented my monetary program for the following year by saying, "We're going to move toward a program of inflation target, and I'm going to use the exchange rate and interest rates to stop this problem," all I would have achieved would have been to make the economy blow sky high. Furthermore, without macroeconomic coordination, the goal would also have been impossible to reach. It is one thing to talk economics sitting around in a consulting firm or giving classes at a university; it is another to actually be a policy maker.

Along these lines, exchange rate appreciation has often been hailed as an anti-inflationary tool, but this should be understood as a partial focus. In a broader view, particularly regarding long-term macroeconomic stability, the evaluation of this factor clearly takes a different turn—or it does, at least, in the particular case of our country.

In an economy with evident distortions—which are the product of the worst crisis in history and with predominately fiscal, financial, and external traits—the effect of foreign exchange appreciation on the sustainability of all economic variables cannot be taken lightly. The gradual deterioration of Argentina's fiscal situation in recent years has had a negative effect on the degree of freedom with which the country's monetary policy can be handled.

The same is true on the foreign front. This happened recently in many other countries (not just emerging countries like Chile and Brazil, but also, highly developed ones like Switzerland) with strict inflation guidelines and excessively restrictive monetary policies—which boasted that they didn't bother to watch the exchange rate—and it ended up generating a foreign exchange bubble that forced the authorities to intervene on the foreign currency market. Successive rounds of capital inflows did nothing more than bolster expectations of currency appreciation, stimulating excessive spending and credit, which ended up being detrimental to the economy. It is easy to see, then, that policy dilemmas are, in themselves, challenging. And they become even more complex in economies such as ours that have experienced severe and frequent disruptions.

* * *

As a self-criticism, perhaps we could have done more to explain and convince people of our policy, even people within the administration, because the anti-inflation policy required a joint, coordinated, and convergent effort on the part of all branches of the economic policy: fiscal, wage, competition, and income policy makers, along with our own effort.

On August 27, 2008, I attended a seminar organized annually by the Council of the Americas in Buenos Aires. There, I said,

"Only through the joint and coordinated efforts of fiscal, wage, income, and competitive policies, in harmony with what we are doing in terms of monetary and financial policy, can macroeconomic sustainability and a necessary reduction in the inflation rate be guaranteed." Clearly, for an answer to the problem of rising prices, one has to look beyond the Central Bank.

* * *

Finally, it would be imprudent to judge our policies if they are not evaluated under the timing of our economic history. The experiences of neighboring countries teach us that flexibility and gradualism, in both the design and implementation of policies, is the appropriate path to take.

At the monetary and banking meetings held in 2007, Chile's former Central Bank president, Vittorio Corbo, highlighted the sequential process that the economy of his country had gone through in the 1980s. On that long road, a fundamental factor was the consolidation of fiscal solvency as an anticyclical tool, the reestablishment of sustainability in the external sector, the restructuring of liabilities, and the shoring up of the financial system. Once all of these issues have been solved, advances were made in consolidating the monetary program, which today enjoys a high level of credibility. This was how Chile managed, over a fifteen-year period, to transform an annual inflation rate of around 30 percent into the low levels that it is now recording (3.7 percent in 2005, 2.6 percent in 2006, 7.8 percent in 2007, 7.1 percent in 2008, and deflation of 1.4 percent in 2009), after following a patient road to the building of trust and institutions.

This transition was characterized by a flexible program that made use of instruments including foreign exchange intervention—at first through the Central Bank and later through operations between state-owned companies and the Treasury, thus allowing that country to meet the challenges of both domestic and foreign shocks.

On the domestic front in Argentina, I am convinced that price developments between 2005 and 2009 were caused by multiple factors that were beyond the control of the Central Bank. In addition to the context of a transition economy we experienced pending adjustments in relative prices as a result of the devaluation. Up to then, the adjustment had been practically nil within the first three years following the end of Convertibility for services such as education, health, and transport. But in 2005, these were refloated with a vengeance. Hence, the foolish attempt to underestimate these hikes in indices, together with the erroneous government policy move to subsidize public service rates, which, instead of helping low-income users, focused on the interests of companies. It was a policy move that was not sufficiently sophisticated as to distinguish among the different social sectors, so as to target, for instance, which ones could pay a higher price for a bus ticket.

A similar phenomenon occurred with nearly frozen rates for natural gas, electric power, and water in the metropolitan area, since in most of the provinces, the prices for these services rose significantly, generating a major distortion in favor of the most well-to-do sectors of the population.

As mentioned earlier, there was also an "imported" inflation factor, resulting from the high price of raw materials. This was particularly true for agricultural inputs, which had a strong impact on rises recorded in nationwide food prices, one of the key factors in the Consumer Price Index.

Monetary policy played its role within this context: Strict control over means of payment each year and their gradual reduction facilitated compliance with the monetary program and the disappearance of spurious monetary printing. Or it did, at least, prior to the creation of the Bicentennial Fund for Debt Reduction and Stability, which provided for intensive utilization of Central Bank reserves to pay off debt, and thus also for the issuing of pesos to cover the fiscal deficit, making use of Central Bank financing.

Slowly but surely, interest rates adjusted to the amount of money in circulation, albeit without falling to extremes. Many highly recognized analysts advised following the same road as Brazil, which had made use of the exchange rate as an anti-inflationary tool. But that suggestion failed to take into account the depth of that South American giant's capital market.

The criterion we employed, *a priori*, in managing interest rates was to keep them higher than the "expected" depreciation of the peso, which represented the main basis on which people saved. In 2009, for example, the devaluation rate was 9.9 percent, while interest rates ran higher than 10 percent throughout most of the year.

This said, if the percentage of savings in dollars hadn't declined in recent years, it was also because the recollection of previous crises was still fresh in people's minds, and the INDEC scandal continued to undermine the credibility.

At any event, when I took over at the Central Bank, our policy rate was at 2.5 percent. We were coming out of an expansive period and we decided to take a gradual path. Moreover, we were seeking to achieve a more correlative ratio between the Central Bank interest rate and the rates paid on certificates of deposit. But since we were just getting started restructuring the system, there was no correlative comparison between them.

I have serious doubts about any analysis that suggests that had we increased interest rates, people would have quit consuming and inflation would have been lower. Since there was a high level of consumption that had been repressed by the 1998–2002 recession, the effect of this tool in stemming price hikes would have only been marginal at best.

While our policy, in monetary terms, was becoming more sophisticated, fiscal and wage policies were pushing aggregate demand within a period of major economic growth, instead of spearheading the anti-inflation effort.

In the last three years, the fiscal surplus had dropped below the level that it should have, considering total output. This is true to such an extent that by 2009, we had reached an operational deficit of 2.5 percent of the GDP.

Meanwhile, nominal wages doubled during this period. Within this context, implementing a more restrictive monetary policy would only have generated sharp inconsistencies, prompting yet another inevitable crisis in the historical cycle of crises that our country had been forced to live through.

In order to confirm our analysis, a team of researchers at the Central Bank carried out a technical exercise and came to the conclusion that with the same monetary and exchange rate policy that we had developed, but with a consolidated fiscal surplus of about 5 percent—as had been recorded in 2003–2004—along with wage growth of 10 percent per year, the annual inflation rate would have been held to a single digit. There would thus have been no need to have resorted to Moreno, either for his largely ineffective price accords or for his intervention at INDEC.

Chapter 6

The Pressure to Devalue

I came very close to presenting my resignation on October 31, 2008.

Three days before, the government had announced the elimination of the private retirement system, arguing that, in the face of the international crisis, there was no guarantee that future pensioners would ever be able to collect on private pension payments.

According to the administration, the system run by private pension management firms, known as AFJPs, had shown itself to be less than efficient. I agreed with this point of view, but thought that the way to correct the situation was to improve the supervision of the AFJPs. Furthermore, just the year before, citizens had been given the option of returning to the social security, and only 11.5 percent of the people had done so.

Because of that government decision, the Central Bank ended up losing US$3.5 billion in reserves. We were locked in an arm-wrestling match with the market just when Cristina Kirchner decided to announce the creation of the so-called Argentine Integrated Pension System. She did so with almost the same glee that the country's default was announced on December 20, 2001. Sitting beside her when she made the news public was the man who was willing to make all of the Kirchners' dreams come true: Amado Boudou.

The Friday before, I had been called to the presidential residence in the northern suburb of Olivos. I went in through the

Calle Villate entrance. A few meters inside the green gate, there is a security checkpoint where there are always several men standing guard. As usual, they asked me to park on the right. A policeman stooped down and used a mirror to check the underside of my car. The security check was very thorough. The inspection with the mirror had a sole purpose: To make sure there were no explosives under the car. Afterward, he signaled me to advance.

The street inside crosses the ample grounds of the residence and leads to a large house with a red tile roof and white walls that is known as the Headquarters Building. President Cristina Kirchner, like her predecessors, used it for work meetings, since it has several offices and a conference hall. Far off to the left, one can see the outline of the white, two-story presidential residence. The entry hall, which is entered through a door made of iron and glass, has a marble floor and two double doors, to the left and to the right. Through the right-hand doors lies a small living room containing three love-seat sofas and Néstor Kirchner's relatively austere study. To the left is Cristina's office, built on two levels: a small living room with armchairs in white leather and a step up to her very modern office, contrasting with a large library in burnished wood that covers an entire wall.

Across that office is the entrance to the cabinet room, which, contrary to the presidents that preceded them, the Kirchners never used.

As soon as I walked into the entry hall, Néstor Kirchner, who was wearing sports clothes, opened the door. I could feel the tension in his gestures.

"Come in," he said, "the President wants to see you." His tone was dry and short.

When I went in, I was surprised to see the numerous files cluttering the desk in front of Cristina. The second surprise was

the nature of those files: file upon file from the Internal Revenue Service (known as the AFIP), all to do with the purchase and sale of dollars for that week. This gave me the first clue.

Just then I recalled the words of Néstor Kirchner before he handed over the presidency to his wife. He was trying to put my mind at ease, since I had never had any dealings with her, having seen her only fleetingly at official functions.

"You're going to get along well with Cristina," he had said. "She's a lot more studious than I am."

* * *

In point of fact, I'm not so sure the word is "studious." No doubt, she's a lot more avid reader than Néstor, who catches on to things quickly in conversations and then asks for no more than a couple of pages explaining the topic.

As President, his wife, on the other hand, demanded greater quantities of written information. Memos of fifty pages don't scare her in the least.

When I was studying for my master's degree at Harvard (1984–86) one of my courses focused on leadership. There I found specific reference to the administrations of the different presidents of the United States. I recalled one passage that pointed out that Jimmy Carter was a very talented engineer who had a passion for detail, but that he was not terribly effective as President because he failed to take "the big picture" into account. They compared Carter, of course, to his successor, Ronald Reagan, who was of much lower IQ, but who could handle four ideas at a time and then turn them over to his staff so that they could work on them.

From that time on, I've mulled over the idea of which kind of president is the most effective. I still don't have an answer, but I tend to imagine that it would be someone with a broad vision,

but who was capable, at the same time, of also seeing the smallest details.

Cristina realized that I was distracted and surprised me with a blunt question. "Martín," she asked, "does the Central Bank have money deposited in Citibank? Because I saw some accounts in the data the AFIP brought me."

"Cristina," I responded dryly, "the Central Bank doesn't deposit money in any private bank, since all deposits are made in the Bank itself and in other central banks abroad."

That day, the conspiracy theory about big financial interests being out to halt the nationalization of the pension funds was present in all of its glory. The Kirchners began to pore obsessively over any kind of data that came under their noses, in many cases without any strict expertise. And Cristina had clearly gotten mired down in the details.

The truth was that, prompted by the AFIP, the President had become confused over an operation in which Citibank handed over securities to the Central Bank and we provided them with liquidity in return, in what was essentially a common repo (repurchase agreement) operation. The error was clearly the product of the climate that was pervading the residence in Olivos. Later, when I talked this over with AFIP Director Claudio Moroni, he didn't hesitate to respond, "They're overwhelmed right now."

* * *

The Kirchners were angry with me, it seems, because I had sold US$525 million in reserves. The fact was that the entire market was making a run on the peso, and we rolled out the big guns to defend it.

Two days before, we had come on strong when the run peaked. I decided to go down to the Bank's trading desk myself

as soon as the currency trading round began. On the most hectic days, I personally monitored all movements.

The rate market desk is a transparent stall that looks sort of like a huge fish tank, where operators are located in two thirty-foot-long rows of desks. In one row are spot and futures market operators. In the other are traders dealing in Central Bank and government securities. It's a really stressful environment. It order to lower their stress level, the people that work in there tend to keep a running dialogue going. They joke around constantly, despite the huge volume of transactions that they are handling on a daily basis. The technical team is a really sound one, headed up by Juan Basco.

All Central Bank operations carried out on both the foreign exchange and bond markets are handled using "blind" computer screens. That is to say, the seller is invisible to the buyer and vice versa.

Each trader has two columns on the screen: The left column is for potential dollar buyers and the right column is for sellers. The transactions are electronic and are registered on the open electronic market (known by the initials MAE—*Mercado Abierto Electrónico*), so as to prevent any sort of maneuver. No less important is the fact that these traders are the only ones authorized to handle these transactions.

Frequently, when the trading round starts at ten in the morning, an institution will offer to buy a certain amount at certain prices—say, ARS (pesos) 3.86 per dollar—and later, lower values will appear—perhaps ARS 3.859. Half an hour after the start of operations, one can tell what the demand trend will be for the day.

On the supply side, for example, there may appear an operation for, say, a volume of around a million dollars at an exchange rate of ARS 3.861 per dollar. Faced with these two columns, the first thing one does is make sure that supply and demand are balanced. But in the days following the President's controversial announcement, it was all about demand. On Wednesday, October 22, at quarter past ten in the morning, when operations had just begun, we already had an order for US$70 million, while the other column was blank.

When these imbalances occurred, traders would start filling the other side of the screen with our own quotes. The great advantage here is that the market has no way of knowing that the quotes are coming from the Central Bank, since they can be seen by only those who click on the MAE's screens.

The first attempt we made was to quote a bid of US$5 million, in order to see if the two columns started to balance out. But that didn't happen. Then, one of the leaders on the exchange table boldly asked, "Shall we show the market that we're up for anything?"

My answer was conclusive: "Put a quote of a billion dollars on the offer side of the screen."

Up until then, there was demand totaling US$150 million, and all there was in the other column was a bid from the Bank of US$20 million. The dollar stood at ARS 3.43, up 7 centavos from the previous day's close.

At that precise instant, the market came to a standstill. Traders began desperately calling the MAE at its building located at *Calle San Martín 344*, a block from the Central Bank to ask if the amount was a mistake, because it had too many zeros to fit on the screen!

Juan Basco didn't hesitate to answer, "There's no mistake. It's a billion dollars and they're available."

From that moment on, the speculative surge eased, and the dollar closed at a value of ARS 3.39, only a few centavos higher than the quotation for the day before, with the Central Bank's having sold US$200 million in reserves.

We kept a close eye on the market until Friday, the day the major test of strength came. As soon as the market opened in the morning, we put US$500 million up on the screen. But the great difference from the previous Wednesday was that the market absorbed all of that amount and a bit more…a major sum of money totaling US$525 million.

As soon as the foreign exchange round was over, the phones started ringing. The calls were from the Presidential Residence in Olivos to connect me with Cristina.

In a number of conversations over the course of that entire month, the Kirchners questioned me on the foreign exchange policy. They didn't agree with the sale of reserves as a means of lowering people's level of distrust. Without a doubt, they were thinking about a higher value for the dollar.

One of the officials who brought the most pressure to bear in this sense—both in public and in private—was the then-president of the National Bank (*Banco Nación*), Mercedes Marcó del Pont, who was to end up being my successor. This economist, who acted more like a congresswoman than a major official of the Executive Branch, had struck an alliance with the "intellectual father" of Argentina's heterodox economists, government official Aldo Ferrer, to convince the Kirchners not to intervene any longer in the market by selling Central Bank reserves, letting the exchange rate seek a new level.

Every time the hypothesis was presented to me, I responded that because of the high level of dollarization of savings among both large and small investors, any decision not to intervene would lead to a mass run against the peso.

I also warned that if the foreign exchange market were permitted to run wild, it would end up destabilizing the government. Instead of placing a billion dollars on the table, we would have to bet US$5 billion in a single day—a sum that was entirely too major to risk if the tension over the elimination of the AFJPs were to drag on for too long.

I believed that I had convinced the Kirchners of my argument. That's why I stood my ground so firmly that black Friday. But clearly, although they had tolerated my exchange rate strategy, they didn't like it. Face-to-face with the president, I once again explained to her the need to provide the exchange rate with upward and downward movement, in order to keep the markets from thinking that there was easy money to be made from it, as had happened in programs with semifixed exchange rates—like Martínez de Hoz's "little table" or Cavallo's Convertibility. However, such movements had to be limited, so that people wouldn't panic.

It is important to get two things straight: First, the Kirchners never came to me and said, "We want the exchange rate at such-and-such a level." Nor would I have permitted them to have that kind of conversation. Second, they never talked to me about the dollar while the market was still operating. All of their calls came after three in the afternoon, when the exchange market had already closed for the day.

What they questioned most was our strategy with regard to futures contracts on the dollar market. To mention just one example, let's say that the Central Bank sells at an exchange rate of ARS 3.90 to the dollar for three months from now. If, when that futures contract comes due, the value of the dollar is ARS 3.94, you have to pay a 4-centavo difference to whomever that contract was made with.

But that payment is made in pesos, despite which, many economists—some of whom had the President's ear—started suggesting that there was a need to calculate and discount the exposure represented by these futures contracts from the Central

Bank's reserves, as if the Bank had liabilities in dollars. And this concern redoubled in the second half of 2008, because of the fact that there were a lot of people holding futures contracts of up to a year's duration.

Perhaps the confusion here stemmed from the Asian crisis of 1997, when the Central Bank of Thailand, in particular, had accumulated a significant number of futures contracts, but in dollars, so that, contrary to our case, at the end of each month the Thai institution had to hand over considerable sums in U.S. dollars. The other advantage that we had was that a major portion of the futures contracts were in the hands of financial institutions and could easily be renewed when they came due, so as not to bring pressure to bear on the foreign exchange market.

We always operated on a sequential basis: first, on the futures market and later, if necessary, selling reserves on the spot. This allowed us to bolster confidence and save dollars, thus providing a sound base to our managed floating policy. This is something that appears to have extended beyond my administration and remained standing as a professional way to manage the exchange rate.

Be that as it may, on that black Friday the President insisted once more, "Martín, we've got to change the market intervention policy."

"If we don't sell," I said, "the exchange rate will run wild."

"Then let it," she said, seeing my bet and raising it.

My response to this was clear and categorical. "If you want to do that," I said, "you can do it with a different Central Bank president."

At this point, I wasn't going to let anything stop me. I simply wasn't in agreement with the measures they were taking.

The fact was that I'd had several talks with pension fund managers in which I suggested that they should take a more proactive attitude toward the productive sector, since they were focusing too much on using the funds on a short term basis. And I warned them that their purchase and sale strategy for government bonds appeared less than transparent. But from there to suggesting that pension management should be renationalized, the gap, to my mind, was abysmal.

That was why I pointed out to the President, "If you can simply sign an order and wipe out a retirement system that was created by law, then people are apt to believe, and rightly so, that just about anything can happen with their savings."

And I warned, too, of other fears that were afoot: fears of devaluation and default, which made it important that we ease people's fears regarding these sensitive issues. But the President tried to persuade me that these fears weren't valid.

"Martín, all our lives, we Kirchners have been very responsible in managing money," she said. "That's been our history in Santa Cruz Province. So, I don't know what doubts anybody can have."

"The doubts exist," I responded, "so it's best if we can dispel them."

On the first issue, devaluation, the President told me that we would continue talking about it the following week. Her answer about doubts regarding possible nonpayment of government debts, on the other hand, surprised me.

"I'll sell the residence of Olivos before I default!" she exclaimed.

* * *

After having that conversation with the President, I spoke to my fellow central banker in Spain, Manuel Fernández Ordóñez, and to other European colleagues, even though I wasn't particularly at ease myself. "This ends here," I told them. "It doesn't continue with the re-nationalization of banks, as some of them feared."

While at first the President's words of conviction about not defaulting had comforted me, later on I was invaded by a disquieting feeling: Might the Kirchners be capable of going to any lengths to pay the debt?

The Kirchners only grudgingly accepted my position. Rumors of my resignation were rife throughout the entire last week of October. Then the rumors dissipated, but my own unease, which had begun a little over a year before, only grew.

* * *

In the United States, the real estate bubble burst in 2006, although the American financial system didn't feel its full effects until September of 2007, in the form of a major domestic liquidity crisis, which later expanded to international scale. This was immediately considered to be the worst economic crisis since the Great Depression, which had been triggered by the New York Stock Market crash of 1929—a crisis that had enormous economic and political consequences.

In 2007, a considerable crisis was generated by an increase in raw material prices, followed by the slowdown in purchases of emerging country bond issues, and two major slumps in world stock markets (one in January and another one in October of 2008).

Contributing to that financial earthquake were also higher oil prices, inflation, and the stagnation of credit. The first instance of panic came in March 2008 with the precipitous fall of the Bear Stearns investment bank, which, without having shown many signs of weakness, had been liquidated on the open market within a matter of days. Following this, in an unprecedented move, the Federal Reserve jumped in and set up a rescue, which ended in the acquisition of the institution at a "bargain basement sale price" by J.P.Morgan Chase.

In order to try to counter the fear that this caused, the Fed and the European Central Bank tried to reinforce the markets with an abundant supply of liquidity, injecting cash into banks and cutting interest rates.

But distrust reigned, due to the fragility demonstrated by the most important banks in the U.S. and European financial systems. The money stopped flowing, and the population in the world's highly developed countries, beleaguered by the bursting of the speculative bubble and incipient recession, quit spending their money.

In addition to the lack of public confidence, there was an even bigger problem: Banks quit lending money to each other for fear of not being able to recover these loans, and the interbank interest rate soared to unthinkable levels.

All of these negative situations—layoffs, bank closures, and fears surrounding mass bankruptcies ended up feeding on each other.

The U.S. dollar suffered a process of sharp depreciation against other hard currencies like the euro and the yen, and the competitive edge that a cheap dollar might have provided in international trade was entirely wiped out by the terms of trade that soaring oil prices dictated.

Millions of U.S. families lost their homes, and it became seriously difficult for major firms such as General Motors, Ford, Chrysler, and several airlines to keep their operations functioning. Consumer confidence indices—a key indicator in the U.S. economy—dropped to their lowest levels since the 1950s.

The desperation expanded in Europe when the Northern Rock Bank in the United Kingdom asked the government for an emergency loan in order to remain standing. This produced a run on the pound and the withdrawal of £2 billion in deposits. Prime Minister Gordon Brown's administration decided to nationalize the institution, and other European nations, like Ireland, had to adopt similar measures.

There was a brief respite during the northern spring until negative real economy figures and financials in the United States forced major stock markets worldwide to post double-digit declines. Featured among a number of events triggering these reactions was the crash of the IndyMac Bank, the second-largest bankruptcy of a financial institution in the history of that country, which came to reinforce fears that other regional banks might end up in the same spot.

The looming danger redoubled when the country's two largest mortgage institutions, Freddie Mac and Fannie Mae, which between them represented half of the mortgage market, started suffering a speculative assault on their shares as a result of the real estate market freefall. At the beginning of July, the U.S. Treasury and the Federal Reserve were forced to announce a bailout.

At the time, a major debate emerged. Should banks be bailed out, serving to confirm the idea that the government would prop them up so that they wouldn't fail? Just as had occurred during the crisis of 2001–2002 in Argentina, seven years later the world debate regarding a banking salvage operation went from one extreme to another. On the one hand, the predominant view was that good money shouldn't be thrown after bad by using taxpayers' hard-earned contributions. But, on the other, there were fears that if a major institution were allowed to crash, there was a risk of its pulling the economy as a whole down with it.

In September 2008, the 158-year-old Lehman Brothers investment bank declared itself bankrupt and officially petitioned for credit protection, following a failed attempt by Bank of America and Barclays to acquire it. Meanwhile, Bank of America acquired Merrill Lynch for half of the latter's real value. U.S. presidential candidates Barack Obama and John McCain, as well as the press, started talking about a "financial panic," an "economic crisis," and even a "collapse."

George W. Bush's administration let Lehman fail, in a sort of "moral punishment" action, and caused an unthinkable implosion in market confidence. Wall Street's leading indicator, the Dow Jones Industrials Index, posted its worst loss since the 9/11 attacks of September 2001, losing 4.42 percent.

The debate was immediately fired up again. Had things gone too far? While the different sides of the issue were trying to reach some semblance of an agreement, AIG (American International Group) quickly hit the skids, effectively increasing the losses of all investors, from Norwegian pension funds to the Reserve Primary Fund, a U.S. money market fund, which was supposedly as safe as cash money. In just a few days, the chaos also dragged down other Wall Street mainstays like Goldman Sachs and Morgan Stanley. But before these could fail, the much-questioned Treasury Secretary Henry Paulson and Fed Chairman Ben Bernanke agreed with President Bush on a US$700 billion bailout to keep the financial system from collapsing at a systemic level, in the greatest state intervention since the crisis of the 1930s.

The great difference between this crisis and that one—which gave birth to the New Deal but also led to World War II—was that, this time, it was not just the United States that acted swiftly and with all of the heavy artillery at its disposal, but all of the other major world economies as well, which made coordinated decisions ranging from contributing funds to shore up failing institutions to a joint reduction in interest rates, in order to avoid a deep, worldwide recession capable of sparking another conflict of unforeseen consequences.

This was also the first time in decades that Latin American countries, instead of being the focal point for the crisis contagion that spread to other regions, ended up being the victims of the burst "bubble" that resulted from the irresponsible behavior of developed economies. Officials of the world's wealthiest countries that contributed to the crisis pointed out, of course, that when the money was flowing everywhere in the world before the crisis broke, nobody was complaining about the "excesses of capitalism."

But the truth is that Latin America had learned a great deal from its own problems and demonstrated macroeconomic soundness combined with an anticyclical reserve-accumulation policy that permitted it to deal with the reduction in the portfolio flows, tension over raw materials prices, and the decline in international trade.

The blow was also absorbed by the phenomenon of robust growth in the economies of China and India, neither of which, in the past, had counted as players with serious weight.

Due to this improvement in their relative position, shared with other emerging economies, the Latin American countries began to garner greater respect when they raised their voices in international forums. This was true, furthermore, because we had greater experience in handling major crises than officials from the highly developed countries did.

Thanks to this constellation of factors and to the measures we adopted, we were able to take advantage of opportunities provided in the world's main venues for debate and decision making to show that, even in a country that was so little appreciated in the rest of the world, our Central Bank had been up to the challenge of facing no less than four brutal crises in less than two years with a sufficient level of success as to keep Argentina from once more falling into ruin.

* * *

The so-called "central bankers club" doesn't exist as such, but that's what it's called by the economists who gain access to this post, which, in some countries, ranks higher than that of finance or economy minister. It is a fairly closed clan, although, thanks to my former experience in the private sector and in trade negotiation, I was able to strike up several personal relationships.

It was in this way that I met Dominique Strauss-Khan of France and Robert Zoellick of the United States, who later ended up as the respective heads of the IMF and the World Bank.

Pascal Lamy also presented me to one of the most influential personalities in that group: namely, his compatriot, Jean Claude Trichet, former president of the Paris Club, executive of several French banks and second president of the European Central Bank following Germany's Wim Duisenberg. Mario Draghi, Italy's Central Bank president as of 2006, I met when he was executive vice president of the Goldman Sachs bank, following his role as the architect of the privatization of some of his country's major firms in the 1990s.

I made contact with the guiding light of central banks, the U.S. Federal Reserve, through the man who knew more than anyone else in that organization about emerging countries: Terrence Checki, executive vice president of the New York Fed, the most important of twelve branches of the Federal Reserve System.

Checki had joined the Fed in 1983, and had gone through every technical rank until he reached the highest line position in the institution. Throughout all of those years, he had kept a close eye on Argentina's evolution and on several occasions took part in its debt negotiations and in the development of closer economic ties between the two countries.

It was Checki who introduced me to Timothy Geithner, his boss, who had previously been undersecretary of the Treasury during the Clinton administration and head of the IMF's Department of Development and Policy Review. With the arrival in office of Barack Obama, Geithner, a graduate of the prestigious School of International Studies at Johns Hopkins University, was appointed Secretary of the Treasury at the height of the economic crisis. Checki was also the one who suggested a working session between the Argentine Central Bank and New York Fed officials as soon as I took up the Bank's presidency.

From that moment on, the question I always asked myself was what I could bring to the table in such a special group of officials, particularly coming from such a peripheral country and one with such a bad reputation following its default at the end of 2001.

I arrived at the understanding that we in the emerging countries were in the midst of a paradigmatic change. So I devoted myself, along with my team, to researching and publishing studies regarding the main traits of this transformation, which reflected a new pattern of growth, as of China's consolidation as a new customer for our raw materials. In this task, I enjoyed the collaboration of an economist who had developed his entire professional career within the halls of the Central Bank. It was this young economist, Martín Castellano, who pleasantly surprised me with his rigorous professionalism and vast intellectual capacity. After an internal competition I appointed him chief of staff of the Central Bank.

The venue that turned out to be the best one in which to present these viewpoints was the Bank of International Settlement (BIS) in Basel—an institution that had been operating since 1930.

Traditionally, the central bank club meetings were kicked off by the Fed chairman: first, Alan Greenspan, and later, Ben Bernanke. Then would come Trichet, sometimes with the comments of Germany´s Weber and France´s Noyer, followed by the Japanese Central Bank president (Toshihiko Fukui until 2008 and then Maasaki Shirakawa), and China's Zhou Xiaochuan, with the rest of the time being divided up among officials from the emerging nations.

I always asked for the floor at meetings to address issues of importance to developing countries. In some cases, I made reference to macroeconomic changes and policies affecting fiscal and monetary equilibrium, and the ties that the Asian and Latin American countries were developing with the rest of the world.

I also focused on the performance of emerging market bonds in both public and private debt issues. Along these lines, one of the contributions I made was to demonstrate the correlation between emerging market bond yields and high-risk debt issue yields on the U.S. market until recent years, when the perception with regard to our countries began to improve to such an extent that we managed to pay a lower interest rate than that for the most speculative of American bonds.

In March 2006, I was the first to refer to the link between the prices for raw materials and inflation. What I sought to do, in particular, was to underscore the fact that, while it was common practice to discuss raw materials in general terms, it was important to mark the difference between the development of prices for "heavy" (industrial) and "light" (agricultural) raw materials, since, in recent years, industrial prices had tripled compared with those for agricultural raw materials.

Trichet always generously gave me credit for having been the first to raise the issue of the impact that structural changes in the world raw materials market could have.

Also functioning in Basel is the Financial Stability Forum, which, as of 2009, G-20 decision makers decided to call the Financial Stability Board. In 2009, both the Bis and this board placed great emphasis on ways to reduce the high risk level posed by the currency mismatch (borrow in foreign currency while perceiving earnings in pesos of Eastern European banks, on the basis of how we had managed to eliminate this phenomenon in recent years in Latin America.

By having researched deeply into these issues, I ended up being a guest at a number of international forums (in Malaysia, Indonesia, China, Italy, France, and Britain, among others) as an expert on emerging markets. If I had limited myself to talking about Argentina, it would have been impossible to generate peer relationships with the rest of the central bankers. And this kind of interaction definitely brought benefits to our country, like the swap agreement we signed with other central banks like China and Brazil in the midst of the worldwide financial crisis.

* * *

January 26, 2009, marked the fiftieth anniversary of Bank Negara Malaysia, as the Central Bank of Malaysia is known.

As of the 1997 Asian crisis, this bank had adopted several measures regarding exchange rate market intervention, which we adopted in Argentina as of the 2002 crisis. The year before, its president, Zeti Akhtar Aziz, an economist with a doctorate from the University of Pennsylvania, had attended the monetary and banking seminar that we organized annually in Buenos Aires and that had become an interesting reference point for international officials, former officials, academicians, and private analysts.

When I traveled to Kuala Lumpur at the beginning of 2009, the global situation remained critical. I recall that my Australian counterpart, Glenn Stevens, was blunt in his assessment, saying,

"In the last quarter of 2008, there was a waterfall effect on all of us." That image of abundant water pouring over every country, not as a blessing, but in the form of a terrible flood, was highly effective in describing what we were all suffering. In Japan, the world's second-most important economy, the gross domestic product had dropped by 12 percent between October and December of 2008.

We were all very concerned. At lunch, I was seated next to China's Zhou. He had a very high opinion of our work, and also because we firmly supported China's admission as a shareholder to the Inter-American Development Bank (IDB), a goal that, as of the beginning of 2010, had still not been achieved.

During lunch, I once again explained how Argentina and China were complementary, not competitive, economies and should become closer on a practical level. Zhou, for his part, stressed that he was very much focused on signing financial agreements with other Asian countries. Indeed, as of December 2008, such swaps had been signed for a total of US$95 billion with South Korea, Malaysia, Indonesia, Hong Kong, and, in an extension of China's geopolitical strategy, the Republic of Belarus.

Curiously enough—since Chinese officials usually speak in their own language, making use of interpreters in such conversations—we both communicated with each other in English.

I took advantage of this sign of trust to explore the possibility of also signing an agreement for a currency exchange swap between our two countries. This would allow us to bolster our foreign support in the midst of the cataclysmic world financial situation.

I was especially interested to do this since the U.S. Federal Reserve had signed similar agreements to assist the central banks of Australia, Brazil, Canada, Denmark, Britain, the European Union, South Korea, New Zealand, Norway, Singapore, Switzerland, and Japan.

Since we had been left out of this list, we needed to find an alternative, since our default and manipulation of government statistics had barred us from the capital market.

Faced with this situation, I said, "Why not Argentina?"

With a smile on his lips but without abandoning his parsimony, he said, "Let's explore it."

* * *

No sooner had I returned from the exhausting trip to Southeast Asia than I got together with the members of my team and started working on a draft proposal for an accord. They, of course, suggested that perhaps the agreement could be extended to include not only financial backing, but also trade. But I had my doubts about this. Allowing China, which exported its products to the rest of the world at really low prices, into the Argentine market with additional advantages might well prove detrimental to the export trade recovery that Argentina had been recording since pulling out of the 2001–2002 crisis.

I explained to them that the agreement should be a show of trust between the two central banks, a line of contingent liquidity—or, in other words, money available to us but not necessarily for effective use.

Within a climate of great secrecy, we signed several drafts and, at the beginning of March 2009, several members of my team— Pedro Rabasa, Juan Basco, and María del Carmen Urquiza—traveled to China to draft the final agreement. In the middle of that month, the economy ministers and central bank presidents of the G-20 countries met in the small city of Horsham, located some thirty miles from London and first mentioned in the tenth century as an important southern market.

Those of us participating in the meeting agreed that some more convincing action had to be taken in order to restore world growth and the growth of credit. We also agreed that reform measures for the global financial system had to be reinforced. At that meeting, Zhou and I finished hammering out an agreement on the terms for the financial swap, by which each central bank would open an account in the other, renewable every six months for a period of three years. The idea was that either central bank could request up to US$10.2 billion (66 billion yuan or 36 billion pesos) in the domestic currency of the other country if we were to lose reserves as a consequence of pressures resulting from international or local crises.

When I returned on March 16 from that meeting, I explained the deal to the President. As usual, she asked me for a memo. She expressed certain doubts. I don't know whether they arose from her lack of understanding of the deal or from the fact that the idea hadn't come from one of her closest allies, following the frustrated bilateral economic cooperation agreement that had been imagined in 2004.

Zhou and I decided that we would advance toward a final document during the IDB meeting in Medellín, Colombia, where the multilateral agency would be celebrating its fiftieth anniversary. A Colombian himself, IDB President Luis Alberto Moreno was planning to make the meeting a truly splendid affair.

I asked Zhou to maintain strict confidentiality, because if I were to present it to the board ahead of time, there was a risk it would be leaked to the media, which could end up compromising its being brought into effect. My e-mail message to him said, "Let's not close the agreement just yet, because I still haven't presented it to my board. Let's do a preliminary draft and then let me walk it through the formal channels, which should take me another week." But the news somehow got to the media, and I ended up having to admit publicly that the accord would provide "an open possibility for cases of illiquidity that would contribute to generating mechanisms for cooperation."

On Sunday, March 29, we met in that attractive Colombian city to close the final details and sign a preliminary draft. We shook hands, and I insisted that I still had to make my way through the administrative and political channels in Argentina. But when I got to the convention center where the main meeting was to take place on Monday the thirtieth, a throng of new people rushed me to ask if it was true that I had signed an agreement with China. For the first time in my career, the news had been leaked, not from Argentina, but from China. The state news agency Xinhua was reporting that "the preliminary agreement is aimed at helping ensure the stability of our monetary systems and at containing financial risks resulting from the global crisis."

I immediately made it clear that this document was not similar to the one we had with Brazil. I also made a statement to Xinhua underscoring the idea that "the agreement will generate liquid resources in our domestic currencies in order to promote financial and monetary swaps between our central banks."

In order to strengthen bilateral ties, I also lent my public support to a complex strategy to promote the positioning of the yuan among the world's hard currencies, along with the dollar and the yen. "Argentina is going to work with China," I said, "in pursuit of this type of alternative to find new referential currencies. I don't believe that there should be a single referential currency, but several."

While the U.S. discourse that defended the hegemony of the dollar might appear an arrogant stance, however, I realized that the battle to dethrone the American currency was much closer to a quixotic crusade than to anything like an alternative reality.

The real commotion, however, was taking place in Buenos Aires, where the Argentine Industrial Union (known by its Spanish initials as the UIA) lodged complaints with the President and with Minister of Industry Débora Giorgi, fearing, as it did, that we were facilitating the mass entry of Chinese products onto the local market. I immediately contacted Giorgi and UIA leaders to explain the scope of the agreement. I also made a commitment to go to the headquarters of the UIA, to personally explain the accord at length.

I also called my friend Henrique Meirelles (Brazil) to explain him that the agreement was different than the one signed between our two countries.

In retrospect, I think the Chinese leak stymied the possibilities for continuing to advance with them toward a currency compensation system between the two central banks. Perhaps I should have found a means of explaining the accord earlier on, thus simultaneously complying with the objective of the agreement's coming to fruition.

Clearly, as I later explained to Zhou, China is seen by other emerging nations as highly aggressive—practically as a predator—in trade terms. So when the Chinese develop this kind of project, they need to advance tamely, since they are bound to raise fears in the productive sectors of other countries.

In terms of its foreign policy, China should really be seeking to transmit the idea of complementation, rather than emulating the European countries that colonized Africa, for instance, by absorbing natural resources without leaving behind any added value in exchange.

At any rate, for us this was a major achievement, especially coming, as it did, from the world's fourth largest central bank. It thus had a positive effect on the foreign exchange market, which, at the time, was still sensitive to the elimination of the pension fund system. In the end, the agreement turned out to be an umbrella, since we never requested delivery of any funds.

Meanwhile, another swap was worked out with Brazil, for a total of US$1.8 billion. In order not to raise any second thougts, I allowed Boudou to quarterback the announcement of the bilateral agreement with Brazil during a lightning trip to Brasilia in August 2009. Our two central banks then ratified the deal.

Meirelles and I also set up a system to permit companies from the two countries to make bilateral trade deals in reals and pesos, without the dollar as a go-between, thus lowering the cost of these transactions. Although we foresaw growing participation among small firms, we didn't expect any major interest in this setup from big business, which generally preferred to deal in dollars so as to cover themselves against exchange rate variation risks.

While in percentage terms the savings gained by this appeared small, working out to about 2 percent or 3 percent per operation, for private companies that didn't have the major financial backing, it was hardly a benefit to be spurned.

In order not to upset the major foreign trade operators, who lobbied fairly strongly against the measure, we made it clear that the de-dollarization of trade with Brazil would be optional. This took strength away from the plan, but provided a concrete signal to the effect that, after so many years, the two main Mercosur partners are taking steps to intensify their relation.

* * *

Another highly qualified guest at our monetary meetings in 2007 was my Russian counterpart, Sergei Mikhail Ignatiev. Born in 1948 in Saint Petersburg, he took up the presidency of the Russian Central Bank in 2002, twelve years after that institution's creation. I always found him to be a very sincere person with regard to monetary policy, and the problems he faced in his own country.

Since he and I enjoyed a good level of personal dialogue, he began to insist, as of 2006, that private Argentine bankers and the leadership of the Argentine Central Bank should travel to Moscow in order to reinforce the still-scant ties between our two financial systems.

Despite the fact that bilateral trade had been growing without pause since 2002—from US$218 million then to US$1.72 billion in 2008—and that the balance favored Argentina, we couldn't muster much interest among our bankers in joining the mission.

As I will explain in the next chapter, local financial leaders have tended to follow a policy of reaction rather than action since the country emerged from its crisis.

Ignatiev, on the other hand, met with greater success in convincing the Brazilian bankers who accompanied Meirelles to promote a greater volume of business. Indeed, before traveling, I asked Henrique how it had gone for him in Moscow, and he answered without hesitation that the trip had been worthwhile.

I had always believed that, in order to be a good economist, you had to be a good historian and a good sociologist, so as to be able to understand the behavior of each culture. And Russian history had always interested me, since it was the story of a country that had plunged from czarist imperialism into communism and then into capitalism, with the crumbling of the socialist bloc in Europe at the beginning of the 1990s.

I arrived in Moscow on June 26, 2008, in the middle of one of those long days of Russian summer. I was to provide private bankers with an assessment of how the emerging markets were coping with the crisis and of the challenges that were still pending.

We were still in the midst of the world financial crisis, but by this time, the worst was already over. Russia, like Argentina, had witnessed major capital flight. In Russia's case, it was sparked by plummeting oil prices, which also prompted a sharp devaluation of the ruble.

A decade before, Russia had been forced to devalue the ruble by 71 percent against the dollar when its government could not meet a US$40 billion debt with foreign creditors, and world markets collapsed in what was known as the "Vodka Effect"—which followed the "Tequila Effect" and the "Rice Effect" and preceded the "Caipirinha Effect" and our own 2001 "Tango Effect," as it was known to the world financial community.

The meeting was in the majestic building that is home to the Russian Central Bank. The Baroque and Renaissance-style building on Neglinnaya Street, near the 4.5-mile-long river of the same name, was rebuilt between 1890 and 1894 by the famed Konstantin Bykovsky.

I began my talk with a sentence in Russian that I had learned phonetically, and which briefly compared the history of the two nations. There was an immediate "click" with the participants at the meeting, despite the fact that what I said wasn't a terribly complicated concept.

Language aside, my main message was that, for the first time in a decade, we in the emerging markets were not at the epicenter of the crisis, and I had no doubt that we would come through the situation strengthened and positioned as much more relevant actors on the world economic stage.

Chapter 7

Double or Nothing

In my five years at the Central Bank, I had a scant three conversations with Kirchner that were strictly about politics.

I now think that it was a mistake to have lived so encapsulated in technical affairs, even if many economists have overestimated my handling of the political issues. I always believed that my work should speak for itself. That was a mistake.

In fact, a well-known Argentine ambassador posted abroad once pointed out that, due to my approach, "one would think you were the president of the Swedish Central Bank." Perhaps because of my nature, I tend to abstract myself from anything that is beyond my control, as if I believed that if I can't resolve something, it's best not to waste my energy on it, unless I'm called upon to give an opinion.

Whatever the case may be, the first political conversation I had with Néstor Kirchner was not long before the presidential elections of October 28, 2007. It was about eight in the evening. He was having a cup of tea and I was drinking coffee, while he showed me province-by-province political surveys. He demonstrated noteworthy personal knowledge of each district of the country.

Kirchner was leaving the presidency with a popularity rating of nearly 60 percent. But far from willingly stepping aside, he was clearly prepared to quarterback his wife's presidency from the shadows, particularly when it came to economy-related issues.

In the week prior to the presidential elections, the exchange rate market was very volatile, operating at record volumes. We had to be fairly persistent in our interventions to keep the exchange rate from topping ARS 3.20 per dollar.

In the end, the Cristina-Cobos ticket won out comfortably in first-round voting with 45.29 percent of the ballots, versus 23 percent for Elisa Carrió-Rubén Giustiniani and 16.8 percent for Roberto Lavagna and Gerardo Morales.

There was an air of expectation surrounding the potential for improvement in institutional quality as of the change of administration. Issues such as INDEC, moderation in public expenditures, and other actions to promote increased investment as well as greater integration into the world scene were among the affairs that many believed would be among the priorities of the president-elect.

But then there were others, like Minister Peirano, who caught on from the outset to the fact that any chance of implementing a different platform from the one previously followed by the new leader's husband was illusory, and thus decided to step down.

I, on the other hand, stayed. Besides wanting to complete the six-year term, validated by Congress, which wasn't to expire until September of 2010, I realized that we were in the midst of the worst international crisis since the 1930s. It was worthwhile showing that our focus was preventing the kind of economic meltdowns that Argentina had previously suffered in recent decades.

* * *

I could have staged a kind of testimonial walkout. But I always figured that I should and could fight my battle from the inside, as I had done with regard to the collateral effects of the elimination of the private retirement system, or when, prior to December 14,

2009, I blocked discretional use of reserves on three occasions. I'll refer to this last in greater detail in the next chapter.

The second conversation I had with Kirchner and Cristina, which was also on political topics, came in the week prior to the elections of June 28, 2009, when, for the first and only time, I was in the residence where they actually live, the presidential compound in Olivos.

The elections were originally slated for October of that year, but on March 13, the President announced their rescheduling for an earlier date, supposedly because "within the context of the world crisis" it was "suicidal to have a lame-duck situation until October." But the fact was that the administration felt it would be in its best electoral interest to get the jump on the negative signals that the economy was beginning to demonstrate to an ever greater degree. Paradoxically, that analysis ended up hurting the administration.

Since Cristina was concerned about opinion polls that had Néstor Kirchner losing his bid for a congressional seat for Buenos Aires Province to Unión-Pro businessman Francisco de Narváez, she didn't want to add another battlefront in the form of the struggle to maintain the dollar-peso exchange rate, which could harm them in the voting booth, where they hoped to retain political power until the end of her term.

In the living room of the Olivos residence, without the formality of a desk between us, the President asked me what could happen with the dollar in those days. And although she didn't tell me so, I got the feeling that perhaps she had information regarding possible shocks on the economic front due to a "market attack" of some sort.

That didn't happen. Naturally enough, there was the kind of nervousness that precedes any election, and this consumed nearly

US$400 million in reserves, although the value of the dollar only rose by 2 centavos in a week, going from ARS 3.79 to 3.81.

What indeed happened, however, was that Kirchner lost his bid, and the government lost its majority in Congress. There was talk of a presumed betrayal among the former president's allies in the outskirts of Buenos Aires who got more votes for their district lists than they did for the congressional list.

Some weeks after the elections, it was he who called me to come to Olivos for a talk. I entered the headquarters building at the residence at eight on the evening of July 14. There wasn't another soul there except for Kirchner's faithful secretary, Daniel Muñoz. I had a hollow feeling. I waited in the glassed-in reception hall for a few minutes, until Muñoz ushered me into the presidential office. Cristina was at Government House and Kirchner asked me to take a seat on the white leather sofa. He opened with an unexpected catharsis.

"We lost in Buenos Aires Province," he said, "because Daniel (Scioli) is putting in a poor performance as governor, with all of the insecurity and unemployment, especially in the second metro loop. So what we have to do is increase public spending in order to recover that vote."

"Néstor," I said, "after the crisis we economists have become Keynesian. But there are consistent and inconsistent Keynesians. If we don't generate the confidence necessary to obtain voluntary private credit, it'll be tough to finance any increase in spending."

I tried to illustrate my argument by comparing the situation to a twin-engine plane: one is overheated (consumption); the other (investment) isn't functioning right; it starts up and then falters. This, I explained, was causing inflationary tensions.

But Kirchner clearly wasn't much interested in my reflections, since he came back with "OK, so bring me alternatives."

That was, in fact, what he said every time he wasn't in agreement with me. But this time I decided not to wait.

"An immediate one would be to start selling off the shares the Social Security system is holding in private companies like Telefónica and Tenaris," I suggested. "That's US$2 billion that could come in right away."

He didn't like my proposal. He made some vague references to the value of those two companies, and I inferred immediately that he wanted to keep them under his control since they were both key players in their respective sectors.

The conversation left me worried. I should be contributing clarity at a confusing time. I had the feeling that time was running short.

* * *

My tenure at the Central Bank can be clearly divided into two periods. The first (2004–2007) was one in which we took advantage of the macroeconomic strength that was still prevalent in order to accumulate reserves within a context of genuine growth, a fiscal situation which, if somewhat weaker than before, was still generating positive figures—and certain signs that Argentina might be able to reconnect with the credit markets. During this period, we recapitalized the bank with 80 percent of the earnings that it obtained and transferred the remaining 20 percent to the Treasury.

The second period was 2008–2009. When the positive variables began to blur in 2008, we inverted the ratio: That year, we ceded 80 percent of the Central Bank's earnings to the Treasury and capitalized 20 percent, in a true demonstration of anticyclical policy.

Throughout the five years, however, there was one path that never changed: that of promoting long-term credit, with the aim of doubling it in the next decade relative to national wealth.

We were particularly active in implementing measures designed to reactivate loans to small and medium-size companies. We did this by making their debt classification and the information required for credit requests more flexible, and by promoting credit guarantees, promoting small loans, expanding the lending capacity for dollar deposits, and generating interest rate swaps, so as to provide greater predictability.

We should have done more to develop credit. Such criticism would be totally valid: It's always possible to redouble the efforts. All the same, it is worth noting that 88 percent of the Argentine economy is handled outside of the banking circuit. The existence of such a distorting tax as the one levied on checks—or, as it is better described, on credits and debits in current accounts—has done much to contribute to the low level of banking in the country's economy.

I referred to this during a seminar hosted by the IDEA organization in 2005. The next day the media reported on my presentation, saying, "In closing the Forty-first IDEA Colloquium, Redrado proposed a gradual and progressive reduction of this tax, since he considered the check tax as one that is 'a burden on people' and added that it was 'one of the most distorting taxes in the entire Argentine tax system.'"

During that talk, which I delivered in the coastal city of Mar del Plata, I said, "One of the factors that limit banking in countries like Argentina, Brazil, Colombia, and Ecuador is taxation of financial transactions, taxes that usually originate as temporary or as emergency measures (implemented during episodes of fiscal crisis), but the use of which tends to extend over time…They are taxes that distort the decisions of citizens, encourage the excessive use of cash and, in this way, promote informality in economic activities, which, in the end, negatively affects tax collection."

I spoke with Kirchner, of course, about reducing this tax, but he asked me for alternative sources of revenue to replace it, in a clearly static vision of tax collection. To my mind, if the ratio were reduced progressively, it would encourage formal economic activity, people would pay more taxes, and, in this way, an initial loss of revenues would be compensated for in the short term.

The other alternative was to implement a tax reform—something Kirchner always rejected—which could have included a capital gains tax. I was, on the other hand, against applying a tax to the interest on certificates of deposit, since it would generate scant returns in exchange for causing major detriment to incentives to get people to place their savings in the local banking system.

The idea of taxing financial yields always sounds great in political terms, but the numbers have always tended to show that the actual revenues to be gained by this are relatively reduced.

At any rate, I found it noteworthy that the debate over proposals always emerged on the side of the government and never on that of bankers. The banks justified their not offering more credit on the basis of the bitterness left behind by the 2001–2002 crisis. They claimed, furthermore, that deposits remained in the domestic system for too short a time to permit them to grant long-term loans. The truth was that bankers tended to have the attitude of followers rather than leaders in processes of change.

As of 2002, the relationship between financial institutions and the government could be divided into two stages.

In the first stage, the institutions focused on asking the Central Bank to provide them with a safety net and solutions to two specific problems: the excess government bonds that they had in their portfolios—generally speaking, they complained about having been pressured to buy them at the end of 2001 (despite my telling them that "nobody can make anybody do anything")—and the "pesofication" agreed to at the beginning of 2002, pursuant to withdrawal from the Convertibility System.

As a consequence of this controversial measure, banks had asked for compensation totaling nearly US$12 billion, with the final agreement being negotiated at about US$10 billion, by means of new bonds that the government issued. Added to this were appeals filed with the courts against the so-called *corralito* and *corralón* (measures imposed during the 2001–2002 crisis to block depositors from withdrawing their savings). In this case, bankers sat back and waited for solutions from the government, while they themselves presented no alternatives.

When the aftermath of the devaluation was left behind toward the end of 2005, the banking system had begun to absorb its losses and was showing signs of recovery.

In recent years, banking has concentrated on four areas: consumer loans, current account advances, discount checks, and wage payment services. This is typical of our country. To argue that the banks have been the only ones responsible for not lending long-term money is to take an overly simplistic view of the situation, particularly considering that Argentina is a country where confidence flags on a cyclical basis and where there is no long-term currency.

During my administration, I carried on a professional dialogue with bankers, although, admittedly, I observed that the banks didn't have a proactive approach.

To be bluntly graphic, in a meeting with bankers at the Central Bank, I told them, "Less Valeria Lynch and more industry, or business or project financing," in reference to the popular singer's ads for consumer banking services and the energy with which the banks place commercials.

This lack of a proactive attitude led to the drafting of a reform for the Financial Institutions Law, something the banks had long been fearing. As had occurred with the pension administrators, when you leave an empty space, somebody else is bound to fill it.

Without a doubt, there are profitable real sectors to which loans could be made. Some are emblematic, like biotechnology as it applies to the agro-industrial sector, the pharmaceuticals industry, or software development, to mention just a few. But the bankers were few indeed who struck out among companies in search of projects, with the sole exception of a single executive who, every time I called for him, was in the interior of the country visiting clients. Argentine banking suffers from the same illness as the rest of the country: "short-termitis."

Another factor that has contributed to this flaw has been a history of deposits being drained from the system in what is generally known as "capital flight," although, to a great extent, these cash resources end up "under people's mattresses." From July of 2007 until the end of 2009, this kind of hemorrhaging totaled about US$46 billion, divided into four major episodes: July–October 2007 (when suspicions regarding the government's tinkering with official statistics became generalized coupled with the subprime crisis); April–May 2008 (during the standoff between farmers and the government); September–December 2008 (at the height of the international crisis and with the decision to nationalize the retirement system); and March–May 2009 (in the run-up to legislative elections held at the end of June).

Our strategy—in order to try to moderate the erosion of deposits—was, first, to stabilize the foreign exchange market; later, to strengthen the demand for pesos; and, finally, to provide all of the liquidity necessary by acting, for the first time, as a peso lender of last resort.

True, we did continue to apply exchange controls that had been applied since 2001, and we regulated the distribution of dividends by banks, in accordance with the solvency of each institution. But I never accepted the proposals of certain board members, like Arturo O'Connell, who wanted to create new and more complicated regulations for the purchase and sale of dollars, since I knew that this would only serve to create a parallel market that would do a greater volume of business than the legal one.

In the past, this split was formalized by creating a commercial dollar rate and a financial dollar rate. The consequences in terms of the pace of devaluation of the peso were highly detrimental and usually led to hyperinflation.

The President never asked me to take this kind of measure. But my successor, Marcó del Pont, was in favor of lowering the ceiling on dollar purchases from the standing two million to just one hundred thousand for both companies and individuals. If the financial situation should become complicated in the future, that's the approach that can be expected.

* * *

In addition to the introduction of statistical intervention mechanisms came the effects of the international crisis and the continuous expansion of government spending, which accelerated in the run-up to the October 2007 election process. It was for this reason that a solution to the fiscal problem was being sought, arising from a big technical error committed by the Economy Ministry under Martín Lousteau, who replaced de Peirano.

On March 11, 2008, the Economy Ministry put out its Resolution 125, which increased export tariffs on soybeans and sunflower seeds, also establishing a mobile system for these tariffs. The administration presented a progressive argument for what was, in point of fact, an appropriation of resources that was practically an expropriation affecting one of the most dynamic areas of the economy in the last two decades.

The escalating clash between the government and farmers included strikes of varying durations organized by agricultural leaders, carried out between the launching of the measure and July 18, following a "not positive" vote by Vice President Cobos, in his role as Senate president, when the administration finally announced the repeal of Resolution 125.

Both sides of the conflict organized public demonstrations. The farmers' Joint-Action Committee—gathering all the representatives of the *Federación Agraria*, the *Sociedad Rural*, CARBAP, and Coninagro—put together two massive demonstrations in the Palermo district of Buenos Aires and in the city of Rosario. The administration tried to organize a similar one in the northern city of Salta on August 25, on the same day that farmers rolled out their second sign of strength, but the government-backed affair turned out to be a flop.

Participation in the farming strikes was so high that they affected national and international trade, mainly in the areas of food, fuel, and supply lines to major cities.

In the midst of this confrontation, in early April, I traveled with Lousteau to the annual Inter-American Development Bank summit in Miami. Following the exhausting sessions at the conference, I met up with the minister on the twelfth floor of the Hyatt, where we were both lodged. We decided to go have a cup of coffee together. It was one of the few times we had an extended conversation together. It was very direct and frank.

"How could you make such a mistake?" I asked him.

"You have no idea," he said. "Moreno wanted to do something even worse! He wanted to impose a floating tax of 60 percent!"

It's my belief that inexperience and arrogance were the combination that led Lousteau to make that decision, and it ended up costing him and the government dearly. Granted, it was necessary to generate a better level of resources, but anybody who had gone through the university or who had any common sense should have known that taking away 95 percent of the farmer's earnings—if the price of soy were to go over US$600 dollars—was clearly confiscatory. After that, everything turned into more of a power struggle than any discussion of resources. This administration simply refuses to tolerate power disputes, and especially when the media reflects in such conflicts.

The administration's idea is always double or nothing, never take a step back. It was for that reason that, although different cabinet members and the four farming organizations met for talks on several occasions, no agreement was ever reached.

Over the course of the conflict, reforms to Resolution 125 were announced on two occasions: on March 31 and on May 29. In the first case, the government set reimbursements and subsidies for small farmers, as a means of trying to drive a wedge into the solid front that had been established with major agricultural producers. In the second case, marginal withholdings affecting the futures markets were reduced.

During that battle, the President suffered two casualties in her cabinet: The logical one was Lousteau, who resigned on April 24, and the other, more resounding one was Cabinet Chief Alberto Fernández, who, because of his reflexive and executive role in the clash, gave up his post on July 23.

A few days before, a crack emerged within the government. This happened after the bill was rejected in the upper house of Congress in the wee hours of July 17, when Vice President Cobos, as Senate president, was called upon to break a tied decision and announced, with historic ambiguity, "My vote is not positive."

This tremendous political shock brought a correlative financial reaction, in addition to the effects of three months of conflict, which had caused capital flight totaling US$7.159 billion. This was a bigger capital drain than that seen in the third quarter of 2007 in the wake of worldwide financial turbulence.

In that second quarter, we had to sell off US$2.74 billion in reserves and use another US$850 million to buy local Treasury bonds so as to stabilize the market in both pesos and foreign currency, and to grant daily liquidity to banks in order to stave off an incipient run.

The flight of deposits was caused by a combination of the reality of a critical situation and speculative operations that seemed to foreshadow catastrophes like the 2001–2002 restrictions on withdrawals, or the so-called "patriotic bond," or a split exchange market, which were not, in fact, among the alternatives being weighed.

I made sure that the citizens' savings were protected within such a turbulent context. It was for that reason that I had a talk during those days with executives in the Argentine Banking Association (ABA) at its offices on the eighth floor of the building at *Calle* San Martín 229. The meeting had been requested by that group's president, Mario Vicens, and included the five major foreign banks in the country.

One of these directors talked to me frankly about fears of a new restriction on withdrawals, like the so-called *corralito* implemented by Economy Minister Domingo Cavallo at the beginning of December 2001 on the request of some of the domestic banking institutions. My first response left him perplexed.

"Look," I said, "the biggest problem that's going to crop up if there's a run on deposits is that I'm going to be in your seat."

"What do you mean?" he asked.

"It's simple!" I said. "In that case, the Central Bank will return people's money to them rather than you. Because this is an economy that, fortunately, has sufficient pesos and dollars, if people should decide to flee from those pesos. If there's a run, we're going to provide all of the liquidity necessary," I stated with absolute conviction.

At the Central Bank, we were certain that, if there were a run on deposits, we were going to give all of the necessary pesos. We remained highly active in showing people that there were pesos and dollars to cover any public demand.

As a means of mitigating the crisis, we worked in sequential fashion. First we stabilized the futures market and made it clear that all of the dollars were available on the market to satisfy public demand. Then we generated all of the liquidity necessary by repurchasing our own bonds (Lebacs) on the electronic OTC market.

Each day, we made credit lines in pesos available to the market, to show that we were acting as a lender of last resort, while employing maximum expertise in each of the buyback bids put out for the Lebac bonds, for example, if there were a billion pesos up for renewal, we took only half, so as not to exert any greater pressure on the market. In short, for the first time ever, we showed that "the safety net was there"—or as U.S. President Harry S. Truman had said, that "the buck stops here, clearly at the Central Bank."

Without a doubt, we were being examined daily, and especially during those first convulsive months of the crisis. By the beginning of April, the rate for the peso against the dollar had reached ARS 3.24, with the Central Bank's sale of dollars having first reached US$100 million a day, then doubling that amount and, finally, tripling it.

Clearly, this had turned into a political test of strength, and the exchange rate was the battlefield. We had to show that we were capable of putting a halt to a run.

While we had indeed stopped the one recorded in the run-up to elections, during the clash between the administration and farmers, we had run into problems with liquidity, since exporters were reticent about bringing dollars into the country. Faced with this situation, we had to show that we knew how to implement an anticyclical policy and provide the market with all of the dollars it needed. Since this move could mean an important loss of reserves, the decision would require an explanation within the administration.

On May 13, I worked with my team until ten at night. That was what time it was when the President called to tell me that she wanted to see me first thing in the morning. She gave me an appointment for nine the next morning at the Olivos residence. The seriousness with which they were taking the situation was clear, since both of the Kirchners met with me in one of the rooms in the HQ building at the residence. I presented them with a critical outlook and explained that the trend that the foreign exchange market was showing would tend to generate greater political instability. I gave them a brief rundown, pointing out that exchange stability plus monetary stability were equal to political stability. And I added that if the Central Bank didn't show that it was capable of controlling a run, we would have political instability for sure.

We had a good talk. I told them not to be surprised, that my vision of the Central Bank was as a strong player that could appear to be a retaining wall against the prevailing tension. And I added that although we had worked with total independence up to that moment, I didn't want to give them any surprises.

I sought to find out what kind of backing I had for a strong play like this one. Their response was immediate. Cristina was the first to answer, saying, "Do what you have to do."

"But don't spend much money!" Néstor said.

I left there comforted by their backing to sell as much as I had to. I had always felt that I had that backing, but this was the first time that I had been able to confirm it.

When you're alone with your technical team and you've got the markets on your screens deciding whether you'll be offering them US$300 million or US$400 million, it's not easy to be calm. That's why it was important to start sharing the costs that Resolution 125 was starting to generate, but bringing them up for debate.

From that point on, when the exchange rate began to calm, reports that started in Olivos began to circulate to the effect that Néstor Kirchner was swearing he would teach the farmers a lesson by pushing down the price of the dollar so that they would lose money. And, in point of fact, the rate for the dollar dropped to almost ARS 3.00—we managed to break its fall at ARS 3.03.

In response to those rumors, the reality was that we had the intention to demonstrate firmness and that it was the result of our own technical design. Had we not done this, expectations would have overwhelmed both the Bank and the administration.

Furthermore, I didn't favor any sort of idea aimed at giving the farmers a lesson via the exchange rate. The farming sector had undergone a major technological revolution. The invention of the bag silo changed the dynamics of export liquidations by permitting storage for a longer period of time.

At any rate, although we won the exchange rate battle, the clash with farmers marked a clear point of deterioration in expectations and deepened the process of short-term decision making. It also created a fragmented society, which expanded the friend/enemy dichotomy, creating greater intolerance.

For the first time, I began to perceive a climate of hatred among our society. All of this had a correlative effect in the level of economic activity. The most noteworthy manifestation was the sharpest drop in investment witnessed up to 2007, with the slowdown starting to be seen in key sectors.

Another lesson to be learned from that conflict: what for the government was "the element of surprise" in the decisions it made—with the administration's aim being to nip news leaks in the bud—appeared to the citizenry to be discretional power. And what discretional power breeds is a reduction in the creation of long-term projects.

If people are unsure whether they might be hit in the pocketbook within the next two or three months, they'll think it over long and hard before they trade cars, buy a major home appliance, go on vacation, or save money in pesos. This is a contributing factor to savings in dollars and capital flight, because the only medium-term refuge in Argentina over the last thirty years has been the greenback.

* * *

After the failure of Resolution 125, I began to receive requests from the President to come up with alternatives for obtaining voluntary financing. I immediately prepared a report in which I proposed the repurchasing of public debt issues, a mechanism utilized at critical points in time and which tends to generate major savings and improved expectations among investors when it's done seriously.

I received no response. Not, that is, until August 7, 2008, when Venezuelan President Hugo Chávez sent Argentine bond quotations tumbling with a highly questionable maneuver.

Nobody in the administration protested aloud. But off the record, Cabinet Chief Sergio Massa, who had made the finance issue one of his top priorities, asked the President for the support he needed to start working on a schedule for normalizing the debt that was in default. Venezuela's "backing" was becoming a burden in both political and economic terms.

On August 12, I sent both the President and Massa a report regarding the debt buyback strategy, the main points of which were as follows:

- **Volume:** "It is important that this be a heavyweight strategy. A parallel can be drawn with the supply of reserves when the demand for pesos drops and the speculative demand for dollars rises. A tepid intervention is of no use, since it could stimulate the flight of the bondholders who are left before a rally can be established. In this sense, US$500 million could prove insufficient."

- **Type:** "Given doubts regarding financing over the course of the next eighteen months, I would concentrate on intervention affecting maturity dates for that period. Today the market is focusing on shorter-term financing (especially in dollars), as witnessed by the recent inversion of the yield curve."

- **Timing:** "This should be perceived as a persistent rather than merely opportunistic strategy. Otherwise, the effect might last only a week. If it is perceived as a random strategy in which it is unclear when and how much the government is going to buy back, we run the risk of putting up money that the market will absorb in a very short time, with no lasting effects. Contrary to this, a buyback program that extended until the end of the year, with set amounts, dates, and bond series, could end up providing the certainty being sought."

- **Program**: "This financial engineering could prove even more effective if it were accompanied by deep-reaching measures: announcement of expected developments in government spending and the fiscal surplus, for example. Otherwise, it could end up providing only temporary relief."

* * *

Nine days later, Massa called me. It was five in the afternoon on a Sunday. I was having tea at a place near home in Belgrano with my wife and children.

"Please," Massa practically begged me, "write something about the buyback for me to put out in a statement, because the Ministry of Economy hasn't given me a single solid paper that I can use."

"Give me an hour to get home," I said.

By seven thirty that evening, the statement was already out, explaining what we were going to do. When I sent it to Massa, he was beside himself with appreciation.

"This is great!" he said. "See what I mean? You should be economy minister. In the province (Buenos Aires Province) we used to call Carlos Fernández 'Bernando the Mute' after the character in the *Zorro* TV series. We need somebody like you."

"No," I said firmly, "Just let me stay at the bank."

The complete report, which I sent to him and to the President, was called "Financial Strategy 2008–2009" and it included the following concepts:

> *"The government should initiate a second stage in the debt buyback program, as part of a strategy aimed at reducing the burden of financial services over the course of the coming months, taking advantage of the savings opportunities emerging from prevailing conditions."*

The intention from then until the end of the year was for the Economy Ministry to carry out a weekly government bond repurchasing program for issues with short- and medium-term expirations, so as to achieve fiscal savings.

> *"The financial program should foresee an efficient use of existing liquidity on the local market, pension capitalization system generates an annual savings flow of more than ARS 12 billion and this flow in the insurance companies is of between ARS 4 billion and 5 billion."*

Later, I underscored the importance of maintaining the model of fiscal and foreign surpluses as the cornerstones needed to guarantee repayment of debt with low-cost funds.

> *"The national public sector has a major stock; plus potential sources of financing on the domestic market of more than ARS 25 billion a year."*

I immediately remarked on the goals that could be reached in under five months:

"The continuation and broadening of the debt buyback plan will permit more efficient liability management, as well as ratifying the capability and will of Argentin to pay its obligations."

In order to place this idea in context, I clarified two final points:

"Measures of this type are normal public debt management operations carried out by the treasuries of emerging nations in recent years. These operations allow a means of taking advantage of the opportunities offered by the market to generate fiscal savings."

But even though I immediately met with Lousteau's successor, Carlos Fernández, his ministry implemented a timid buyback program that showed no conviction whatsoever—and reflected differences between the departments of finance and treasury—which ended up, in just a few short weeks, withering an initiative that could have provided the administration with major benefits.

At that same time, in a meeting I had with Fernández, the President, and Sergei Massa, I brought up the subject of INDEC. Cristina limited herself to answering, "Yes, we have a problem with INDEC's credibility."

While the President, Massa and I were still thinking about the options for gradually returning to the market, Néstor Kirchner had struck out on a tangent of his own: total onetime payment of the Paris Club debt.

Following the last debt placement in Venezuela, Kirchner called me. As soon as I arrived in Olivos, he took me off to one side and said, "I want to talk to you! We want to pay off the Paris Club."

"Well, I think that's a good signal," I said rather naively.

"Yes, but we want to do it with reserves."

"Why with reserves?" I asked. "I mean, what you want to do is generate a reinsertion into the club and a position in which those countries will restart lending you money."

"No, no, this is a political issue," he said. "The administration has to take the initiative after the crisis with the farmers, and this will give Cristina the same kind of lift we got with the payment of the IMF."

"But the circumstances are different," I said. "There's room to negotiate, and they're not imposing the kind of conditions on the country that the IMF was. Here what you need to do is get the export and investment credit agencies in Europe to start lending us money again. I'd forget about the reserves. If you want, I'll present some ideas to you about how to restructure our debt."

The conversation ended there, but I didn't drop the issue. I remember that I had a friend, Daniel Cohen, who was a tenured professor at the University of Paris and who also worked for France's Lazard Freres bank, which had taken part in some Paris Club renegotiations.

We had a long talk. Cohen told me that there was room for a negotiation, and we started to take a look at the precedents for the elimination of charges for nonpayment and at what kind of possibilities there were for debt reduction.

Later, at a meeting of the Financial Stability Board, the oversight group in charge of reformulating global regulations, the French Paris Club Secretary General Ramón Fernández gave me a message that was friendly in tone but harsh in substance. "I'm still waiting for a concrete answer," he said, "because all the ones I get are coming through the newspapers."

* * *

In a meeting at the Olivos residence, I proposed negotiating a minimum monthly payment plan for the Paris Club as a means to start the negotiations.

The first experience I had in the public sector was in April of 1990, when Argentina had gone through nearly a decade of default. Following the 1982 crisis, the country began to fail to comply with its commitments.

I had met Economy Minister Erman González back when I was vice president of the Security Pacific Bank in the United States and he was finance minister of La Rioja Province in Argentina (1988).

When Menem took office, his first two economy ministers were Miguel Roig—who died almost immediately after taking office—and Néstor Rapanelli, an executive from the Bunge & Born Group, which had contributed heavily to Menem's electoral campaign.

After a bout of hyperinflation, Erman became the Menem administration's third economy minister, with Javier González Fraga as president of the Central Bank. The two of them jointly had to quell the hyperinflation and sought to do so with their "Bonex Plan," which compulsively swapped certificates of deposit for ten-year government bonds.

They had barely taken up their posts in April 1990, when they called me to join the economic team in a weekend brainstorm aimed at finding alternatives to normalize government debt payments. The proposal that was finally agreed on was to start by making payments of US$40 million a month to the commercial banks that were Argentina's main creditors.

At that time, González Fraga offered to make me Argentina's financial representative in New York, since prior to the appointment of Domingo Cavallo as economy minister, debt management was the responsibility of the Central Bank. I was in the midst of a very good year at Security Pacific and answered, "Make me that offer again at the end of the year, when I've cashed my bonus." I had an excellent compensation coming for all of the projects that I had handled in 1990.

But in December, everything blew up in Argentina, as prices once again stampeded out of control. Six months later, Cavallo, who had taken over the Economy Ministry post in January 1991, offered me to make me Chairman of the Securities and Exchange Commission.

Now, in 2008, my proposal to Kirchner, as a means of rene-gotiating the debt, was to resurrect the kind of partial payments that had led to the Brady Plan (named for U.S. Treasury Secretary Nicholas Brady), signed in April of 1992

"We need to make a commitment to the Paris Club," I said. "And what they are waiting for is some gesture from us. Let's pay interest from now on. Something that won't be a burden to Argentina, but that will show goodwill."

But I got the feeling there was very little willingness to accept the idea.

I also made a proposal to make a new offer to the bondhold-ers with which we remained in default, but it faltered due to the inexperience and lack of expertise of the economic team.

Bent on carrying his own plans through, Kirchner hastened to announce payment of the Paris Club. While we at the Central Bank were hosting our annual monetary conference, at noon on September 2, 2008, Cristina Kirchner went onto the nationwide radio and television network to announce that she had instructed Economy Minister Carlos Fernández to make use of "freely avail-able" federal reserves totaling US$6.706 billion to pay the coun-try's debt with the Paris Club. I wasn't told until just a few minutes before the announcement was made, since they knew full well that I wouldn't validate the decision, despite their trying to compare it to payment of the IMF, as I will explain in a later chapter.

Twelve days later, on September 14, the effect of the announcement was wiped out when Lehman Brothers crashed and changed the entire world of finance.

It was at that moment that Kirchner also decided to make his move against the private pension funds, the elimination of which would be announced a month later.

Up to then, successive crises (the subprime, elections, the clash with farmers) had all failed to provoke any alteration in the monetary and financial system, despite frequent cases of nerves on the foreign exchange market. But the nationalization of the pension fund dropped the crisis in the middle of my desk, sparking a strong wave of capital flight that ate up US$6.649 billion just between October and December and that totaled US$23 billion for the year.

On October 22, 2008, I explained to the President, in a telephone conversation, that there was a major feeling of uncertainty with regard to what might come next. Rumors were rife: confiscation of deposits, the opening of safe deposit boxes…any rumor at all seemed credible.

Be that as it may, there were no mass protests as there had been in the case of the 2001–2002 freeze on deposits or during the conflict with farmers, because people simply didn't perceive the money of the pension funds as their own savings, which, indeed, it was. I recall that at one point, I suggested to the AFJP Association that people should be permitted to use the money they had deposited in the system as collateral for loans, so as to make them realize that these retirement payments were tangibly useful assets.

About the time that all this happened, I had a meeting with an important American investor. "If this had happened in the

United States," he said, "all hell would have broken loose. Why doesn't anything happen here?"

"Because in your country," I said, "people know that they can use their retirement plan as a tangible asset. They can take it out, touch it. In Argentina, people don't have that. His words reflected the feeling of breakdown that this caused in the rest of the world.

Here, what was seen was a show of discretional behavior, a serious grab at funds to finance the fiscal deficit. Far from comprehending this concern, the administration went on the defensive and set out to hunt down those purchasing dollars, to see if they could detect some illegal maneuver.

The weekend before the announcement, without telling me about it, Kirchner called Guillermo Moreno to tell him to call up companies and find out why they had bought foreign currency. This persecution went on for several days. On Thursday, November 6, I went to talk to Néstor Kirchner to warn him about the boomerang effect that this kind of muscling would cause.

"Look," I said, "this isn't the way. If you all want to do it that way, go ahead, but you're going to get a reverse effect."

Kirchner argued that there was a conspiracy against the government, designed to overthrow the nationalization of the pension funds by promoting powerful speculative exchange rate action.

But I offered him another alternative. "The best way to respond to speculation," I said, "is with serenity, and showing them that you have broad enough shoulders to handle the situation. We have to show the market that it can end up losing money. That's the only language the market understands, not scare tactics. Market controls are like water leaks. You stop them up one place and they seep through another."

Kirchner agreed to ask Moreno to stop and he obeyed.

Chapter 8

A Country without Credit

It doesn't make much sense for me to keep on explaining all of the mistakes made in recent years if I don't first explain that, as of 2007, the country had no access to voluntary credit, even in the domestic market.

Most countries have the policy of accessing the credit markets to renew principal amortization and pay down interests due, so as to gradually reduce the debt/product ratio.

Therefore the concept of having access to credit was a logical one, to the extent that the administration started putting out reasonable signals. The one who, undoubtedly, understood this concept right away was Cabinet Chief Sergio Massa. But the question underlying this goal was precisely what kind of conditions would have to be met first.

And the answer to this question was that the administration wanted to go back to the capital markets, but without first doing its homework. Kirchner would ask what was the critical path for obtaining financing, and then, time and again, the decision to do so would be postponed.

Both Kirchner and Cristina grasped the concept, but every time they ran up against some condition that they didn't like, the discussion of it was removed from the table—for example, the normalization of INDEC and the moderation of unproductive spending, among others.

Faced with this outlook, and in view of the electoral defeat that the administration suffered on June 28, 2009, I would have recommended the government come up with an economic plan and a team to implement it. I knew full well—considering the traits of the political decision makers involved, who considered appointing an economy minister with proper technical skills to be tantamount to creating an "economy czar"—that developing such a plan would be impossible.

Politicians were imbued with a fear of the so-called "Cavallo syndrome" (in reference to all-powerful 1990s Economy Minister Domingo Cavallo), rejecting a replay of the days when economy ministers were provided with excessive powers. And, indeed, I share that view: ministers shouldn't have an overabundance of power, but rather, they need to be able to agree on a plan with the President, who should provide them with his or her vision, and then step back and let the minister comply with the agreed-upon plan.

In the absence of changes capable of improving productivity and competitive levels, and without tax changes aimed at prompting a wave of new investments, what would permit us to have smooth sailing until 2011? Only voluntary financing.

I don't think that I was the only one with whom the Kirchners discussed these ideas. The fact is that Amado Boudou took office in July 2009 knowing from the outset that he had no chance of being a strong minister with independence to impose any plan of his own. But he set two logical and attainable goals: to restore credibility to INDEC and to return to the capital markets.

The INDEC issue put him on an immediate collision course with Moreno, and he ended up resigning himself to making cosmetic rather than substantive changes. In the second case, it looked like he might meet with success, and, for that reason, I lent him my conceptual support, because it was what I also recommended. Beyond my own impression of Boudou on a personal and professional level, I felt that if he maintained a good level of dialogue with the presidential couple and could find a way back into the credit markets, it would be a welcome move.

Boudou had the advantage of being the first economy minister to present himself to investors since Lavagna met with them for the last time in 2005.

In the absence of previous contacts and in the presence of an economy minister and a Central Bank president who were both saying the same thing, the intention of recovering Argentina's credit standing came off as a forceful message.

Our relationship was, however, negligible when it came to technical discussions. We had a clear vision of our separate tasks, though, especially at international meetings. I spoke inside the boardrooms, and he took direct contact with the media, which were, without a doubt, what attracted him most.

Boudou was fully aware that those sitting in the meeting rooms—for example, representatives of the G-20 or of the IMF—knew and respected me. A categorical demonstration of this was during the G-20 Summit at Saint Andrews. When the official meeting was over, Boudou put together a teleconference with our local media, and I stayed behind talking to the official delegates about a proposal to create global insurance with reserves administrated by the IMF.

One of the few face-to-face discussions we had was in early September 2009, regarding the selection of the superintendency for financial institutions. The post had remained vacant following the resignation of Waldo Farías, and the government didn't appear to have any intention of filling it, despite the importance of that job.

Boudou convinced the President of the attributes of Sergio Chodos, who was appointed to the board of the Central Bank at the beginning of 2009. Both of them had worked together in the nationalization of the pension funds. My candidate, meanwhile, was Zenón Biagosch, without a doubt the man of greatest intellectual capacity on our board.

I was called to Government House for a meeting on the evening of September 4, 2009, at eight o'clock. While we were waiting for the President in the room adjoining her office, far from arguing with Boudou over his naming Chodos, I encouraged him to advance on the road toward returning to the markets:

"Amado," I said, "the day you place a bond on the voluntary market, you can take a bow, because you will have done your job."

"Well, we're working on it," he said. And then he filled me in on the details of how he had rekindled a relationship with the French investment bank Lazard to see if there was any chance of an agreement without an IMF audit's being implemented.

Something that struck me was that, all this time, he had been saying publicly that he was negotiating with the Paris Club, when, in fact, he was negotiating with Lazard, which came up with the proposal to place a bond with creditor countries instead of striking a traditional refinancing accord, as a means of skirting the IMF. Boudou made this idea public, but then he ended up having to backtrack, since he hadn't actually put it through the proper channels.

When we were both ushered into the President's office, she wasted no time getting to the point. "We're up against this anomaly in the superintendency," she said, as soon as we sat down together at her desk, "because the post has remained vacant."

"I'm certain that we must name a superintendent," I hastened to respond.

"It has to be Sergio Chodos," she said quickly.

"Sergio's a creative fellow," I said, "but he has never had a line management job, and the superintendency has a staff of nine hundred professionals. Besides, I don't see him in that post because of his profile. He's a lawyer, but he has no auditing, accounting, or supervisory knowledge. If you want to train him for the job, he'll require coaching, and that's going to take time."

I explained how the organizational structure of the superintendency worked: that it had a division that supervised the banks; another one that covered compliance and control, which granted authorizations and drafted indictments under the criminal exchange regulation system, an internal and external auditing division; and other data systems.

I was surprised that, throughout my entire explanation, Boudou never opened his mouth. He presented no objection whatsoever. It was I who added a word of praise, saying, "It seems to me that Sergio has shown a capacity for hard work."

So then we started discussing different names, but we couldn't come to an agreement. That was the same day that the United States Congress ratified Ben Bernanke in his post at the head of the Federal Reserve, after a tough review of his actions in the midst of the international financial crisis. More than a few Democrats wanted to replace him with former Treasury secretary and former Harvard University president Larry Summers. When I mentioned this, Cristina exclaimed, "No way! It was Summers who made that chauvinist comment at Harvard and had to resign!"

Clearly, it was also Summers who, when Barack Obama became president, was named to head the Council of Economic Advisors.

Since I saw that we weren't getting anywhere, I proposed Carlos Sánchez, a low-profile technician from Santa Cruz Province.

"He has demonstrated common sense," I said, "and he merits your confidence."

In the face of the minister's silence, the President immediately accepted.

His failure to provide an enthusiastic defense of his candidate demonstrated to me that Boudou lacked strong convictions, even when he knew which road was the most advisable one for the government to take.

In this sense, we both agreed that it was necessary to normalize relations with the IMF, since following payment of the country's debt with that agency and the manipulation of government statistics, the administration had refused to accept any review of the country's economy, something which other members of the Fund permit on an annual basis. So it was clear to everyone that the administration didn't want anyone setting it down in writing that the administration had a problem with its statistics. The IMF had started to show in its annual economic report, the differences between government figures and private data. In several meetings that I had, respectively, with Managing Director Strauss Kahn and with Nicolás Eyzaguirre, Director of the Western Hemisphere, we tried to find a framework that would allow us to eliminate the prevailing distrust. Both of them demonstrated a willingness to carry on a rational dialogue with Argentina far from the eyes of the media.

I transmitted this message to the President in such a way that she could understand that it meant an opportunity for her to establish a direct one-to-one relationship with Strauss-Kahn. Eyzaguirre took the initiative and came to the Council of the Americas meeting held each August in Buenos Aires, and although he ended up holding meetings with Boudou, with businesspeople and economists, and with me, what he was really expecting was a meeting with the President. Unfortunately, she didn't receive him.

I made several different attempts to generate an encounter. I even thought of getting them together in a secret meeting through Chilean President Michelle Bachelet, since she and Eyzaguirre had been colleagues in the cabinet of Socialist President Ricardo Lagos.

So I asked the President if she trusted Bachelet, and she answered, "Yes, yes, absolutely."

She promised me that she would talk it over with her Chilean colleague at a meeting the two of them would have in Maipú for the signing of the Strategic Association Treaty. But later she told me that the opportunity hadn't arisen and the chance was lost.

We agreed to seek mechanisms for the building of bridges of trust, and Cristina suggested the idea that she and Eyzaguirre could get together in some other country. That opportunity was also lost when she traveled to Rome to meet with Pope Benedict XVI and Bachelet, on November 28, 2009, to commemorate the twenty-fifth anniversary of the Peace and Friendship Treaty between Argentina and Chile. Although I insisted once more, Cristina preferred to elude the issue entirely.

What I observed in the Kirchners was great mistrust of any kind of IMF monitoring. My own feelings about Strauss Kahn's plans to reform the institution were positive, but the information the Kirchners had was that any report the IMF put out on Argentina, especially from a technical standpoint, would be negative. It is true that most of the reports that the IMF puts out are critical, without this implying that the countries are bound to strictly adopt the recommendations formulated.

I also came up with the idea of allowing the IMF to conduct a surveillance on our financial system, known as the Financial Stability Assessment Program (FSAP), I was sure that due to the advances made since 2003 the report would have a positive impact. Furthermore, we were the only G-20 country that hadn't carried out this analysis.

I underlined this issue to Cristina: We had to demonstrate positive actions while taking some kind of step toward establishing a technical dialogue, which the Central Bank never quit having with the IMF. My own policy was always to hold three-day meetings once a year with them, focused on monetary, exchange rate, and financial issues. The last of these meetings was held in Washington, far from the possibility of any public leaks.

I had learned that whatever didn't appear in the media didn't exist, just as Robert De Niro and Dustin Hoffman had portrayed this truth in the motion picture *Wag the Dog*. At those meetings, which were held in absolute privacy, Eyzaguirre ended up understanding why the exchange rate couldn't be allowed to appreciate. This signified a great difference with his predecessor, Anoop Singh.

Furthermore, these meetings served as a context in which to talk directly with Strauss Kahn:

"Look," I told him at one of the last meetings we had together, "the political authorities are worried about any report that might come out of the IMF."

"It wouldn't be in the best interest of either the IMF or Argentina for there to be a situation of greater tension once we've sent out our reports," he responded.

"Well, if there should be a very negative report, that would oblige the economy minister, or the President herself, to put out an immediate response," I explained.

"I don't want that!" he repeated.

Later, the spirit was a good one at the meeting that Boudou and I had separately with Strauss Kahn and Eyzaguirre in Istanbul at the Annual Meeting in October 2009. The French official—who had had a shoe thrown at him during his talk at a Turkish university, like the incident in which an Iraqi tried to bean U.S. President George W. Bush with a shoe during a press conference—told us that there was a willingness to "explore mechanisms" that would permit Argentina and the IMF to return to a normal relationship.

But on October 6, Minister Boudou let it slip to the press that we were very close to an agreement, and as soon as his feet touched our soil again, the Kirchners got hold of him from their residence and made him take it back. This turned out to be strategically counterproductive.

When my own meeting with Strauss Kahn was over, I, on the other hand, made mention in public of a couple of things that were of no great importance but that gave the impression that there might be hope for rebuilding a relationship of trust if a review of Argentina were carried out applying strictly technical criteria and with the lowest profile possible.

I think that this, once again, suggests Boudou's inexperience in handling international issues. When you're negotiating, you can show a good face in public, but you can't show the substance of what's being negotiated.

In Istanbul, I also received proposals that would permit Argentina to attain financing once again. The Friday before the start of the IMF meeting, I gave a talk at a seminar together with my colleague Nouriel Roubini. On Saturday, I had lunch with the CEO of the Merrill Lynch, at which we talked about the abundant liquidity available for emerging markets, just a year out from the worst of the global crisis. Within this context, they made a comment that was supposed to be flattering.

"Even Argentina could go out and issue debt."

"At what interest rate?" I asked.

"At 13.5 percent per annum for ten years."

"That sounds really expensive to me," I said. "I guess we'll have to keep working hard to lower that rate."

In the midst of these conversations, and after presenting a budget to Congress that provided no details of how the country would finance itself in 2010, two measures were taken that promised a sharp increase in spending: a plan to provide support to one hundred thousand labor cooperatives and a universal per-child family allowance.

I'm all for helping nonpayroll workers and unprotected children, but getting involved in the coop plan only served to expand the patronage system, and the per-child subsidy was launched with noteworthy improvisation.

It was while I was in Saint Andrews one Saturday, at the latest meeting of the G-20, that Cristina called to tell me that the head of ANSES (the social security administration) had told her that a Central Bank regulation made it impossible to distribute the funds for the child allowance through the banking system.

I explained to her that no such restriction existed. Immediately after we hung up, she called Boudou, who was sitting right beside me and repeated the same message to him. The minister gave her the same response I had, but added a scornful comment about his young successor at ANSES.

Since she still didn't trust our answer, she called Banco Macro Chairman Jorge Brito, a close contact of the Kirchner camp, to see how the benefit might be distributed. He suggested using the network of branches of the different banks and providing beneficiaries with a debit card.

These random queries showed—and indeed show—the level of improvisation that exists in the administration's social welfare strategy. What really mattered to Néstor Kirchner was to win back the confidence of the voters in the second loop of the

Buenos Aires area and to get the jump on the opposition in the public agenda battle, where the child allowance had already been advanced as a priority issue for 2010.

When in April the IMF approved capital expansion to offset the crisis and sent Argentina US$2.5 billion that corresponded to it as a stakeholder in the fund, we carried out an exhaustive analysis as to whether those funds should go to the Central Bank or the Treasury. After completing a study that encompassed a number of historical precedents, we came to the conclusion that governments were the shareholders in the IMF, so it was the government, in the end, that should decide what to do with the resources.

A heated discussion arose, however, between the Central Bank and the Economy Ministry, since the ministry wanted to convert that money from the IMF into pesos, and we refused, because that would have meant issuing ARS 10 billion over the course of December in a country where the currency in circulation only totaled ARS 90 billion. In other words, issuing those pesos would signify increasing the amount of money in circulation by 10 percent in a single month, and there was no calculation we could think of to show that the demand for pesos would increase by that much. What this meant, then, was that such a move would generate inflation, and this time, by monetary means.

In a note I sent to Treasury Secretary Juan Carlos Pezoa, I pointed out that such an operation would have a disruptive effect on the economy. I proposed that the Central Bank should not issue pesos in exchange of those dollars so that the operation would have a neutral monetary effect. In the end, Pezoa took my advice and sold the dollars on the open market, with excess pesos being used to pay costs and without there being an increase in currency in circulation.

Other countries, meanwhile, took advantage of those additional resources to pay off debt, rather than financing current costs. So it was that the much-maligned IMF ended up helping Argentina to cover its expenditures in 2009 with a fiscal surplus that would otherwise have gone up in smoke.

Argentina's failure to forge closer ties with the multilateral institution also reflected the limitations of the degree of commitment the administration had assumed with the G-20. All of the other countries involved met to seek joint solutions to the international crisis, but, from the outset, on the basis that they would share information, something that Argentina was only grudgingly willing to do.

The President was perfectly comfortable with having her picture taken with her peers at the G-20 summits. But she didn't feel that those meetings were of any benefit in concrete terms of opening the way to financing. And that was totally logical, since Argentina had not complied with any of the premises for achieving that objective.

And then, too, perhaps I overestimated the ability that this core of developed and developing countries might have in "containing" the Kirchners in the direction they were taking.

Independently of Argentina's particular situation, the G-20 managed to erect a retaining wall to stop the freefall that the world economy had begun following the Lehman Brothers bankruptcy, when we in the emerging countries considered that the G-7, made up of the world's wealthiest nations, was no longer a sufficient framework within which to contribute ideas capable of guaranteeing sustainable growth.

Once the sensation of a deep global crisis began to wane, however, the role of the G-20 became diluted and, today, it seems to have stalled midway to its objectives.

Still undefined is an outline for balancing countries like China that have a strong surplus with those like the United States that have a major deficit in their foreign accounts. The United

States wants and needs for China to spend more. Most countries tend to agree that Uncle Sam's being so far into the red has been the main factor in triggering global imbalances.

Pressure is being brought to bear on China for its currency to appreciate against the dollar as a means of increasing consumption of products from the rest of the world. In terms of today's international debate over foreign exchange policy considerations, this is the main issue. Anything else is practically anecdotal.

Chapter 9

The Temptation for the Reserves

In mid-February of 2006, a few months after Roberto Lavagna resigned, I went to visit him at his office on *Avenida* Diagonal Norte, very near the Federal Courthouse. We talked for about an hour and a half regarding the challenges that a scenario dominated by the Kirchners implied. When I was leaving, he accompanied me to the elevator and, as I was about to get in, he let fly with this explosive statement: "Watch out, because Kirchner wants to buy back YPF using reserves."

On December 31, 1990, the administration of President Carlos Menem issued Executive Decree No. 2,778, turning the fully state-owned Yacimientos Petrolíferos Fiscales Sociedad del Estado into a public corporation called YPF SA. The sale of the oil company was completed in October of 1992, when, under Federal Law No. 24,145, the firm available capital was privatized.

While this sparked harsh debate in the Chamber of Deputies (Lower House) Congresswoman Cristina Kirchner managed to push through a bill that she had authored, ratifying the Law on the Federalization of Hydrocarbons and the Privatization of YPF.

Oddly enough, in 2007, at a meeting held in the South Hall of Government House, Néstor Kirchner was to say, "We know all too well about the genocide that has taken place in our petroleum industry, that incredible privatization...If YPF had remained in our hands, we would now be taking in...between US$20 (billion) and US$25 (billion) or perhaps even US$30 billion a year."

But the fact is that he was one of the ones who, fifteen years earlier, permitted Menem to get the votes needed to push through the privatization, despite staunch resistance not only by deputies from the opposition Radical party, but also from his own Justicialist (Peronist) Party.

As President of the Federal Organization of Hydrocarbon Producing States (OFEPHI), grouping the provinces of Chubut, Formosa, Jujuy, La Pampa, Mendoza, Neuquén, Salta, and his own Santa Cruz, Kirchner lent his support to that privatization in exchange for the federal government's promise to pay those provinces royalties that had supposedly been "badly liquidated."

As former Radical Senator Rodolfo Terragno would recall, on August 30, 1991, Menem, along with ministers Domingo Cavallo and José Luis Manzano, signed a curious "conciliatory" pact with Santa Cruz, whereby they recognized a debt of US$480 million, in an accord contingent on passage of the law privatizing YPF. In effect, if the privatization didn't go through, payment of that liability would remain "without value or effect of any kind whatsoever," according to the final agreement that Menem and Kirchner signed.

On Tuesday, September 22, 1992, Kirchner, as governor of Santa Cruz, and the other OFEPHI governors held a press conference at the Government House, during which he called for support for the YPF privatization, urging dissident congressmen to at least provide the necessary quorum for the session that would consider this controversial bill.

Following the passage of that law, sale negotiations got under way in 1998, and a deal was sealed in 1999, when REPSOL, the Spanish oil company, ended up with YPF's share, for which it paid US$15.168 billion.

Kirchner's dream began to come true, meanwhile, just as he was leaving the presidency. In December 2007, stock totaling 14.9 percent of the oil company's shares was acquired by the Petersen Group, headed up by banker Enrique Eskenazi, who had close ties to the outgoing president, having been an ever-present figure in Santa Cruz's public works sector, and purchaser of the bank.

Eskenazi had also acquired the provincial banks of San Juan, Santa Fe, and Entre Ríos. His buy-in at Repsol-YPF was the result of the Spanish group's desire to sell off part of its assets in Latin America, but especially in Argentina, where regulatory issues have disrupted the development of the company.

Fifteen days after my talk with Lavagna, at the beginning of March 2006, I had one of my regular meetings with the President. Before he could beat me to the punch, I said, "Look, the operation with the IMF was a onetime deal, because it was a part of the Central Bank's liabilities, it had a neutral monetary effect, and the market handled it OK because it was perceived as a onetime transaction…Do you have anything else in mind?"

"We need to find a way for the reserves to be invested here," he said. "Why not YPF, I wonder?"

"We'll analyze it," I said, "but I doubt it. I don't see any central bank in the world buying stock. Generally speaking, their investments are highly conservative."

I saw how he reacted to such sincere questioning of his wishes when I laid out the technical unfeasibility of it for him. I knew right then that when such discussions came up, I needed to be able to offer him viable alternatives.

But in this particular case, I didn't even bother to analyze his suggestion with the Central Bank's teams, because I knew that the feasibility of a move like this was completely indefensible.

Shortly after that, Kirchner doggedly pursued the issue, asking me, "So? Did you have a look at the YPF thing?"

"There's no legal way to do it with reserves," I said.

In mid-2008, the daily *El Cronista* ran a story saying that Legal Secretary Carlos Zannini had started exploring three ways to comply with his boss's wishes.

One was to buy 25 percent of the shares of REPSOL for US$3 billion, taking advantage of the fact that while, in the rest of the world, oil was selling at US$90 a barrel, in Argentina it was price-regulated at under US$40 a barrel.

A second, more complicated option was to take over 10 percent of the shares that were currently in the hands of YPF workers, as a result of an agreement between YPF and the oil workers union, which ended up being rejected by company employees. Their objection turned into a lawsuit filed with a federal judge, so that Plan B was eventually rejected.

Then there was the most daring plan of all. It consisted of declaring the entire privatization of YPF null and void, alleging that there had never been a public tender or auction, two of the systems generally used to sell off a company of the dimensions of Argentina's biggest oil producer. But the high cost of the diplomatic tension that this kind of expropriation would generate with Spain eventually led the administration to shelve it.

Nevertheless, on October 22, 2008, when elimination of the private pension funds was announced, the option of renationalizing YPF came up again, and with it, REPSOL's share price dropped 15 percent on the Madrid Stock Exchange. The administration and YPF ended up having to officially deny the possibility to keep the company's value from tumbling still further. Still, the feeling remained afloat that the Kirchners would seek to take back what they had contributed to privatizing in the Menem era a decade before.

* * *

On May 5, 2007, the mass circulation daily *La Nación* reported that the top brass of the Construction Industry Chamber (CAC)—which represents a sector that has become the bastion of Argentina's economic growth and with the greatest backing of the administration—had been received by President Néstor Kirchner, who had given the group a message of support. According to the report, the President had told them that "the government is accumulating reserves to invest in public works."

The news story explained that Kirchner's support was based on a reform of the Central Bank's charter, drafted by Congresswoman Mercedes Marcó del Pont, who wanted to add the intention "to maintain a high level of activity and ensure maximum employment of available human and material resources, within the framework of sustainable economic expansion."

Accompanying the CAC's Wagner was the organization's secretary, Gregorio Chodos, father of Sergio Chodos. I immediately asked for a meeting with the President and spoke with Cabinet Chief Alberto Fernández. I was so upset that I didn't even recognize my own tone when I said, "Alberto, this is crazy! Why don't we start a development bank? That way, we can each do what we're supposed to."

"Take it easy, I'm going to talk to him. You do the same on your own," Fernández said.

When I saw the President, I tried to comply with the idea of presenting "alternatives."

"There are a lot smarter options, Néstor," I said. "You've got the pension funds with which to work on long-term financing. And the National Bank is practically paralyzed, but it should indeed be a tool with which to create a development bank."

Right away, I presented some ideas for how *Banco Nación* could unify the stock of public funds so as to take better advantage of them. I pointed out that each public agency, had its own financial manager, with no coordination among them. None of this had ever been unified, even though the Treasury had then captured these resources in order to make debt payments when faced with increasing fiscal weakness and the impossibility of access to voluntary credit.

* * *

On September 2, 2008, when we were in the second day of our Monetary Conference, an announcement by the President regarding payment of the Paris Club using Central Bank reserves caught me completely off guard.

Some members of my team even believed that the announcement had been made precisely on that day because the debate at the meetings in the Central Bank had garnered too much media coverage to suit the administration's style.

That suspicion grew even deeper when the President lifted a statement I had made the day before at the meetings as justification for full payment of the Paris Club. "Today," she said publicly, "I read something in the newspapers that Central Bank President **Martín Redrado** had said about how the past condemns us, and he's right."

Many analysts took this to be a slap in the face for me as an official of previous administrations. I had, indeed, said this the day before, but in another context, when I explained that Argentina couldn't consider itself exempt from the global financial crisis because "our past condemns us," due to the mistakes we made in that past which oblige us to "dramatically reverse the burden of proof." And I added, "It isn't realistic for us to think that we can disengage ourselves completely from what's going on in the world, if the external context should continue to deteriorate."

Despite this fact, in her eagerness to deny domestic problems and lay the blame on others, the President had categorically minimized any possibility of infection from the foreign crisis. She had even gone as far as to try to impose the term "jazz effect" that she had coined to describe the worldwide market crash arising from the crisis that started in the United States.

I let Cristina's statement roll off my back, although I did send the couple a report on a number of different options that they might consider. But they never called me.

I tried to react as serenely as possible in public, stating that the decision to pay off the Paris Club formed part "of an overall strategy aimed at gaining access to the voluntary debt markets" and reinserting Argentina into the international financial community.

I believe that, just as happened with the Bicentennial Fund a year later, they already knew how I was going to react. After this announcement, there were some very tense moments, because the Central Bank was accused of planting the negative reports that came out in the news media in the days that followed saying that the markets hadn't approved of it.

The truth is that, following the government's clash with farmers, a strong feeling remained that the country was having problems paying its debt, to the extent that it prompted two rating agencies to lower Argentina's grade.

It was for that reason that, after the President's announcement, far from going up, our bonds remained weak as the market awaited other signals, like the debt repurchasing plan that was finally implemented in such a lukewarm way that it ended up failing entirely. Additionally, we once again suffered tension on the foreign exchange market, because of the perception that it would be hard for us to recover the foreign reserves that would be used to cancel the country's debt with the Paris Club.

In order to execute this idea of Kirchner's about paying off the Paris Club in order to allow Cristina to regain the political initiative they used an executive decree, like they had in the case of the IMF. But their big mistake was to compare the Paris Club with a multilateral institution. The Paris Club is actually a group of countries that make use of a joint negotiating format, but then final negotiation must be closed with each individual creditor.

That's why, a few days later, they had to resort to a DNU (Decree of Necessity and Urgency), which was submitted for discussion of the congressional committee.

Parallel to this, we at the Central Bank submitted the DNU to the board for discussion, and out of this came corresponding legal and technical reports.

Meanwhile, the Paris Club leaked information to the effect that Argentina's debt came to US$7.9 billion, instead of the US$6.7 billion that the President's decree ordered to pay.

For its part, the administration began to backpedal, saying that the onetime payment to the club would only include past due arrears The rest, with due dates in the future, would be canceled in installments later.

But, in the end, the crisis generated by the fall of Lehman Brothers—which managed to convince the government that, even if it canceled its debt, the world's more highly developed nations wouldn't lend it any money—and the administration's lack of personal contacts in the Paris Club kept that operation from materializing.

The failure of the move crystallized on February 9, 2009, when the government publicly admitted that payment of the Paris Club had been placed "on standby." Reality itself, then, had confirmed my position regarding reserves.

* * *

Perhaps the most stark-raving mad attempt of all to lay hands on the Central Bank reserves was Moreno's scheme to build "a popular and Peronist automobile" on the strength of Central Bank rediscounts that we would be expected to provide, free of charge, to the banks to finance consumer purchases of the car.

Toward the end of November 2008, the drop in new car sales was threatening to bring mass layoffs in the industry, so the administration called on the Commerce Secretary to come up with a "creative solution" to keep this from happening. The first brick wall Moreno ran into was posed by the car companies themselves, who told him that it was impossible to manufacture a special car. The alternative, they said, would be to put out more basic versions of existing models so that people could buy them at a more accessible rate.

Pigheaded as usual, the Secretary convinced Néstor Kirchner to appeal to rediscounts from the Central Bank, arguing that this was "money for free." Right away, in the first week of December, Cristina called me and asked me to go to Olivos to talk about it.

"You've got to put up the rediscounts in order to push this idea," she said.

"Look, the Central Bank is a lender of last resort," I explained. "When all of the dominoes topple over, we have to still be standing. If we put up money for cars, then somebody will come along and say, 'Why not textiles?' Besides, in a context in which people are fleeing from the peso, you can't go throwing cash onto the market, because you're going to give people an incentive to buy dollars."

Without showing any great conviction, she asked me to write up a memo "to get the ideas straight," and I immediately complied.

The next day her husband called me on the phone and, taking an angry tone, said, "I don't agree at all with your policy!"

"Let's talk about it," I said. "Let me invite you to a cup of coffee."

"All right," he said, "I'll call you within the next forty-eight hours."

He never called, and the idea of the rediscounts dissipated.

On Saturday, December 6, the administration presented a plan "to facilitate access to a first new car" based on financing from the social security administration. This plan was headed up by Amado Boudou and presumed to use retirement funds in an investment scheme that was almost certain to be detrimental to the savings of future pensioners.

Automakers signed the agreement, but in practice, it turned out to be a system that was entirely too complex, so in the end, each company opted to offer its own discounts, without any state subsidy. In February, a revival of economic activity in Brazil ended up being the factor that kept the auto industry afloat.

Once again, genuine economic growth replaced Moreno's arbitrary willfulness.

* * *

Another attempt to grab "free" money, in March 2009, was not on foreign reserves, but on the effective minimum reserves deposited in the Central Bank by the country's banking institutions. Finance Secretary Hernán Lorenzino first posed the possibility to me of issuing short-term T-bills of up to one year, which would permit the government to take advantage of that liquidity. We discussed whether this idea might not override our sterilization program, whose clients were precisely the same institutions as the target of the proposed program. I asked Lorenzino, in any case, to proceed using good judgment.

"As long as you do it in a voluntary manner," I said, "you might give it a try, if the effects on the rest of the economy are also coordinated."

Economy Minister Carlos Fernández called me to try to convince me that we needed to take advantage of the possibility of issuing a bond that could be used as banks' regulatory reserve requirements. But I explained to him that those reserves were frozen by the Central Bank as part of a liquidity safety net, a retaining wall, in case of a run like the one that had affected deposits during the domestic crisis.

What this meant was that converting these reserves into bonds could end up tying our hands later on. The President called me later, of course, to try to talk me into it, but I played my hand to the limit in order to make sure the initiative didn't prosper.

"That's the same thing Cavallo did in June 2001," I exclaimed, "and that year we ended up defaulting!"

End of discussion. At the Central Bank, we kept on analyzing options that might permit us to generate some solution that wouldn't lead to reheating inflation. For this to happen, there would have to be a fiscal program that was consistent with recovering the credibility Argentina had lost.

This concept was explained by Central Bank Director Carlos Pérez in July of 2009 in one of the few radio interviews that he ever granted as an official.

The response from Olivos consisted of asking me to obtain Pérez's resignation. It was a request I wasn't willing to grant them, to such an extent that I never told Pérez about it. They were simply eluding discussion of the real issue in question.

This reaction made me realize that the Kirchners would do whatever they had to in order to increase spending, with their only aim being to maintain their grip on power.

They were prepared to do whatever it took…and more.

Chapter 10

A Battle Is Not a War

At this point, I want to share with the reader my daily thoughts and feelings as of the moment that the administration decided to appropriate the Central Bank's reserves. Or, in other words, from the moment when our country started living with *No Reserve*. This is the chronicle of a story that remains open ended.

December 14, 2009

At midday, Minister Amado Boudou announced the creation of the Bicentennial Fund for Debt Reduction and Stability, making use of Central Bank reserves, with the aim of clearing away "uncertainty" and "lowering the interest rate for both the government and the private sector, simultaneously generating less stress on the fiscal front." He made no mention at all of the administration's fiscal problems, which were what actually prompted this decision. Beside the minister was Cristina Kirchner, in an event that was broadcast in a nationwide network television presentation. The message that we at the Central Bank put out made it clear that we had certain qualms about this initiative. A board member who would later claim party loyalty to change his position commented the following in a private meeting:

"We need to maintain the strategy of returning to the voluntary debt markets, which includes carrying out a swap for bondholders with whom we remain in default.

- "We must meet the fiscal surplus guideline for 2010, following a year that ended with a deficit, disguised with money from ANSES and the IMF. Otherwise, the low interest rate available right now will evaporate within a few months.

- "We have to handle the demand for money carefully in a world that will grow more, and, in particular, in a country that will be facing greater inflation.

- "We must preserve institutional backing through congressional ratification of the DNU that will modify the use given to reserves."

At first, the markets took the announcement as a positive sign, since the government was ensuring payment of its debts, even if by whatever means it could—something about which bondholders, of course, couldn't have cared less. Be that as it may, the announcement didn't produce anything like euphoria, nor did it bolster the scant volume of business negotiated in previous sessions. Over the next three days, the country's risk rating dropped, but by the same measure that it did for other emerging countries. In other words, this was a global phenomenon that wasn't attributable to the Bicentennial Fund.

In any case, that day it became clear that Néstor Kirchner wanted to transform the Central Bank into a development bank. The fact is that Argentina should indeed have this kind of an institution, but with specific funding of its own drawn from the Treasury, as in the case of those in Brazil or Mexico.

Regardless of all this, there were two main elements of the DNU that worried me: the exclusion of the concept of neutral monetary effect that had indeed been included in the legal provisions for payment of the IMF, and the disregard shown for embargoes imposed by foreign creditors.

It was just a matter of days before the administration began to compare the move to payment of the IMF. Néstor Kirchner even went as far as to tell radio anchor Víctor Hugo Morales that if I had agreed to payment of the IMF, he didn't understand why I wouldn't accept in this case. The differences, however, were clear. The most obvious one was its inflationary impact. The most subtle one was the effect of this move on the soundness of the Central Bank's balance sheet, since the IMF debt had been a Bank liability.

In the end, the clearest difference of all was that the Bicentennial Fund plan talked about making reserves available "for payment of debt"—or, in other words, any obligation whatsoever.

December 15

The day after the Bicentennial Fund had been launched, I felt that, despite the fact that they had just dropped an anvil on my head, I should go on. I got up very early and, of course, read the newspapers. It surprised me that while the announcement had generated a certain amount of alarm, there appeared to be no sensation of a desperate last resort.

In fact, on that day, even several Wall Street banks put out reports containing mixed conclusions, saying, on the one hand, that the announcement of the use of reserves to pay off debt provided guarantees for Argentine bonds, but, on the other, warning that this move ratified the administration's scant will to put its fiscal house in order. I can't say that this reaction came as a surprise to me. I know Wall Street from the inside. I began my professional career there, and I know that it is obsessed with next-quarter earnings. It has a strongly speculative profile, and the Argentine government was proposing a good deal for it. Native progressivism was staunchly defending foreign banking interests. What paradoxes life can bring!

At J.P. Morgan, Vladimir Werning, the bank's research director, indicated that "with this measure, [Argentina] is trying to provide positive signals, in order to cover up its incapacity in other affairs that were launched to please the market, like the negotiation with the Paris Club and talks with the IMF about monitoring its accounts."

Investment house Goldman Sachs made the closest review, which underscored the fact that "although positive in regard to short-term credit, it is clearly negative in institutional terms, since it weakens the Central Bank and provides the government with incentives to expand its spending." Goldman Sachs analyst Alberto Ramos went on to say that "this undermines the Central Bank balance sheet and provides the government with all the wrong incentives."

Contrary to this, Argentine Banking Association President Jorge Brito, who was totally aligned with the administration, said that the Bicentennial Fund "...provides Argentina with certainty...permits the lowering of the country's risk rating...[and opens possibilities] for more investments to come in..."

I knew that the world would be awaiting my statement following the government's announcement. So I focused on the talk that I had prepared for the conference organized by a major industrial group (Tenaris) at the Hilton Hotel. Media representatives were waiting for me in the lobby of the hotel in the posh Puerto Madero district to try to get a statement from me before I gave my talk, but I headed straight for the elevator. In the little room next to the conference hall, I talked with Paolo Rocca (President of Tenaris) and with the company's director, Luis Betnaza.

"How do you feel with US$6.5 billion less in your balance sheet?" Rocca asked ironically.

"It's not gone yet," I said, and then added, "And how did you feel when Chávez expropriated Sidor from you?"

"He hasn't paid me for it yet!" Rocca exclaimed, and then we both burst out laughing.

Then we went into the conference hall to close the event. I didn't make many changes in the speech that I had prepared prior to announcement of the Bicentennial Fund, but I placed greater emphasis on some of the points that I had had in mind and underscored certain aspects of my administration, stressing business that remained pending. A point to which I gave special emphasis was when I said, "Argentina must duplicate its credit in the years to come. It is important for both companies and the public sector to return to the voluntary markets. And here there is no room for shortcuts."

Taking stock, I made it clear that since 2004, we had been guided by technical approach. "Professional criteria," I said, "are what have served as the guidelines for Central Bank procedure."

Later, I returned to my perennial observation regarding inflation, without having any idea that it would be the last time I would state it as head of the Central Bank.

"Inflation has dropped," I said, "but in order for this process to continue, we must keep close watch on two areas: fiscal policy and revenues, including the wage policy. When you see signs of inflation, the problem doesn't stem from the Central Bank. The problem stems from the other branches of economic policy."

December 16

Amado Boudou stated that Argentina "would now be in a position to garner single-digit interest rates," as he was going into a meeting of the General Business Confederation of the

Argentine Republic (better known as the CGERA). But the truth was that, beyond pure propaganda, no such conditions existed. Furthermore, at that point in time, the debt swap to free the country from its default status had run into technical difficulties, due to the incomplete presentation that the Economy Ministry had made to the U.S. Securities and Exchange Commission (SEC). In this same audacious style, the minister announced that the following week, the government would start using reserves, when this had not yet been authorized by law.

December 17

The opposition reacted formally, if somewhat tepidly, against the Bicentennial Fund in a letter sent to me by the heads of the opposition blocs in the Chamber of Deputies (Lower House of Congress)— Oscar Aguad (UCR), Elisa Carrió (CC), Federico Pinedo (PRO), and Felipe Solá (PJ Federal)—in which they warned the Central Bank board not to make use of the reserves:

> *"The Charter of the Central Bank stipulates that the main function of the institution that is under your responsibility is to preserve the value of currency, which is the value of the labor of the Argentine people. It is for this aim that the reserves are allocated under the Law of the Nation. It is also with this aim that the Central Bank has been provided with independence from the powers that be in the Executive Branch, and maintaining same is the duty of its authorities.*
>
> *"You should be reminded, Mr. President, of paragraphs 6, 7 and 11 of Article 75 of the National Constitution that grants exclusive authority to   Congress to regulate the functioning of that Bank, for settling payment of public debt and for setting the value of currency.*

"Consequently, in our capacity as heads of the opposition blocs in Congress, we hereby demand that you comply with your legal duties and abstain from releasing Central Bank reserves to the Treasury, over and above the limits set in the Charter, until such time as this is authorized by a formal law from Congress."

Parallel to this, a discussion ensued over composition of the joint congressional committee for Decrees of Necessity and Urgency (DNUs), whose job it was to review the decree dictated by the President. The governing party made a preemptive strike against the logical call of the opposition to have a greater number of lawmakers on the committee, reflecting the new situation that prevailed in Congress. They wanted to maintain the group with four governing party legislators and four from the opposition. Faced with this challenge, the opposition swore that it would fight to chair the committee, since the chair would have a tie-breaking double vote. With no agreement being reached over who would chair it, the committee was eventually headed up jointly by Luis Petcoff Naidendoff (opposition UCR) and Diana Conti (governing FPV), until the conflict could be resolved, together with Miguel Pichetto, Nicolás Fernández, Beatriz Rojkes de Alperovich, Liliana Negre de Alonso, Jorge Landau, and Agustín Rossi (from the administration's FPV camp), Adolfo Rodríguez Saá (PJ) and opposition members Marcelo Guinle (UCR), Ramón Mestre (UCR), Luis Cigona (UCR), Juan Tunnessi (UCR), Rubén Lanceta (UCR), Enrique Thomas (PUP), and Marcela Rodríguez (CC).

December 18
The final destination of the fund was growing ever more confused. Vice Minister of Economy Roberto Feletti at first said that

the Central Bank reserves would be employed to guarantee debt payment but without actually being used.

But that Friday, at a year-end cocktail party for journalists, Minister Boudou glibly announced that the idea was to spend all of the money made available by the decree.

He also confirmed that the administration had no intention whatsoever of reviewing the sharp rise in spending of the last few years, stating that the Bicentennial Fund would give the administration "more resources, so as to permit it to guarantee the primary surplus for the year to come."

My confusion continued to grow. No two people in the administration had the same discourse regarding the Bicentennial Fund. That night, while draft technical reports began to emerge that would be taken to the Central Bank board for discussion, my wife, Ivana, and I attended the wedding of the daughter of the former secretary of the Buenos Aires Stock Exchange, José Cirilo, whom I knew from twenty years before, and with whom I had started a project in 1999 called *Invertir Online* (Invest Online), which was a pioneering enterprise in Internet investment on the local market.

On our arrival, we were seated at the same table with brokerage Cabinet Chief of the Government of the City of Buenos Aires, Horacio Rodríguez Larreta and his wife, Bárbara Diez, whose daughter, Paloma, is one of our daughter Martina's best friends. At first, we talked a little about the situation in the city, and then I commented about the letter I had received from (opposition leader Federico) Pinedo. In the midst of this discussion, Horacio said, "Why don't you talk to Federico?"

"Be glad to," I responded.

"I'll call you tomorrow," Horacio said.

December 19 and 20

I spent the weekend with my family. I repeated the weekend ritual of going to play tennis with my son, Tomás, at the Vilas Club in Belgrano, taking advantage of the fact that it was a nice early summer day. While I was having lunch, the phone rang. It was Horacio. We agreed to meet with Pinedo at eight o'clock that evening at his house. The three of us were very punctual, and since I have known Federico Pinedo for twenty-five years, there was no beating around the bush.

"Instead of sending out letters, Congress should be taking action," I suggested.

"I agree," Pinedo said. "The thing is, the time of year doesn't help." Then he closed rather mysteriously, saying, "I'm going to think about a legal strategy."

I made it clear that the issue hadn't reached the Central Bank Board of Directors yet and that the corresponding analyses were being carried out. That Sunday, San Luis Governor Alberto Rodríguez Sáa told one of the members of my team that he was planning the next day to make a legal presentation to the courts saying that the use of reserves to pay debt was unconstitutional. This day was the eighth anniversary of the tragic incidents that had brought the Alianza administration to an abrupt end, and, despite this clash over the use of foreign reserves, the country was choosing a relatively calm path.

December 21

The board decided to meet on this day to approve the 2010 monetary program instead of waiting for its traditional Thursday session, since that day was going to be Christmas Eve. The message that we stressed in that program was the need "to consolidate the recovery process seen in the domestic economy over the past several months," which was far from the "autistic" attitude of which certain pro-administration sectors had been accusing us. We committed to expansion of the amount of money in circulation, consistent with the pesos that we projected would be demanded in 2010, taking into account the reverting of the capital flight process seen during the last quarter of the year.

I attempted to make the board meeting like any other one, although I started out with a more displeased tone, using words that were encouraging but preventive. Speaking to the directors, I said, "Let's work, but let's do it in such a way as to make a positive contribution to our economy, but the message should not be the Executive has no limits and so it is going to grab the money.'"

Nevertheless, a news item in the daily *Ámbito Financiero* had caused a stir in the Economy Ministry, since it indicated that I had "sent the Bicentennial Fund DNU to our legal department, with the idea being to determine the legality of the operation and avoid future lawsuits."

Indeed, the article reflected a concern that was shared by all of the Central Bank's board members, even the most pro-Kirchner ones among them. But the administration, with its conspiracy-theory vision of reality, was certain that it was a move to stall them.

December 22

Curiously enough, it wasn't until this day that the Economy Ministry sent us a request for the opening of a Treasury account at the Central Bank, so that we could deposit the money. Payment and Operations Manager Julio Siri received the formal request from the Secretary of the Treasury, Juan Carlos Pezoa.

The fact is that we started processing the request on that same day, December 22. To this end, I asked for the opinions of the

Legal, Economy and Finance, and Reserve Management sections, not in the form of drafts, but as final reports.

How, then, could they be accusing us of stalling, when it had taken them an entire week since the President launched the decree just to put in this simple request?

The Bank's administrative chief, Norberto Domínguez, together with board member Zenón Biagosch, came up with the advice of consulting our external auditors KPMG in order to help us determine the value that should be placed on the note that we would be receiving in exchange for the transfer of funds. The aim here was to exploit the impact of the decree on the Central Bank's balance sheet.

Nevertheless, without waiting for any of the technical opinions, which were indispensable for a step of this magnitude, the Economy Ministry unilaterally decreed the issuing of a single T-note for the US$6.569 billion mentioned in the corresponding decree. The ministry did this in spite of the fact that we had formerly analyzed the possibility of partial and progressive installment carried out each time debt was paid off with reserves. Boudou leaked word that he was taking "revenge" for our supposed message (which never existed) to the *Ámbito Financiero* newspaper. He further resolved that the funds should not be transferred, but that they should remain in the Central Bank, so that the "vulture funds" that had brought several legal actions against Argentina for the still-pending default in the United States and Europe wouldn't have a perfect excuse to attach them.

In the afternoon, opposition UCR National Committee Chairman Ernesto Sanz sent me a letter requesting that we abstain from transferring the reserves, maintaining that decree 2010 "is neither necessary nor urgent, invades an area reserved for Congress, fails to recognize the autonomy of the Central

Bank, and undermines the intangibility of reserves, compromising the deposits of that Bank abroad."

After citing several pertinent legal precedents, he indicated that "the decisive factor here is that there is no motive whatsoever that can be seriously argued for not turning to Congress for a decision on an issue of this nature. There was nothing to keep it from being submitted to the regular sessions for treatment this year, and nothing, either, to impede the calling of extraordinary sessions for discussion of this question."

"Why, instead of so much rhetoric," I asked myself, "don't they just do their job?" I couldn't seem to come up with an answer.

That night, there was a dinner to which sixty top business people were invited at the Olivos Residence. Its aim was to reestablish confidence and dialogue with the government. None of those present remarked to Cristina or Nestor Kirchner on the issue of Central Bank as an institution, or on having the slightest concern regarding reserves.

December 23

Internal affairs were running their own course, but the Economy Ministry again put pressure on us, this time verbally.

I repeat: There was a profound contradiction between discourse and actions. They took a week simply to ask us to open the accounts in which to deposit the reserves. In the meantime, we began to study both the ways and means of the issue, even before we received any formal request.

That Wednesday, Treasury Secretary Juan Carlos Pezoa called me to see if we could speed up the transfer. I stopped him cold.

"Just as you're a very meticulous public servant, so are we. So just wait until the reports from the different areas can reach the board and we can vote accordingly."

Meanwhile, in no other technical contact with the bank had the Economy Ministry reflected this kind of urgency. The Central Bank's general manager, Hernán Lacunza, sent the letters from Sanz and the opposition party leaders in Congress to the heads of the legal studies and reports division.

There was a feeling that the officials' minds were elsewhere. I recall that in those days I had a conversation with Central Bank Auditor Hugo Álvarez. He visited me in the morning to have a cup of coffee and tell me that he was going on vacation for a couple of weeks.

"I'll be back on January 15," he said.

To make sure we weren't going to fall behind on the DNU paperwork, I asked him, "Do you have any sense of urgency with regard to the Bicentennial Fund issue?"

"No," he said. "If I did, I'd stay."

This dialogue begins to take on more importance when one considers the fact that Álvarez had been the auditor at Banco de Santa Cruz in the Kirchners' home province, and, later, director at Banco Macro in representation of the administration. He was finally designated auditor of the Central Bank in March 2009. It was to be assumed that he was a person with a pretty direct line of communication with regard to goings-on in the Executive Branch.

I thus felt that his message meant we could continue to work as we had up to that moment, analyzing all aspects of the issue so as to be very sure before we made any major decision. Clearly, I was mistaken.

With that in mind I called the Cabinet Chief Aníbal Fernández who received me right away at his office on the first floor of Government House.

I began to repeat one of the arguments I had used two weeks before: the possibility that the reserves used to pay off debt might be attached by bondholders abroad. I reaffirmed my position by carrying along a memorandum from the law firm that represented the Argentine government in the United States, Cleary, Gottlieb, Steen & Hamilton, who warned of the possibility of this kind of move on the part of foreign investors.

"Aníbal, this could cause difficulties," I said. "We may get into trouble with the embargoes."

"Look, Martín," he said, "prepare alternatives, but you have to talk to (Legal Secretary Carlos) Zannini. I'm here for when the pizza dough is ready to go, but he's in the kitchen putting the ingredients together."

When I was leaving, Aníbal, with his habitual smile, felt me out to assure himself that I would do what they were asking of me.

"Martín," he said, "you know that the renewal dates for all official appointments are coming up. There's the one for Mercedes [Marcó del Pont] at Banco Nación in early January, and there's yours in September. And you're a shoo-in to continue there. So, you know, any alternatives you can bring us will be appreciated."

If anything had been left to my imagination before, now I could understand everything. They thought that if they promised to renew my appointment, I would give in to them on the use of the reserves. That was why, since 2008, they hadn't bothered to consult me about their use, from the time that I opposed the Paris Club payment.

When Aníbal mentioned the possibility of the renewal of my term, however, I acted like I hadn't heard him and insisted that, first, I had to find a sound solution to the Bicentennial Fund issue.

* * *

Staying was an alternative. But as I was fond of saying, in terms of professional fatigue, six years at the head of the

Argentine Central Bank was equivalent to Alan Greenspan's eighteen years at the head of the U.S. Federal Reserve.

During my term, we had constructed the four pillars of monetary policy to uphold a more normal monetary and financial policy in Argentina. I felt that my mission had been accomplished. It was time to move on to another stage. Even so, had someone asked me in those days, I would have said that long-term in Argentina was eight months. I didn't want to become, as they say in North American politics, a "lame duck" to whom nobody paid any attention in my last months in office.

Furthermore, there were pending economic policy issues, like this obsession with overheated consumption, and the idea of hanging onto political power at all costs, which led me to believe that 2011 was going to be a highly complex year, since the Central Bank could end up being used for just about any purpose at all.

I preferred to complete my cycle, leaving behind a legacy of stability on the seventy-fifth anniversary of the Central Bank's founding, and to be able to state that, for the first time in decades, "the Central Bank is a solid cornerstone of the Argentine economy."

December 24

Without even wasting the day before Christmas, the Bank's Economy and Finance Division, under the direction of Pedro Rabasa, drafted a full report in response to DNU 2010 and to the heads of the opposition blocs in Congress in which it demolished the arguments in favor of the presidential decree, based on two main points:

- The Bicentennial Fund would receive freely available reserves from the Central Bank, but the definition of "freely available reserves" was only economically plausible when the Convertibility System was in effect, and, hence, when the monetary liabilities of the Central Bank were basically the components of the monetary base.

- Therefore, since the Convertibility System was dismantled for the purpose of calculating the definition of excess reserves, one must take into account not only the monetary base, but also all other Central Bank liabilities: reserve requirements on dollar deposits, repos, and Lebac/Nobac bonds. If all of these liabilities are taken into account, the Central Bank possesses no excess reserves.

- In such a scenario, in which economic agents realize that there is no positive net balance, pressure will be brought to bear on the foreign exchange market, as will upward pressure on interest rates. This pressure will increase to the extent that people start thinking that instead of the US$6.569 billion mentioned in the decree, the US$18 billion considered, *a priori* to be "excess reserves," could end up being used.

- Regarding the differences between this and payment of the IMF, the two biggest ones are that the latter was done without producing any monetary effect and with the assurances that reserves would be used on a one-time basis for the payment of international agencies, since it was taken for granted that the country would continue refinancing its debts with the World Bank and the IDB.

- With regard to the urgency invoked in the wording of the DNU, in the first quarter of 2010, services on the public debt would come to nearly ARS 23.213 billion, of which 60 percent corresponds to renewals within the public sector, temporary advances from the Central Bank to the Treasury, and *Banco Nación* loans. Of the remaining 40 percent—about ARS 8.64 billion— the Treasury had deposits in the banking system of ARS 7.7 billion, which could be supplemented with loans from the IDB, the World Bank, the National Bank, and advances from the Central Bank.

- Therefore, no such urgency exists.

With this report in hand, I left the Central Bank to spend Christmas Eve with my family, my parents-in-law, and my brother-in-law, Sebastián, who had arrived from Brazil, where he works, accompanied by his girlfriend, a lovely young blonde who had a lot of trouble speaking Spanish.

December 25

But the respite didn't last long. I had lunch with my mother and her husband and shared my concern with them. "Do what your conscience tells you," my mother said. "You always showed good judgment and it has always gone well for you." In the afternoon, I got together with my team and set to work on what Aníbal Fernández had asked me for: alternatives to the Bicentennial Fund.

I also used the time to call some government officials, whom I thought might be capable of clearing some of the hurdles to a negotiated solution that had run aground midstream.

I talked to Senate leader José "Pepe" Pampuro, who has shown a great willingness to reach a consensus.

But Pepe's first reflection didn't put me at ease. "You've got a serious problem," he said. "And the opposition's stance is more one of rhetoric than of any real power in terms of putting a legal stop to the decree."

"Pepe," I said, "I want to see how you can give us a hand. Above all, by not rushing us. I don't see any urgent debt expirations on the part of the public sector, so with these things, it's better not to rush, because we could end up in more trouble."

Pampuro agreed to talk to the Kirchners, but he never called me back.

My team and I kept working through the weekend of the twenty-sixth and twenty-seventh so as to be able to present the administration with alternative actions.

December 28

At six in the evening, I went to see that man whom Fernández described as having the pan by the handle: namely, Presidential Legal and Technical Secretary Carlos Zannini. With the aim of continuing to demonstrate a willingness to cooperate, I carried with me a folder containing two different options.

When I was starting to explain them, the President called us into her office. I pitched the alternatives we had been working on to both of them.

The first was to use the money mentioned in the DNU as a collateral fund deposited in the Central Bank. An account would be opened to provide guarantees for debt issued by the Treasury, but the actual funds would remain in the Bank.

In this way, debt would be paid off using regular resources of the Treasury or with new financing, with the peace of mind of knowing that the funds were available in the Central Bank.

This would probably be sufficient to reduce the interest rate paid by the country on a ten-year bond to 8 percent per annum, and allow us to advance with the idea of attaining voluntary credit. In point of fact, two investment banks had already agreed to issue an Argentine bond. And furthermore, we could always act as "lenders of last resort" if there were some problem.

The second option consisted of making use of additional resources that could be made available through the National Bank (*Banco Nación*) and the social security administration (ANSES). I proposed that if Kirchner didn't want to sell the shares in Tenaris and Telefónica that the government owned through ANSES, it could put those shares up as collateral for loans. And we, of course, would contribute with the corresponding Central Bank earnings to be transferred to the Treasury, in this case, for about US$2.2 billion. In this way, we could close the discussion over Central Bank earnings for 2009, so as not to generate a negative monetary effect.

All of these resources added up to the US$6.6 billion equivalent to the Bicentennial Fund, divided into three parts: US$2.2 billion from the National Bank in the form of surplus deposits from a number of different government agencies, US$2.2 billion from a loan based on shares in the hands of ANSES, and US$2.2 billion from the Central Bank.

These were two distinct alternatives, but both were consistent and properly prepared from a technical standpoint.

The President appeared to be listening to me attentively. Seeming at ease, she said, "What you're saying sounds all right to me. We'll talk the issue over with Boudou again and see how to reach the objectives."

Needless to say, I had taken a sheet along for her, providing a summary of all the details.

"Leave it with me," she said, "and I'll call you back."

We never talked about the subject again.

December 29

The provincial government of San Luis presented an appeal to the Supreme Court seeking to block the government from making use of Central Bank reserves. It was the last business brought before the end of its regular sessions, and the justices had to decide whether to issue a precautionary measure before they began a month-long recess. The presentation was signed by former attorney general Eduardo Allende and administrative attorney Rodolfo Barra, who had served as justice minister in the administration of President Carlos Menem.

The appeal maintained that Decree 2010/09 was unconstitutional and null and void without remedy for several reasons.

The first of these was that there was neither necessity nor urgency to justify a DNU, since, after the Constitution, the provinces delegated determination of the value of the country's currency to the Congress and to the Central Bank.

A second reason was the government's decision to avail itself of funds from the Central Bank, instead of using the ARS 26.5 billion expressly approved in the last federal budget. What this signified was that the resources approved by Congress would be used to increase public spending, which would produce inflation, which would, in turn, affect the people of that province.

That evening, Minister Boudou stated that the question of reserves was "not subject to judicial review," just as the Kirchners were preparing to leave the next morning for El Calafate in their home province to spend a quiet New Year's holiday.

December 30

On the last working day of the year, I received the report of the Central Bank's Legal Division, headed by María del Carmen Urquiza (a professional with twenty-five years of experience at the Institution). It carried her signature and those of Assistant Manager for Legal Reports Cristian Pujol and Senior Legal Analyst Martín Carreras. It was clear and to the point:

> *"No consideration has been formulated in Decree 2010* [the Bicentennial decree] *that would justify the kind of urgent nature that would permit the Executive Branch to make use of this type of exceptional mechanism."*

It then went on to detail all of the faculties delegated by Congress to the Central Bank through its charter and for compliance with its objective of regulating the quantity of money and credit in the economy and dictating regulations, without being subject to instructions from the Executive Branch of the federal government, since exclusive control over it was a faculty of Congress.

The thirty-four-page report concluded by saying, "…it appears advisable that this institution should await congressional intervention before following up on the process provided for in Art. 3 of Decree 2010…."

* * *

During that tense day, Congressman Pinedo unveiled the legal strategy he had mentioned by making a presentation before an administrative court of appeals. But he made the mistake of failing to request for suspension of the court's summer recess, so the issue was left pending until February. He was accompanied in presenting this appeal by Congressman Patricia Bullrich, Juan Carlos Vega and Alfonso Prat Gay (former Central Bank Governor).

Meanwhile, the Supreme Court declared itself competent in the appeal presented by San Luis Province, but said that it would take up this issue as of the second month of the new year. Nevertheless, the court asked the administration, through Attorney General Esteban Righi, for a detailed explanation, within ten days, of the nature of and the grounds for the controversial measure presented in DNU 2010.

Parallel to this, another action was filed in the federal courts, this time against Boudou and me for presumed misuse of reserves.

That same day, the Minister decided to put in an appearance in Congress before the corresponding joint committee, where he stated that "…this is not an isolated measure, but is encompassed within the framework of policies designed to permit Argentina to access the financial market and achieve sustainable growth." All of these other "measures" that Boudou was talking about had ended up being left by the wayside, and that was why he was now seeking to lay hands on the Central Bank's reserves, as a shortcut to keep from falling into default.

It was in Congress, then, that the first sign came that the governing party and the opposition were running neck and neck with regard to the most sensitive issues involved.

On the one hand, the unified opposition issued a brief invalidating the creation of the Bicentennial Fund, another one rejecting the intention to issue US$15 billion in bonds, and a third one against the President's vetoing of two articles that obliged the smaller parties to comply with certain requirements in order to compete in elections. But the Kirchners' followers issued three opposing briefs approving all of these administration-backed measures.

Year's End

I celebrated the year-end festivities quietly in the company of my family. As we toasted the new year, I was feeling that decisive times were coming. I talked to Ivana about it. She was well aware of everything that I was going to have to face. New Year's Day I spent with my children, Martina and Tomás, in the pool in our backyard. They were eager to know when and where we were going on vacation. Without going into any detail, I told them that until the issue I was working on came to a close, I couldn't leave Buenos Aires.

January 4

I received a report from our Reserves Management, headed up by Juan Carlos Barbosa, indicating that the note that the Economy Ministry wanted to swap with the Central Bank for the use of reserves "fails to demonstrate the characteristics of liquidity required for international reserve investment assets."

The explanation indicated that this financial instrument had no market on which to trade it. It was nontransferable, or, in other words, it couldn't be sold, nor did it provide mechanisms with which to calculate its purchase-sale value. Moreover, it contained no clauses obliging the Economy Ministry to repurchase it. Additionally, it was possible that the external auditor might later object to its being placed on the books, which would seriously affect the Central Bank's balance sheet.

With a considerable part of the technical information now in my head, I was prepared to face the next meeting with the President when she asked for me to see her at eight thirty that evening.

She was relaxed and smiling. She asked my opinion about what lay ahead for the new year on both the local and international scenes. At one point, however, she put aside her parsimony and delivered an admonition. "I need for you to make the Bicentennial account operative," she said.

"Look," I said, "we're carrying out all of the corresponding studies and reports."

"Well, OK…but I need it tomorrow," she said.

"Tomorrow?" I said, "Impossible, because we still don't have the report from Accounting on capital impact or the auditor's report. What's the rush?"

"In reality, there's no rush," she responded, "but this issue of the offer to the holdouts is coming up, and this would help that operation."

"The opening onto the voluntary markets, and the Bicentennial. Fund all move along different lines," I said. "Besides, I think the transaction still needs to be approved by the U.S. Securities and Exchange Commission, because the Economy Ministry never reported the existence of the Bicentennial Fund and that may cause it to be questioned with regard to the proper disclosure to investors."

I thought that I had gotten her attention, so I carried on with my arguments:

"The people coming into the operation have already gotten a good deal, because they bought into these bonds at fifteen or twenty centavos, and the current value for the new bond will be about double that. The holders of these bonds couldn't care less who the economy minister is or who the Central Bank president is. They make a good deal and that's that. So I see these things moving along different paths."

It was at that point that she charged again. "Well, our idea is to present the debt exchange next week. We need to have the fund up and running by Friday the eighth."

"I doubt we'll have it ready by then, but we'll keep working to get all of the analytical work done," I said.

By the time the meeting ended at ten o'clock that night, every trace of a smile had been wiped off of her face. The climate was one of absolute tension.

January 5

I received the final opinion from the legal department signed by Cristian Pujol, since Urquiza, who had made her reservations far in advance, decided to stay on a few more days in Mexico. But she was to be back by January 12.

The report took into account the appeals entered by the opposition legislators and the government of San Luis, and opined with regard to DNU 2010 that "...no situation of urgency emerges from the elements under review that would impede or override the primary and fundamental mission of the institution [Central Bank] to preserve the value of [domestic] currency." The report warned that considering "...the possible adverse effects of provisions therein on the monetary policy and the lack of adequate assets to be received by this institution, should the decision-making bodies be in agreement with said opinions, the Central Bank of the Argentine Republic should not implement the course of action..." that would imply transferring the funds to the Treasury.

That same day, Argentina's attorneys in the United States sent us a report in which they confirmed the danger of an embargo. With this analysis to back me, I prepared to comply with other obligations of the Central Bank: the inauguration of a painting exhibit in the coastal city of Mar del Plata. Since the end of 2004, we had been making a major effort to open the doors of the Central Bank to the entire community, placing special emphasis on education and culture. This, our third painting competition, had a very special meaning for me. When I visited the Swiss Central Bank in 2005, I had been very impressed by the collection of art that it had. And I began to learn about the role of patron that a number of different monetary institutions were playing worldwide.

So this exhibition had by this time transcended institutional bounds: It was to be opened in Mar del Plata, where we began the year. I left Central Bank at three, accompanied by the Manager for Institutional Relations, Adrián Figueroa, and returned at eleven that night. For me it was a matter of taking my office on board with me and switching gears for an hour while I joined Mar del Plata's Mayor Gustavo Pulti for the inauguration of the art exhibit at the Villa Ocampo cultural center.

I had no sooner returned to Buenos Aires than I received a call from Cabinet Chief Aníbal Fernández, who told me he wanted to see me in his office the next morning at a quarter to nine.

January 6

I got up that morning with two scenarios playing in my mind, although I had started imagining them the night before: They would either ask me for my resignation, or Néstor Kirchner had decided to try to work with one of the ideas I had proposed. On the way from my house in Belgrano to Government House, I thought over the different reactions I might have. I was in no mood to improvise.

I entered his office at ten to nine and, as was usual with Aníbal, no time was lost on irrelevant matters.

"Martín," he said, "I've known you a long time and I've got a lot of respect for what you do and for your career. But in this case, you're on a different wave length, and the President has told me to ask you for your resignation."

"I don't think this is proper treatment, Aníbal," I said, "because I proposed alternatives to improve the Bicentennial plan and to give it a better structure. I don't believe that I've made any policy or technical error. If you think there have been errors, then go through the proper legal channels to remove me as Central Bank president. I'm willing to have you make this kind of evaluation, but I'm convinced that from December 14 until now, we took all of the proper legal steps."

"But you're ignoring the fact that the DNU is a law," he said.

"Not at all," I replied. "I'm not ignoring it. Nor has there been any official request from the Economy Ministry for the transfer of funds. The only thing there's been is a request for us to open an account. They didn't even take the corresponding administrative steps."

"Look, Martín," he said. "I have my instructions. I'll communicate what you've told me to the President."

The meeting lasted ten minutes. It was five past nine when I reached my desk. At nine-fifteen, the Central Bank press chief called me and said, "Turn the TV on. Crónica TV is saying that you resigned and that Blejer's coming to replace you."

I went into the room next to my office and turned on the TV. The *Crónica* news network carried a big banner headline reading:

"Cristina Fires Redrado. Blejer Is New Central Bank President."

I remained there in front of the screen for about twenty minutes, zapping through the different channels to see how the news was being covered. I also checked to see how the markets were operating. When the news media started calling to get a confirmation, I told my people that the response should be, "I've been asked for my resignation, but I'm not resigning."

Chapter 11

My Last Stand

The last battle over the use of Central Bank reserves started on January 6. My objectives were clear: first, to get Congress to decide whether it was appropriate to make use of them in a way that was not sanctioned by the Central Bank charter; second, to establish the fact that any type of institutional change had to be endorsed by Congress; and, finally, to explain to the public about the inflationary effects of the Bicentennial Fund, due to the printing of pesos to artificially finance the Treasury. With these concepts in mind, I entered into the most tense and risk-laden struggle of my entire professional career.

That day, after several conversations with the bank's external auditors at KPME, the general manager sent them a formal letter asking them to issue an opinion about the accounting criterion that should be adopted in the exchange of the nontransferable note to be received from the Treasury on the Central Bank's balance sheet.

Also on January 6, the head of the bank's litigation team, Marcos Moiseff, obeyed the request of Sergio Chodos by sending him a written opinion that was favorable to Decree 2010. Since the first of the year found Moiseff in the Andean resort town of Villa La Angostura a thousand miles away, he first responded with a one-page memo that he sent to Chodos from a cybercafé. The idea was to counter the report from the legal division that had opposed the use of reserves without congressional intervention.

But since Moiseff wasn't in charge of the legal reports division, his opinions had no technical validity, as was demonstrated later when the case went to court.

The day before, opposition UCR Party Senators Ernesto Sanz and Gerardo Morales asked for a meeting with me to formally announce that they were presenting a precautionary measure in court against the use of reserves as foreseen in DNU 2010. As I mentioned earlier, Sanz had, in fact, already sent me a letter warning me to abstain from transferring the funds to a Treasury account. But his letter in itself carried no real weight without legal action.

I had my doubts about the pertinence of that meeting, but in the end, I decided it was for the best. Business as usual, keep working on schedule, demonstrating that the climate at the Central Bank was completely normal.

Despite the fact that, just that day, the daily *Crítica* tried to suggest the contrary, there was no kind of prior agreement between the UCR Party and me. Institutionally speaking, however, canceling the meeting would have been more counterproductive than going ahead with it. Politically, nevertheless, it had the opposite effect.

Morales and Sanz arrived at the Central Bank at noon. Speaking to Sanz, I said, "This is an institutional meeting. I'm receiving you in your role as UCR chairman. I'm prepared to listen to what you have to tell me."

"As you know," he said, "we've come to leave you a copy of the precautionary measure that we have filed. Make the Central Bank board aware of it. You and they will know what you have to do."

It was a brief meeting. When they left the Bank at half past twelve, reporters were waiting for them outside the door. Logically enough, they took advantage of the media presence to make statements.

"We came to defend the reserves, to defend the wages of workers," Morales said.

"It doesn't make any sense at all," Sanz added, "when there is a Congress, which must necessarily legislate on reserves, to presume that these things can be done by executive decree."

My concerns were confirmed when Morales went on to say that I had warned them "about a rise in inflation" and about "being careful with fiscal and income policies because they could endanger the monetary policy."

By that time, Cabinet Chief Aníbal Fernández had already officially announced that the President had asked for my resignation, alleging that it was for "obstruction" of the execution of Decree of Necessity and Urgency No. 2010/09. Curiously, the first news release that they distributed through the state's news agency Télam stated that Fernández had asked me for my resignation. But a few minutes later, when they realized they had no legal authority to do this, subsequent news releases claimed that the administration had "accepted" the resignation that I had, on repeated occasions, offered to the President.

Later, Economy Minister Amado Boudou also sought to reinforce this lie when, at a press conference, he said, "He presented his resignation verbally to the President on several occasions. So now I figure he should keep his word."

The truth was that the only time I had ever placed my resignation at the Kirchners' disposal was on Friday, October 31, 2008, when they expressed their disagreement with the Central Bank's foreign exchange market intervention, following announcement of the renationalization of the retirement and pension system.

When I heard these statements, I realized that absolute confusion prevailed in the presidency. Despite this fact, I knew too that operations would be under way to undermine my resolve and my conviction. This was the case throughout that entire afternoon. Throwing their support behind the *Casa Rosada*, both the Association of Argentine Banks (ADEBA), in the person of Banco Macro president Jorge Brito, and the Association of Public and Private Banks of the Argentine Republic (ABAPPRA) called for my resignation "in order to preserve financial stability." Banking's support for the administration made it clear that I was not a representative of the financial system. More specifically, they showed themselves to be servile supporters of the powers that be, while I was showing myself as I genuinely am: independent of any and all pressure groups.

The other support that the Kirchners received came from General Confederation of Labor (CGT) leader Hugo Moyano, who also called for my resignation, saying that I was acting "against the best interests of the people," when the fact was that in analyzing the full scope of DNU 2010's consequences, protecting the people's interests was precisely what we were trying to do.

I kept on working as if it were any other day—although I kept constant watch on the markets, which remained calm.

As of the 2007–2008 crisis, we had activated a system by which, when things turned complicated, we made use of a report that was a sort of daily radar reading from each bank that, every evening, provided us with information on key developments such as deposits, withdrawals, and current accounts, among others.

As of the start of the conflict, we had observed major daily activity in dollar purchases among retail investors: some US$70 million a day in January.

At half past seven that evening, the Central Bank board secretary came to show me the topics under discussion in the Bank's different committees. This was how we formulated the agenda for the board meeting the next day. There was practically nothing of importance in the items he showed me. In earlier summers, we held a board meeting every fifteen days instead of weekly, as was usual, since there were always several members of the group on vacation. Committee 6, which covered operations, hadn't discussed the Bicentennial Fund, so the issue didn't figure in the minutes that the secretary, Roberto Miranda, had shown me. Any and all topics are first discussed in the committees and only then by the board of directors. So the message I gave to Roberto was one of calm.

"Let's leave the board meeting for next Thursday," I said, "unless something urgent comes up. And send an e-mail to all of the board members."

Right then, I received a call from the attorney for the Treasury, Osvaldo Guglielmino, with whom I had always had a good professional relationship.

"Aníbal (Fernández) told me to call you," he said. "I'd like to get together with you at my house tomorrow morning at ten o'clock."

I accepted. I was completely at ease with my own actions, especially since I hadn't let a single variable escape my control.

January 7

Guglielmino lives in a comfortable apartment on the tenth floor of a building across from the plaza located at the corner of Arenales and Paraná in Buenos Aires. As soon as he received me, he took a conciliatory tone.

"Let's try to seek alternatives, solutions," he said. "Nobody wants this to turn into a big deal."

"I'm willing to look for solutions," I responded, "but it looks to me like the Bicentennial Fund is badly set up. Its structure clashes sharply with the Bank's charter."

Just then his cell phone rang. Answering it, he stood up, looked surprised and said to me, "It's Zannini," in reference to Presidential Legal and Technical Secretary Carlos Zannini.

Guglielmino stepped away a few paces and spoke in low tones for a time. Then he handed me his phone. "Carlos wants to talk to you," he said.

"Hello, Carlos, how are you?" I said.

"Ok," he said. "I'm on my way back from Pinamar, because the President called me." Then, without beating around the bush, he said, "You've got to resign."

"Look," I said, "the screw-up isn't on my side. If you all want me to resign, explain to me why. But there's been no mistake on my part. Here, Carlos, I'm handing you back over to Osvaldo," and with that I gave Guglielmino back his phone.

When he hung up, I said, "Listen, I didn't come here so you could gang up on me. I appreciate the conversation, but if…"

"No, that wasn't my intention," he cut me off. "Carlos called because I talked to him a half hour ago and happened to mention that you were coming over."

"Well, that sounds like a squeeze play to me, and under those conditions, there's nothing to talk about," I said, and that was that.

I went back to the Bank. There was a climate of mounting tension. A covey of reporters were mounting permanent guard by the door of the building.

The Bank's general manager sent a copy of all of the pertinent paperwork to the board secretary's office, so that everybody would be up to speed on the technical analyses, in order for us to be able to call a meeting within a couple of days to review them.

I then received word that, at a quarter past twelve, Central Bank Vice President Miguel Pesce was meeting with four directors: Sergio Chodos, Carlos Sánchez, Gabriela Ciganotto, and

Waldo Farías. They had received instructions from the cabinet chief to validate the presidential decision without prior discussion.

Nevertheless, it could not be considered a formal meeting because they needed one more board member in order to have a quorum. The meeting continued while I remained in my office. A little later, Arnaldo Bocco, a board member with whom I'd had a solid professional relationship due to his firm stance in calling for proper application of the Bicentennial Fund, called me. He had even taken part in designing the alternatives that I had presented to the Kirchners. He asked if he could talk to me and came to my office.

"Aníbal's calling me," he said. "They want me to go to the meeting."

"What's your position going to be?"

"I'm going to go see Aníbal, and then I'll tell you."

So Bocco went to Government House and met with Cabinet Chief Aníbal Fernández and Legal and Technical Secretary Carlos Zannini. I found out later that the President had also dropped into the meeting for a minute while he was there. That was enough. When he got back to the Bank, he said, "They put a lot of pressure on me. I'm going to the board meeting to see what's happening."

But he didn't tell me what stance he was going to take.

Nevertheless, it is *my understanding* that the attitude he took was to validate the decree "for reasons of party discipline," in reference to his political belonging to the *Frente Grande* Party, which was part of the government coalition.

* * *

The day before, a close contact of Mario Blejer's got in touch with one of my aides, telling this person to let me know that Mario didn't know anything about what was going on. The message was, "Tell Martín that Mario has nothing to do with all of this and wants to talk to him. He (Blejer) is in Davos (Switzerland). He'll call tomorrow."

His call came in at noon on the dot.

"Martín," he said, "you know I've always had words of praise for your administration. Boudou called me at four in the morning yesterday telling me that you had resigned and offering me the Central Bank. I told him I was willing to cooperate but that we would have to talk about the conditions for it when I got back to Argentina at the end of next week. Later, I found out about what was going on. You're the Central Bank president, and I don't want to interfere. Evidently, the conversation with Boudou was false information. But anyway, I didn't accept. I did accept the idea of talking it over, but under these conditions, I'm not talking at all."

"Look, Mario," I said, "everybody's responsible for the attitude he takes. I appreciate the call, and I hope you have all of the elements you need to evaluate the situation."

After that, we broke all contact. I think that he understood that it wasn't advisable for him to end up being the man who did away with the Central Bank's independence, and that's why he stepped aside.

* * *

The hours ticked on. The illegal meeting called by Pesce, who claimed to be "exercising the presidency," ended at four in the afternoon. At that same hour, I found out that the President had organized a semblance of a cabinet meeting—the kind she hated to hold in order to talk over major issues. All of her ministers were rapidly returning from wherever they were vacationing.

This was reflected in the different anecdotes printed in the mass circulation daily *La Nación*:

"Carlos Tomada traded his flip-flops for a dark suit, while Nilda Garré quickly straightened up her house in Pinamar for the trip back. They traveled together in a Defense Ministry plane in order to comply with the urgent presidential order. Florencio Randazzo had already set out by car, alone, from Valeria del Mar. Was he speeding? They say he made the trip in barely three hours. Agriculture Minister Julián Domínguez showed up at Balcarce 50 [the address of the *Casa Rosada*] *wearing a gray suit and an only half-knotted tie, following his trip back from San Bernardo. Carlos Zannini was the first to sorrowfully bid farewell to the seaside at Villa Gesell. But he didn't entirely abandon his informal wear. For the first time since he has been in charge of drafting the Kirchners' legal briefs, he was seen without a tie, a real feat of daring for him.*

"This was the color story behind a hectic day at the Casa Rosada, which featured an unending parade of ministers who fell into formation to place their signatures on the executive order ending Redrado's term at the head of the Central Bank. The biggest surprise was provided by the ever serious Julio De Vido, who quipped, "I never even went on vacation," as he gave a little twirl, model style, to show off his gray suit, with which he hoped to demonstrate that even in January, when most of the cabinet was taking a break, he had remained firmly in the trenches.

"And what about Amado Boudou? He hadn't been at the beach but was next to the last to arrive, despite being only a few steps away from the Casa Rosada. Taking long strides as he walked, he was practically stepping on the heels of Julio Alak, who

rushed in talking on his phone. All of the ministers received a call from the presidential secretaries between one and two o'clock in the afternoon. Clearly, this couldn't wait. Today was the last day of the week in which to publish the decree removing Redrado from his post in the Official Bulletin, so that it could, thus, come into effect."

At six in the evening, I began to receive the first informal news from the press office to the effect that the administration had drafted DNU 18/2010 to remove me from my post.

With sweeping impunity, Pesce and the directors that accompanied him validated the decree permitting use of reserves, falsifying the time that their illegitimate board meeting took place to make its conclusion coincide with just after the executive order was issued removing me from my post. In this way, they could justify an order to the general manager for the transfer of Central Bank funds to the Treasury's accounts, thus sidestepping the technical reports that suggested that this could not be done without congressional intervention.

From very early on, the instructions that they received from Government House made them aware that there would be an attempt to remove me and that was why they signed a false document. I immediately got into touch with attorneys whom I could trust. We needed the formal text of the decree in order to evaluate courses of action. I finally had a copy in my hands at half past seven that evening.

The decree, which carried the signatures of the President and all of the members of her cabinet, instructed the attorney for the Treasury, Osvaldo Guglielmino, to present a suit against me charging misconduct and noncompliance with the duties of a public official. By doing so, they were ignoring application of paragraph 2 of Article 9 of the Central Bank charter as established under Federal Law 24,144. This article provides that "... the removal of members of the board shall be decreed by the Executive Branch in case of misconduct or noncompliance with the duties of a public official, in which case, this shall be done on the prior counsel of a committee of the Honorable National Congress." Nevertheless, Article 4 of the decree provided that the decision should be made known "to the Permanent Joint Committee of Congress," but without ordering prior consultation. The whereas clauses of the measure stressed the government decision that gave rise to the creation of the Bicentennial Fund and spoke of an alleged "remiss attitude on the part of the President of the Central Bank, who has publicly stated that he would not execute compliance with the measure." This was an absolute falsehood.

For the next hour, I analyzed the decree with the Bank's lawyers, although, parallel to this, I knew full well that I had to find other attorneys to engage in my defense. Among the queries I put out, one name that came up was that of attorney Gregorio Badeni, a great specialist in constitutional law.

At about half past eight that evening, I located Badeni in the seaside city of Quequén, where he was vacationing with members of his family. I laid out the case for him, and he didn't hesitate to accept. "It's going to be an honor to accompany you," he said. "I can be in Buenos Aires tomorrow at midday."

My usual level of anxiety jumped by several notches. "Noon seems a little late to me," I said. "I'm going to try to get you here sooner."

I managed to get a businessman friend of mine who had a plane to pick the lawyer up bright and early the next morning. Almost providentially, as soon as I hung up with Badeni, another great attorney specializing in administrative law, Juan Carlos

Cassagne, gave me a call. I had consulted him on several specific issues previously, and now he was coming to me with the same good predisposition as Badeni.

"My entire law firm, and especially my son Ezequiel, are at your disposal," he said.

Juan Carlos was also on vacation, in his case in the mountain resort of Villa La Angostura. So I asked his son, Ezequiel Cassagne, to come to the Bank.

Meanwhile, I talked to several specialized journalists. I was seeking to transmit a clear message. I quoted a former president who was deposed in a coup, telling them, "As Frondizi said, I do not resign, nor shall I resign." I added, "Let them remove me if they're willing to do so."

At half past nine that night, I got down to work with Ezequiel Cassagne and Beltran Fos in the conference room next to my office. We talked for about half an hour, detailing arguments. They asked for a complete file, with the technical reports, and with these in hand started preparing my defense. They worked nonstop until four in the morning.

Parallel to this, I began to receive messages of support from governors, opinion makers, and friends. "Don't give up," they all entreated.

At nine that night, my wife called to tell me about how my children were taking all of this. "Tomás is watching the news and is really on edge," Ivana said.

"Best you try to comfort him there at home, because here we're packing boxes to leave," I said.

She passed the phone to my son to see if I could calm him.

"Tommy," I said, "the fact is that none of this is very pleasant. Why do you want to come here?"

"I want to be there!" he said. "I want to be there!"

So I agreed to let him come. He arrived a half hour later and stayed with me until three thirty in the morning.

Our daughter, Martina, wept inconsolably. "Daddy lost his job!" she cried. But Ivana was able to contain her and cheer her up. The early morning hours were full of calls, meetings, visits from friends, with everyone expressing support. When we were leaving, carrying the draft presentation that my lawyers had drawn up, Tomás said with conviction, "Dad, we'll be back!"

"I think maybe you're confused," I said. "We'll put up a fight, like always in life, but I'm not so sure we'll be able to come back."

I was able to get only about four hours of sleep.

January 8

I was out of bed at eight. By nine thirty, I was meeting with Badeni in his office at the corner of Reconquista and Tucumán, accompanied also by Cassagne's team, headed up by Ezequiel, whose father was flying in from the South. At ten in the morning, we went to Cassagne's offices in the Retiro district. There, we learned that Judge María José Sarmiento of the Eleventh Administrative Court, who was on duty during the summer judicial recess, had accepted the precautionary action presented by Pinedo, Bullrich, Prat Gay, and Vega, thus halting the transfer of reserves to the Treasury's accounts.

It was the judge's consideration that no Central Bank money should be transferred "until the constitutional and legal terms for this formality and the scope of congressional intervention for Decrees of Necessity and Urgency have been complied with."

She took a tough stance too in considering "the unjustified haste of the Executive Branch in executing the decree, [which] inhibits the institutional play of the Republic by trying precisely to avoid the participation of the Legislative Branch (to such an extent that a new DNU had to be dictated yesterday, removing the President of the Central Bank from his post)."

Sarmiento's arguments were clear:

"The Constitution prohibits the Executive Branch from issuing legislative provisions. This stipulation was specifically established in the constitutional reform of 1994, with the clear intention of amending an omission in the historical Constitution, as a means of guaranteeing the republican form of government established in Art. 1 of the National Constitution...The possibility of the Executive Branch's issuing Decrees of Necessity and Urgency requires the existence of a functional impossibility on the part of the Congress to perform as such, an impossibility that, prima facie, does not appear to exist in this case since, in accordance with the provisions of Art. 99, Paragraph 9 of the Constitution, the President has the faculty to convene extraordinary sessions wherever a grave question of order or progress should so require..."

Meanwhile, by eleven o'clock, we had finished the brief to be presented, seeking another precautionary court action against the decree calling for my removal from office. We signed it and the attorneys were off to present it in the same court.

However, at the same hour that Sarmiento was halting application of Decree 2010, back at the Central Bank, Pesce, in his role as "vice president exercising the presidency," had set to work with Chodos to transfer the reserves to the Treasury accounts. The first thing they did was to appoint Moiseff as the new head of the Bank's legal division, in recognition of his political loyalty.

Next, they called an urgent board meeting. At eleven o'clock in the morning, Pesce called General Manager Hernán Lacunza to ask him to open the accounts in the name of the Treasury. But since Lacunza had heard through news channels about Sarmiento's decision, he refused.

To seek a way around him, Pesce and Chodos went to the office of Silvia Zaragoza, the Bank's accounting manager, and put pressure on her to make the Treasury account operative. But she explained to them that in order to comply, she would need the signatures of the chain of command above her.

The Central Bank vice president insisted, asking her what requirements would have to be fulfilled in order for her to comply with the wishes of President Cristina Kirchner. Zaragoza ended up writing out two paragraphs on her computer, printed out the page, had Pesce sign it, and, at twenty past twelve, the Treasury accounts were officially open. But now one step still remained, and it was no little one: the actual transfer of the funds.

To achieve this, they needed the consent of Operations Manager Juan Basco. But he also refused to comply with this political order. Taking the same intimidating tone they had with the other Bank officials, Pesce and Chodos threatened to fire Basco.

Basco stalled for time, just as a call came through from Sullivan & Cromwell, the law firm that defends the Bank's interests in New York, warning of an imminent decision by the "vulture funds" to slap an embargo on the reserves.

At that point, Pesce and Chodos found themselves suddenly assailed by doubts. What should they do? Push ahead with the presidential order and place the reserves at risk, or wait for some sign from the New York attorneys that things had settled down?

At ten minutes to twelve, the Central Bank reception desk logged in the notification of Judge Sarmiento's decision in the "Pinedo Suit."

Lacunza, who was following the matter minute by minute, explained it formally to the entire board of directors. But everyone wanted to plead ignorance and disobey the court order. That's why, at eleven minutes past one, the general manager left his office, went to the reception desk, and asked to be informed in person of Judge Sarmiento's resolution. An hour and a half later, Pesce informed Lacunza that he had been removed as general manager.

I didn't know that all of this was going on, because I was in one of the offices at the Cassagne law firm, thinking out the different scenarios that I might have to face, while looking out the window of that room on the fifteenth floor at the vast expanse of the River Plate. Around noon, Ezequiel Cassagne called me on the phone. His voice sounded distressed. It was clear why: The precautionary action wouldn't be resolved that same day.

But when he reached the firm's offices at about two, his voice and expression gave out a completely different message. "I didn't want to tell you on the phone," he said, "for fear that the line might be tapped, but we're doing well! We have to go back at three thirty or four o'clock, because they're going to give us the court order!"

I couldn't believe it. Suddenly, I was filled with optimism. And none of this was leaked. At half past three, Ezequiel Cassagne, Gregorio Badeni, and I went to the court, located in the 600 block of *Calle* Carlos Pellegrini. We decided to park around the corner so that no one would see us. We walked half a block to the door of the court, where a single newsman was posted waiting for us. I excused myself, saying, "No comment."

At four o'clock, we were notified of the court order reinstating me in my post. Cassagne personally communicated the court's decision to Government House, where they kept him waiting for a while before the reception desk would stamp the order as having been received. In the meantime, I went back to the law offices.

After he left Government House, Ezequiel quickly crossed Plaza de Mayo to the Central Bank at half past four. When he advised me that everyone involved had been notified, I left the law firm by car.

Only then did I call the people in administration to tell them I was returning to the Central Bank, asking them to notify security. A block before I arrived, in a ritual repeated every time I was about to enter the building, I used my radio handset to ask that they send the elevator down to the garage level. Alicia, one of the secretaries, answered my radio call.

"Alicia," I said, "please send the elevator down to the basement."

"My pleasure, Doctor," she said.

There were reporters posted on *Calle* Reconquista, but they didn't mob my car, because they still didn't know that a court order had put me back in my post. Curiously enough, when I arrived at the Bank, the steel rail gate was closed on the garage and I had to lower my window and ask the security employee to open it for me.

When I arrived on the first floor, some fifty people were waiting for me in the entry hall. They all applauded, and some were visibly moved. Indeed, my return was an emotional one. It's an image that I'll never forget.

The first thing I did was sit in my office and read the screens. Everything was all right. I called Lacunza, who told me that he had been removed as general manager, adding that, since he had refused to resign, he had been attached to the economic research division. Later, I contacted Basco and asked him to bring me, on paper, all data relating to the transfer.

I ran a check on the entire operations division that was tantamount to an audit, seeing what had been done and who had been responsible.

Together with me, I had solicitor and notary public Gustavo Badino, who sought to notify each of the members of the board of directors regarding the judge's decision. First, I called the board secretary and had him draw up the notification to be taken to the offices of each of the directors. Sánchez, Pérez, Biagosch, and Bocco were officially notified. The rest of the board members, according to their respective assistants, were not present in the Bank.

Parallel to this, the government administration notified me of legal action entered against me with the federal court of Judge Norberto Oyarbide for alleged noncompliance with the duties of a public official. I immediately began to look for a criminal attorney to defend me. After checking around, I was convinced that the best choice was former Judge Jorge Valerga Araoz, due to his impeccable background, which included his having been one of the superior court judges who, in 1985, tried and sentenced the members of the former military juntas from the country's last dictatorship for human rights violations.

At five thirty in the afternoon, I notified the media that I had once again taken charge of the Central Bank. Another major wave of tension was generated. Ten minutes after my announcement, journalist Gustavo Sylvestre called my office to advise me that he would be doing a show that same night on the TN network on the subject of Central Bank reserves, and he wanted me to be on it. I hesitated to do that. In principle, I really didn't want to say anything. I wanted sobriety to prevail. Especially since, right then, Ivana called me to tell me that her father had been hospitalized with a heart problem. I was feeling the tension that was being caused *in my own family*. The news cables that the Bank's press chief, Fernando Meaños, brought me reflected a state of major confusion. Someone close to the Kirchners called me to tell me that Cristina was fit to be tied, shouting, "Somebody fix this mess for me!" as she walked the corridors of the Olivos HQ. This, then, made me think that I should bring a message of calm to the public.

Sylvestre arrived at the Central Bank that evening at seven. We had a twenty-five-minute informal interview in which I emphasized the following points:

"No reserves will be transferred until Justice and Congress hand down their decision on the issue.

"I have not been given the right to defend myself.

"For me to be removed, there is a procedure, a law, a process by which Congress is consulted.

"There is currently a level of monetary and exchange soundness like never before in history. The Central Bank guarantees soundness, and the people, who know this, have acted with serenity.

"One of my objectives, for the good of the country's institutions, is to complete my mandate, so that the Central Bank remains a solid pillar of the Argentine Republic."

Afterward, I continued working with my collaborators in order to decide which steps to take next. We ended work on that exhausting Friday at 10 p.m.

January 9

Newspeople began to stake out my house. That morning I went to play tennis with my son, but I didn't go back home because Ivana advised me that there were reporters waiting for me to get back, so we went, instead, to Cassagne's offices.

Meanwhile, the administration was plotting an extortive maneuver to bring pressure to bear on Judge Sarmiento. Even though it was Saturday, the administration expected the judge to receive their formal appeals. Sarmiento, who had reported receiving a couple of anonymous phone calls in the wee hours of the morning, later, at half past seven, saw a squad car (driven by Deputy Precinct Chief Marcelo Méndez of the Nineteenth Federal Police Precinct) in front of her apartment building in the 2900 block of *Avenida* Santa Fe. The police were there to notify her of the appeals.

According to the story run in the mass circulation newspaper *La Nación* the next day, Deputy Precinct Chief Méndez politely advised the judge that "the high command would need to know when you might be available to receive an official notification from the President."

"I don't know what this is about," the judge responded. "I can't answer you."

Méndez returned to the squad car and, it seems, put in a call to Assistant Chief of Police Jorge Oriolo, since Federal Police Chief Néstor Valleca was on vacation. Oriolo asked for instructions from Cabinet Chief Aníbal Fernández. Finally, Méndez went back up to the apartment building and informed Judge Sarmiento, "It's about an appeal against the Central Bank decision."

"I can't receive anything here," the judge responded without hesitation. "I have no jurisdiction in my home."

The judge ordered the officer to leave, explaining that, until Monday, the next business day for the court, she would not receive any request.

Faced with this rejection, however, the administration managed to convince Appeals Court Judge Carlos Grecco to officially accept the appeal in the middle of the weekend and in the middle of the summer judicial recess. This was completely contrary to law, since the procedure should have been for the appeal to be presented before the same judge so that she might admit it and send me the arguments for it, so that I could then present my defense.

Aníbal Fernández maintained that "…the judge's disposition has evident political roots." He accused her of having refused to receive the appeal. From the seaside resort of Santa Teresita, former President Néstor Kirchner upped the ante, saying, "We're staying on our toes. There's a constant conspiration. And if you don't believe it, just look as this shameful judge, who came up with a decision in just two hours [my reinstatement], and who was nowhere to be found when it came to our getting the same opportunity."

My legal team and I all got together at Cassagne's offices: Some analyzed the appeal presented by the government, while Valerga Aráoz and his team looked into the charges presented against me in Judge Oyarbide's court. We lunched on sandwiches and throughout the afternoon attempted to design scenarios, even though we didn't have actual copies of the official government appeal documentation.

This last was the reason why we focused on the profile of each of the three appeals court judges who would take over the case whenever Judge Sarmiento decided to hand the case files over to them. Our specific concern centered on Judge José Luis López Castiñeira, who had close ties to the administration and would surely vote in favor of the presidential couple along with Grecco. The one who might dissent and vote in favor of the lower court ruling was Judge Néstor Buján. Grecco's case was puzzling, because he had improperly received the administration's presentation. But based on that fact, we were pretty sure that he would vote in the administration's favor.

That same afternoon, Graciela Caamaño, a Peronist congresswoman for Buenos Aires Province, called to ask me for information on the situation. From that point on, she played a central role. Her capability and leadership were crucial in defending proper use of reserves. Later I received a call from congressman and former governor Felipe Solá. He and Caamaño, together with Alfredo Atanasoff and two other legislators from Chubut Province, decided to make a court presentation that very next Monday.

That evening, I took Ivana and the kids out for dinner to a restaurant in the Palermo district. I was surprised at the tremendously positive reaction of people there. "Hang in there, Martín!" more than one of them cheered me, with spontaneous gusto.

January 10

That Sunday, we continued to work, especially to see which appeals judges we might challenge, while attempting to look for information on the documentation presented to the court by the administration.

It was our intention to buy the time necessary to be able to present our arguments with the greatest accuracy possible.

January 11

Reporters continued to mount guard in front of my house. I figured that it would be best to provide a message of calm to banking depositors and to the people in general, particularly with regard to the development of the dollar exchange rate. Then I went to the Bank, where, like any other Monday, I met with my team to evaluate the week's foreign exchange supply and demand.

I had to make the decision to name a new general manager. I was already beginning to note a move in the media to wear me down. The message being transmitted was that the board of directors, which had recovered certain functions regarding technical issues the week before, would hem me in to keep me from making any decision.

Over the past five years, I had achieved a good working relationship with all of the Central Bank's professionals. It was a relationship based on respect and knowledge of the issues. That was why I made an emblematic decision. I asked myself, "Who is the most historical professional for the difficult times that are coming?"

With the decision that I was about to make, the idea that I was seeking to underscore was that the Bank's president leads the institution together with the operative line, regardless of whether the board decides to go off in a different direction. That was why I designated Raúl Planes to take up the post of general manager. I asked him that same morning.

"Raúl," I said, "you have to stand with me on this."

He had been about to retire. But because of his vast experience, I had contracted him to stay on until the end of my term.

The truth is that inside the Central Bank itself, I was in control of the situation. I've always said that, in the Central Bank, it's the President who signs and who makes the decisions. It is simply a matter of legal capacity. In spite of my mandate, I had always attempted to ensure that the directors took charge of specific matters, like Bocco when it came to external issues, or Arturo O'Connell in all affairs having to do with the G-20, or Ciganotto in dealing with matters pertaining to the Mint House.

Returning to the routine of that Monday morning, the foreign exchange market, which is the first barometer for analysis, was functioning with relative normality, despite some major purchases in the retail segment. Once I saw that the dollar was holding fairly steady, I called our attorneys in New York in order to assess the risk of our accounts being embargoed. I pointed out to them that we needed to emphasize to the courts that the judiciary in Argentina was working to ensure that the Central Bank funds were well safeguarded and that, therefore, the system of checks and balances was working well.

On the local legal front, given the complexity that the matter was acquiring, affecting Central Bank deposits abroad, we requested that Judge Sarmiento transform our precautionary measure into a regular lawsuit, in which there would be a greater scope of debate and evidence. Sarmiento partially granted our request, turning the action into an urgent summary proceeding—a sort of abbreviated regular lawsuit.

Even before she found out about this change, President Cristina Kirchner accused Judge Sarmiento of making a "political" rather than legal decision—a typical knee-jerk reaction by the administration, which consistently applauded favorable court rulings and labeled as destabilizing any that were contrary to its will.

"It's a political decision," the President opined, "when a judge makes a decision to reinstate or remove a public official, when the only one with the right to designate them is the President."

Strangely enough, considering that she was an ex-legislator with ample knowledge of legal affairs, the President should have known full well that the judge was acting in accordance with the Constitution and in keeping with rule of law, in which individuals who feel affected by a political or administrative decision have the right to legal recourse in order to exercise their legitimate defense. This is a constitutional guarantee of which the country's maximum authorities cannot be ignorant.

"Not even under water will we give in," Cristina added, during an event held at Government House, as if intransigence in itself were a virtue.

January 12

When I booted up my computer, I was surprised by an e-mail message from a friend in New York. "Look at the *Financial Times*," it said. My surprise was even greater when I saw that a front page story in this prestigious daily was praising our attitude in preventing the use of reserves without the intervention of Congress. Other articles followed, in *El País* of Spain, France's *Le Monde*, *The New York Times*, Britain's weekly *The Economist*, all of them referring to how positive the steps taken by the Argentine Central Bank had been.

* * *

It was midmorning when word came of a decision by South Manhattan District Court Judge Thomas Griesa to embargo the Central Bank funds on the basis of a request by the Elliott and Dart funds, in a suit in which the two creditors were claiming nearly US$2 billion.

Since the lawsuit had been filed in 2007, the judge had never made any such major decision, due to the insistent arguments of our lawyers, who confirmed that the Central Bank did not act as the "alter ego" of the government administration. A relevant point in our defense that was also being emphasized was the autarkic nature of the institution, which had a different legal status from that of the Argentine Treasury.

But that day, the other side had managed to convince the judge to the contrary, with President Cristina Kirchner's two executive decrees (DNU 2010/09 and DNU 18/2010) being used as the most abundantly clear proof that the "alter ego" theory proposed by the creditors was a valid one. This theory, upheld by the investment funds, was applied in cases in which an institution was not independent from the central power of government. It means just that: that the institution is an alter ego of the government, that they are one and the same. As such, Judge Griesa ordered a precautionary measure, attaching US$1.834 billion deposited in a Central Bank account in the New York branch of the United States Federal Reserve. In addition to that measure, the judge ordered an embargo on all moneys passing through bank accounts of the Argentine state in that U.S. district, as well as all of its properties and holdings up to the sum of US$3.11 billion that five creditors were claiming.

This judge, who, since 2002, had become a true nightmare for Argentina in the face of the government's delay in resolving the issues it had with the bondholders with whom it remained in default, was categorical in his findings, saying, "All of the evidence presented shows that the Central Bank is acting as the alter ego of Argentina…The country has made of the Central Bank a primary source of funds with which to pay foreign debt…The Argentine Central Bank accounts that are subject to this order are not protected by sovereign immunity."

This dealt a harsh blow to the reserve defense strategy that we had maintained for nearly five years and was yet another demonstration of how the administration's bungling had consequences that placed the country's foreign reserves at risk.

January 13

We worked hard to appeal the embargo, particularly in terms of explaining that the precautionary measures adopted by our courts meant that we were indeed not functioning as an alter ego of the administration, since the reserves had not been released to the Treasury. My return to the Central Bank and the court order against use of the reserves constituted a strong argument for use by our attorney, John Newhouse of the Sullivan & Cromwell law firm, in seeking a reversal of the decision.

Focus was also placed on the "operative problems" that the court's embargo caused for a country "nearly 90 percent of whose commercial operations are negotiated in dollars," and which were carried out through those accounts. Therefore, the damage caused was not only to the state but also to private companies and other governments.

Meanwhile, in order to avoid the embargos, the foreign exchange operations desk quit making use of the accounts affected by the measure, since both the transfer of foreign currency and effective minimum requirements that the banks carried out via New York were done using the Bank for International Settlements in Basel.

In Congress, the administration's backers gave another demonstration of intolerance by rejecting an opposition proposal to have President Cristina Kirchner call extraordinary sessions, so as to permit the legislature to decide by law how debt payments would be met for the current year.

The Kirchner bloc demanded, as a preliminary step, backing for the Decree of Necessity and Urgency that had removed me from my post.

News wasn't all that good on the local legal front, meanwhile, where the superior court of appeals was now in a position to analyze Sarmiento's findings. There was no letup in the pressure that the administration brought to bear on the judge, and she eventually decided to transfer the case to the appeals court and to let that be where I would be permitted to respond. The pressure was truly major, with front pages in the pro-administration media being devoted to the judge, like the one for the electronic version of the daily *Página 12* that showed Sarmiento walking in slow motion.

Be that as it may, since—as a result of our having challenged him for accepting the government appeals on a nonworking day—Grecco had been taken off of all of the actions filed for use of Central Bank reserves, including that of Pinedo, who had also challenged López Castiñeira. That appeals tribunal was not, then, in any shape to hear the case, since the only one of its members left was Buján. That day, I was at the federal courthouse. Our attorneys wore themselves thin presenting requests that I be permitted to respond to the administration's accusations. But no responses were forthcoming, and high-ranking officials were on parade there, as were other judges who had been on vacation. It was only hours later that I realized that the opposition was negotiating a possible agreement with Justice on the question of reserves in exchange for my head. One of the appellate court judges handling the case even suggested this to one of my lawyers, who rejected any deal of this nature. Finally, Pinedo turned down the agreement proposed to him by Guglielmino and the judges, and refused to withdraw his challenge against López Castiñeira. That appeals court ended up having only one competent judge in the case: namely, Buján, who then decided to return the case to the court of first instance, which would permit me to exercise my defense at that level.

So it was that we were able to present our responses before Judge Sarmiento.

January 14

In complying with a presidential directive, the Economy Ministry committed a serious error when Finance Secretary Hernán Lorenzino told international news agencies that the administration had managed to get the reserve embargo lifted, when this had not yet actually taken place. "The question of the Central Bank's accounts has, in fact, returned to the status quo prior to the embargo," he said, thus achieving a rise in the price of Argentine bonds for the rest of the trading day.

Government House had ordered the ministry to ensure that the positive spin of this situation not end up benefiting the Central Bank, so it quickly went public to say something.

The truth was that, on that very day, the American judge had suggested that the attorneys for both parties in the dispute should sit down and negotiate an agreement.

This meant that I was forced to also make a public statement clarifying the situation. "For right now," I said, "the judge's decision still stands. But we are confident that our arguments will permit the freeze on the account to be lifted...We have to be very cautious about what is said regarding our arguments."

A little later, after the markets closed, Lorenzino came out again, clarifying that "the measure adopted by [U.S. Judge] Griesa still stands and a period is in place in which both parties must present the judge with some form of consensus to render the measure operative."

* * *

Meanwhile, members of the board of directors continued to indulge in puerile chicanery designed to show the administration that they were pruning my faculties. Our meetings are held in the part of the building that faces onto the 200 block of *Calle* San Martín. There is an internal patio there with a lot of natural light, and on the first floor over it is the board room, presided over by a stately round table. It's an ample, quadrangular, carpeted room furnished with armchairs and with a chandelier that hangs from the ceiling. When I first took office, there was a historical book there which carried the signatures for every public loan taken out by Argentina as of the one agreed to with Baring Brothers at the beginning of the nineteenth century. After my first year in office, I ordered that this book be removed from the board room and placed in the Central Bank Museum, where it could be better preserved. In its place I put a small scale to represent the need for balance. I have said on many an occasion that in order to be president of the Central Bank, one needs to be highly balanced.

This time, it appeared there was no interest in preserving any type of balance, when the board proposed that I could no longer travel abroad without its consent—as if such missions had been for my personal enjoyment.

At a meeting that had started at eleven in the morning, we discussed routine issues. When that meeting was about to end, at half past one, Gabriela Ciganotto said, "I want to table a motion: that any trips made by officials must have the approval of five members of the board and must be previously announced."

The message here was obviously leveled at me. The previous weekend had been an important one, since I should have attended the traditional meeting held in Basel every second Monday of every other month, which, in this case, fell on January 11. It was usual for me to travel the Saturday before the meeting and to return on Monday evening. Because of the state of affairs in Argentina, however, this time I had decided to cancel the trip. I called European Bank President and host Jean Claude Trichet and explained the situation to him. I also asked BIS Director General Jaime Caruana to explain the situation to my other colleagues. I was to have made a presentation in that forum regarding the challenges posed by speculative capital flows in monetary policy management.

The idea of the kind of decision that they had made didn't bother me as such. What did bother me was the aggressiveness of the proposal. So I said, "I think the form of the motion is improper. If a motion is being brought to the table for discussion, it should be previously distributed among the directors, as is the case with other topics. Bottom line, I think it would be good for all of us to know about the trips each of us makes and with what authorization."

But with the relish born of having the majority, they went ahead and approved the motion. Emboldened, they later wanted to formally reinstate Moiseff, whom I had removed from his post. During his "presidency," Pesce had returned him to his post within twenty-four hours by a board vote of seven versus three abstentions—Biagosch, Pérez, and myself.

They immediately leaked these decisions, hailing them as a great triumph, even though they had let pass the opportunity for the board to discuss something as important as Decree 2010 issued by the President a month before. Not a word was mentioned on this topic.

January 15

Before leaving home, I said something to the reporters camped out in front of my house that really angered the Kirchners and their followers with regard to the offensive that the administration was mounting against me.

"They think they're killing me," I said. "I think they're committing suicide."

It wasn't a random comment. I thought of it while I was reading the newspapers during breakfast that day. The reports reflected all of the attacks they were hitting me with. It was an aphorism by Italian writer Antonio Porchia that was popularized by broadcast newsman Bernardo Neustadt, to whom I had always been grateful for the airtime he had given to me when I was a young university student leader.

That was the only day that my emotion overrode my calm and reflection. But I don't regret it. When my team of collaborators criticized me for it, I was more sincere with them than practically ever before. "I've got blood in my veins," I said, "not water. There comes a time when you get ticked off."

* * *

In New York, in the first hour of that afternoon, Judge Griesa accepted an agreement between the Central Bank and the vulture funds which implied the lifting of the embargo on the Bank's account in the Federal Reserve, but preventing us from operating through private banks in that country.

Throughout the morning, I was following this issue by means of teleconferencing. Attorney John Newhouse would come out of the meeting and explain each step, until we finally reached an agreement. They sent us a draft copy. With the cooperation of María del Carmen Urquiza and Juan Carlos Barbosa, we gave it our blessing.

Nevertheless, Boudou once again spoke publicly, stating that the decision to lift the embargo came thanks to the hard work put in by the administration, adding that this had nothing to do with the independence of the Central Bank. The logic behind this statement was self-evident. If the frozen funds belonged to the Central Bank, the Economy Ministry was in no position to do anything in the New York District Court. This was, in the end, yet another sample of Amado Boudou's shockproof audacity.

I limited myself to explaining the measure publicly, as a demonstration of the importance of our independence and the defense of it that Congress was exercising. "All of the funds that the Central Bank has worldwide might well be endangered," I said, "because of continuing litigation, and what remains to be demonstrated is that the Central Bank is not the alter ego of the Treasury." I did this to ensure that no one could claim a victory that was far from being a definitive one.

In the second half of January, with Judge Sarmiento on vacation, Ernesto Marinelli took over the lower court case and defended the action of his colleague, who had been so harassed by the administration. The only decision that Marinelli made was to refer the case to the appeals court opened for the second part of the January summer recess with Judges Clara do Pico and Marta Herrera presiding.

Half of my energy was focused on managing the Bank. The other half was centered on recognizing the fact that in as little as six hours, the appellate court could revoke the decision of the lower court and remove me from office. Until then, I was trying to bring peace of mind to my team of collaborators, but, in point of fact, the road ahead was looking considerably foreshortened.

January 16 and 17

The weekend was relatively calm. We had already presented our response to the appeal that Guglielmino had entered on behalf of the administration. There was little work for the attorneys, except for a meeting on Sunday afternoon at half past five in Cassagne's offices in order to set up the framework for the following week's work and to study the profiles of the two appellate court judges who, in the end, were to analyze the case.

We had ambivalent feelings: calm, on the one hand, because we had done everything that was within our capacity to do, but alarmed, too, on the other hand, by the increasingly aggressive verbal attacks by the administration, including the President, who had accused me of being a "squatter" at the Central Bank.

So, although I went to play tennis as usual with my son, unease was again being transmitted to my family. Ivana and I finally decided that Tomás should go on vacation with my mother to Iguazú Falls, and that our younger daughter, Martina, should travel to Punta del Este, in neighboring Uruguay, with a schoolmate, so as to remove them both from this climate of tension. We knew that what we were going to have to face was going to be difficult. So we wanted to do it alone, together.

Meanwhile, the brief presented by the administration on a request from the court in the lawsuit initiated by the provincial government of San Luis became public. In it, the administration admitted that, without the Bicentennial Fund, it couldn't execute the spending provided for in the national budget, nor could it acquire the funds it needed to comply with the government's creditors. In spite of the fact that the administration had boasted about finishing 2009 with a fiscal surplus, the black hole on the country's fiscal horizon seemed to have materialized from one day to the next.

January 18

In order to contribute to the tranquility of my own home, I decided after Friday not to talk to reporters any more when I left the house.

"From now on," I said, "we'll talk from the Bank. This is an institutional matter and all communications that must be made are going to be made from the institution." So ended my dialogue with the media at the door of my home.

A few hours later, I realized that, just as my attorneys had warned the week before, the opposition was negotiating a possible deal with the courts with regard to the reserves in exchange for offering my head to the administration. In fact, one of the court of appeals judges in charge of the case suggested this to one of my attorneys, who rejected any possibility of reaching a deal that wasn't within the letter of the law.

In this sense, Mendoza Senator Ernesto Sanz criticized the administration for being "stubborn" for not permitting congressional debate of the decree although he considered my own situation to be of little importance. The UCR chairman added, "If the administration puts aside the first decree, the one creating the Bicentennial Fund, and opens Congress, Redrado's situation is totally secondary."

January 19

While Pesce was acting as interim president, on January 8, a decision was made that the interest rate at which Central Bank bonds (Lebacs and Nobacs) were tendered each week would be decided by a board committee. We met at half past five in the afternoon. I asked Juan Basco and Raúl Planes to come. Basco always brought a proposal for a cutoff rate. As soon as we started to discuss the issue, Pesce interrupted us, saying, "Is this a formal or informal meeting of the board?"

The truth was that I hadn't called a formal meeting to discuss this issue, so I responded, "Since this is a natural function of the board, let the board discuss the cutoff rate."

In the end, as usual, Basco's proposal was accepted without changes. Later, we discussed how the foreign exchange desk functioned and established that it should keep on operating as always, but that the board should be kept informed of exchange market developments every half hour.

Another tense moment arose, although it ended up being almost ludicrous, when the vice president again interrupted.

"There's a request," he said, "by the majority of directors on the board that you remove your message to Congress with the 2010 monetary policy from the Internet site."

In that report, I had stated that the administration shouldn't take shortcuts in seeking financing, in an elliptical reference to the use of reserves. "Which part of that report are you in disagreement with?" I replied calmly.

"It's nothing specific," he said. "It's the tone."

"Bring the document," I said. "We'll look at it paragraph by paragraph, discuss it concept by concept."

Then Chodos piped up, "We don't agree with the spirit that you give to the issue of inflation."

I wasn't about to grant him this ambiguity, so I took the discussion a step further, saying, "I'm prepared to discuss absolutely everything, but be specific. The board of directors has nothing to do with the Web site," I added. "That's in keeping with Article 10 of the charter, which has to do with the management faculties of the institution. If you don't tell me what it is you're not in agreement with, then I'm letting it stand."

Pesce took another tack, seeking a point of agreement, but with no supporting arguments. "Martín," he said, "I'm asking you to please take it off the site."

"Miguel," I said, "give me sound reasons, because the board has no faculty to remove it."

We debated the topic for an hour, at the end of which the monetary program was, obviously enough, not removed from the Web site.

January 20

As I said before, while my lawyers managed to successfully challenge Grecco, Guglielmino came up with a proposal to try to cut a deal with Pinedo and appellate court judges Buján and López Castiñeira. It consisted of their lifting all of the precautionary measures in exchange for the administration's not touching the reserve funds (the Pinedo case); my post (the Redrado case) was, as I had suspected, the trade-off. But although they reached an agreement, it was later broken because, as frequently happened to officials of the Kirchner administration, once a deal had been cut and they took a consensus proposal to Olivos, they ended up being left holding the bag. Furthermore, Pinedo, at the last minute, mistrusted the judges and his friend Guglielmino, whom he had left alone together at a meeting called to close the deal. In reaction, the prosecutor charged Pinedo the next day with procedural fraud.

The day's most significant and astonishing event was when the President announced that she would not be heading up a very important mission to China because of her fear that, in her absence, Vice President Julio Cobos might take over the Executive Branch.

"It's too big of a time lapse," she said during an event at Government House, "especially when the person who is exercising the vice presidency doesn't comply with the role assigned him by the Constitution." According to her, Cobos "has not only become an opposition party leader, but also directly opposes measures that are the sole concern of the President of the nation."

Throughout this entire conflict, the vice president had played a moderate role, but he had asked on repeated occasions that Congress be permitted to rule on the DNU that gave the administration the power to pay debt with reserves. The government was pleased as could be to repeat that there was a conspiration among Cobos, myself, and what they referred to as "the judicial party"—or, in other words, all judges whose rulings were not in keeping with the desires of the powers that be—as well as the Clarín Group media firm, with which the Kirchners had been in powerful conflict since the crisis resulting from the government's clash with farmers.

Suspension of the President's trip seemed improper to me, since it denoted a defensive attitude on the part of the head of state and also because it showed incomprehension with regard to the importance of consolidating international relations by means of a state visit to the country that would surely battle the United States for the role of top world power in the decades to come.

During this same public event, the President had to give up ground by saying that she would seek the nonbinding counsel of Congress to remove me from office. Toward this end, she ordered Cabinet Chief Aníbal Fernández to send a note to the chairman of the Lower House, Eduardo Fellner, asking him to form a special committee to provide her with advice on my situation. However, she once again refused to call special sessions of Congress so that the Legislature could make a pronouncement on the validity of the two emergency decrees that had given rise to the worst fight that the administration had been forced to face since its conflict with farmers.

January 21

Before the month was out, we were expected to comply with the commitment we had assumed with the G-20 by—like all other countries in this world forum—sending in Argentina's economic data so that the IMF could study the information on the group as a whole and determine some measures aimed at preventing any new major episode in the global financial crisis. To this end, we worked on some figures for the close of 2009, which showed that the economy had declined by 3 percent, investment by 15.1 percent, and private consumption by 5.1 percent. Also mentioned in the report was an unemployment rate of 11.6 percent, which was sharply higher than the 8.4 percent recorded by the national statistics bureau (INDEC).

These were not final figures, but they made their way into the newspapers, and the Economy Ministry came out saying that it would send the G-20 only the figures contained in the national budget. The fact was that not even the ministry itself used those figures for official government projections.

In the budget bill sent to Congress, mention was made of GDP growth totaling 0.5 percent, a rise of consumption of 0.9 percent, and a drop in investment of 8.9 percent. Despite the fact that the G-20 had no faculties to permit it to formulate objections to the numbers presented, the truth was that all of the rest of the countries in the forum were aware that the only country refusing to show a willingness to have the IMF analyze its statistics was the Kirchners' Argentina.

January 22

The day finally arrived. The court of appeals validated Judge Sarmiento's lower-court decision assuring that no extraordinary reasons existed that could justify taking over reserves by decree without first consulting Congress. As to my continuing to head the Bank, the decision was more ambiguous, maintaining that it was a matter to be resolved between Congress and the Executive Branch. So began an interpretative battle over whether or not I could remain in my post. The only limit imposed by the court was that the administration abstain from naming another Central Bank president until such time as the consultative process was completed in Congress.

Appellate court judges Marta Herrera and Clara do Pico backed the opposition's questioning of the legitimacy of DNU 2010/09, by which the Bicentennial Fund was formed to pay off debt for a total of US$6.569 billion by culling the resources from Central Bank reserves.

Among other considerations, the decision stated that such a decree could not be justified simply by making mention of its urgency and necessity, but rather, required a situation *of sufficient concern* as to make ordinary procedures impossible. They recalled, furthermore, the importance of the other two branches of government's controlling the Executive Branch's use of Decrees of Necessity and Urgency.

The judges made it clear that their decision did not imply that they were questioning the jurisdiction of each of the branches of government, but sought to adapt them to the law. In this way, the court elliptically responded to the President, who had criticized the Judicial Branch, claiming that the courts were taking on attributes that were the province of the Executive Branch.

With regard to my continuing as Central Bank president, the court pointed out that in dictating Decree 18/2010, the President had failed to first convene a joint committee of Congress to provide a decision on whether or not I had failed to comply with my duties, but since that error had been corrected later, there was no need for the court to continue to intervene in this question.

I interpreted the court decision as "constructive ambiguity." In the paragraphs that preceded the decision, the appeals court judges said, "The President has taken measures that tend to amend the errors of Decree 18." Although amends were not entirely made, the question was, then, did DNU 18, which called for my removal, have the validity to stand?

As soon as the court handed down its decision, Cassagne and Badeni came to my office. We prepared a statement that was made public at half past five in the afternoon, maintaining that the court's findings ratified our position to the effect that my removal had been unconstitutional. It was necessary, then, for DNU 18 to be repealed, so that the Joint Congressional Committee would be free to act by giving the President its counsel in keeping with Article 9 of the charter. If, that is, there were grounds for my removal.

"Legal procedure demands," the statement said, "that prior to removal, the President must first ask for the intervention of the joint committee, so that it can, in effect, issue a report on the existence or not of causes sufficient to justify such removal, if that should be the case. The appellate court decision recognizes the fact that this procedure has not been complied with.

"It is clear from all of this that the appeals court does not consider that the president of the Central Bank has been removed, and that, since there is a willingness to rectify the measure that ordered the removal of the head of the Bank, it will be a sufficient precaution for no definitive replacement to be designated.

"The only reading possible for this court decision is as proof of the fact that Art. 9 of the charter is fully in effect. The appeals court judges fully provide for this."

I left the Bank at nine o'clock that night. According to what I was told afterward, it was only moments later that the administration tried to notify me that the government's interpretation was that the precautionary court order was no longer in effect and that I could, therefore, no longer enter the Central Bank. They drew up official proceedings with Pesce to try to imbue him with an aura of greater legitimacy.

At ten o'clock, Aníbal Fernández was on television renewing the attack on the judges for impeding discretional use of reserves. "We're going to appeal," he said. "The 'judicial party' is taking functions away from Congress. The judges want to govern.

"The President has given me instructions to the effect that Redrado is not to enter the Central Bank ever again."

I talked to my attorneys to see if the cabinet chief had the faculties to make such a decision. They explained to me that he obviously didn't. And while, in principle, I had let it be known that I wouldn't be going back to the Central Bank until the joint congressional committee made its decision, when I saw the images of federal police posted around the building to keep me from getting in, I decided to put out the word that I would return to the Bank the following Monday.

In point of fact, to keep me from entering the Central Bank, they would need a court order. Under what argument would they be able to get one? They told Pesce to take care of the situation.

January 23

I spent Saturday preparing my presentation for the joint congressional committee, forming part of which were Vice President Cobos, Alfonso Prat Gay, and governing party Budget and Treasury Committee member Gustavo Marconato. *All of the media* published the photo of the police line guarding the entrance to the Central Bank to keep me out. If it couldn't be done with reason, it would be done by force. Be that as it may, my first goal had been achieved: the destiny of the reserves would be decided by Congress.

January 24

That Sunday, I decided to go to the Central Bank in order to generate a surprise effect and avoid the scandal on Monday. My decision had to do with demonstrating that the administration was, once again, acting outside of the law. "Let's show the arbitrary nature of this decision," I reasoned. "Let's get together on Sunday at five thirty in the afternoon and then go to the Bank."

Accompanying me were Badeni and Cassagne, and I also asked Valerga Aráoz to join us because if, as we might very well expect, they barred my entry, I was going to file a criminal complaint with the court for abuse of authority.

There were about twenty policemen with riot shields posted on *Calle* Reconquista. At half past seven, we parked on *Calle*

Perón, walked around the block, and walked in through the door on *Calle* Reconquista. I said hello and kept on walking, wondering when they would stop me. I reached the reception hall and continued along the corridor to the elevator, greeting a policeman on duty there. Then, suddenly, the security chief appeared. "Doctor," he said, "unfortunately, I have to tell you that I've got instructions…"

I asked him who had given him his instructions and if he had a court order in this regard. Since he didn't, I requested that a report of the incident be drawn up in a room on the ground floor. From there, both Jorge Valerga Aráoz Jr. and Sr. accompanied me to the First Precinct of the federal police to file a complaint against Cabinet Chief Aníbal Fernández as a result of my being denied access to the institution.

In a later statement, I explained the reasons behind my filing charges. "The attitude adopted by the cabinet chief constituted a flagrant violation of the precautionary measure ordered by the court of administrative appeals," the statement said, "a failure to recognize the fact that Redrado's authority stands until such time as the joint congressional committee makes its pronouncement."

Fernández later tried to deny his responsibility, stating that it had been Pesce who had made the decision to keep me from entering the Bank.

That night, Juan Carlos Cassagne detailed the reasons for my decision. "The decision of the court of appeals," he said, "supports Redrado's main argument, and that is that Congress did not have intervention before the decree was issued. That is why the judges say that this [congressional] counsel must be awaited. This was the same thing that Judge Sarmiento said. What has changed since then? That the President promised to make this consultation. Therefore, the right Redrado was demanding has begun to be covered, and, until such time as the consultation is complied with, he remains in his post. In a way, the precautionary measure on behalf of the Central Bank president was provided by Mrs. Kirchner herself, when she committed to including Congress in the decision."

* * *

When I returned home that night, I began to think over my resignation. I clearly couldn't continue to hold my post. But besides filing that criminal charge, I felt it was important to stress that, from now on, any decision that needed to be made regarding the Central Bank should be discussed in Congress. This was one of the great achievements of that month of struggle.

Also very important—and by that Friday, this had been achieved—was that the precautionary measure protecting the reserves remained firmly in place. Despite the fact that DNU 18 remained pending, it appeared to me to be of key importance, as a historical precedent, that the issue of the reserves, or of any other change in the direction of the Central Bank, had been taken to Congress.

January 25

The President confirmed that her request that Congress intervene had been a mere formality when she called on the special committee to make the procedure "brief and swift," as if she possessed the faculties to manage the timing of the procedures of another branch of government. "The responsibility of all sectors," she said, "merits making this procedure as brief and swift as possible, because, in the end, I think we have to put an institutional end to this issue." In reality, giving it an institutional end was worthy, precisely, of a deep-reaching study of the reasons for which I was being accused of improper performance of my duties and for failing to advance with the Bicentennial Fund. As has been demonstrated, it was the lack of expertise of the Executive Branch that delayed the process. At the Central Bank, meanwhile, in less than eight working days, we ran the economic and legal gamut to arrive at the unequivocal conclusion that prior to transferring the funds, Congress should give its opinion. This was precisely the institutional path that the President was calling for and that she was not willing to comply with.

January 26

That day, I sent a note to the joint congressional committee in which I maintained that for my presence before that committee to make sense, Decree 18 removing me from office would have to be repealed. This was not some whim on my part, since that decree maintained that the Executive Branch could indeed remove me without prior consultation of any kind.

What sense did it make to present myself before the legislators if the law of the Central Bank charter was not being complied with?

The fact was that when President Fernando De la Rúa had wanted to remove Pedro Pou as president of the Central Bank, he'd had to await the decision of a joint congressional committee, which took two months to prepare it. In the meantime, Pou, against whom there were accusations filed for alleged money laundering and other very serious crimes, remained at the head of the Bank until he was finally notified of his removal following the decision handed down by Congress.

Meanwhile, the joint committee that had to analyze the validity of my removal had begun receiving testimonies. The first to testify were Economy Minister Amado Boudou and the vice president in charge of the Central Bank, Miguel Pesce, both of whom, of course, defended the legality of the administration's actions. State attorney for the Treasury Osvaldo Guglielmino also went to testify. Following that testimony, Kirchner, who was furious over the court decisions, accused Guglielmino of handling the case badly and fired him, although it appeared to the public that the Treasury prosecutor had resigned. Among other reproaches, the most telling one that they launched against Guglielmino was that he had been unable to convince Judge Do Pico to unfreeze the reserves when, months earlier, he had promoted her to the appellate court post that she now held. It was also reported that congressman Marconato was less than pleased with the quality of the presentation Guglielmino made before the committee.

My request that Decree 18 be repealed before I testified was not a condition. It was merely designed to underscore the anomaly to which the Executive Branch was subjecting us. But there began to be speculation about my supposed refusal to go before the committee. Nothing could have been further from my intentions. But the question was, would I appear as the president or the former president of the Central Bank? No member of the committee could respond to that question. This was why I had gotten together with my attorneys and prepared all of the background on the case.

It wasn't my intention to offend the committee members. I just thought that they should be emphatic in defending the laws that were in effect. Otherwise, neither the opinion of these three legislators nor my own had any validity whatsoever, because Decree 18 had not been repealed. But it was indeed important for me to go before the committee in order to leave my testimony in full on the official register of Congress.

Meanwhile, back at the Central Bank, Pesce was losing no time in getting rid of the professionals who had issued reports contrary to the use of reserves without the intervention of Congress, and all of those connected with my administration. The first to be sacked was Pedro Rabassa, followed by Administration Services Manager Norberto Domínguez, Human Resources Manager Santiago Eidis, and Systems and Organization Manager Héctor Biondo, among others.

This was a repeat performance of what had happened at INDEC. Once again, all professional capability was being eliminated from an institution.

January 27

Everything in the joint commission hearing was handled in a calm and friendly tone, like a chat in a café. Nevertheless, I quickly realized that there was, if not an agreement between the administration and the vice president, at least a certain acquiescence on his part. I was struck by how quickly the formalities were handled, especially when, after the four hours that the meeting lasted, he asked me if I had called off the board meeting of January 7 to avoid discussing the Bicentennial Fund, with the intention of stalling it, as the administration accused me of doing.

Here, I pulled an ace out of my sleeve, saying, "Look, here's the Order of the Day as it was brought to me by the board secretary at 7:30 p.m. on January 6, and in which the Bicentennial Fund doesn't figure."

At that point, Prat Gay asked the Central Bank to send around the original of the Order of the Day, which proved once again that the issue had not been up for discussion on that date and that I hadn't called off a meeting in order to elude a sticky question, but because there were only three or four very basic topics on the agenda that didn't justify holding a board meeting on that date.

During the meeting, Vice President Cobos asked very few questions. He was interested, in particular, in the Moiseff affair, especially because of the report that the latter had drafted. I explained that he had merely sent an e-mail, which bore no weight in the issue of the Bicentennial Fund. Marconato barely made a few comments.

To accompany my statements, I took along three files of about five hundred pages each with detailed information on each of the economic and legal reports put out on the Central Bank's reserves.

They asked me why I had asked for the repeal of Decree 18 prior to my testimony before the special congressional committee. Without the slightest hesitation, I responded, "Because I still feel myself to be the president of the Central Bank. I did nothing other than comply with the Central Bank charter, a republican act that is not important in terms of the persons, but of the institutions involved."

That was the only time when Marconato shook off torpor and exclaimed, "To my mind, you're already the *ex*-president of the Central Bank!"

At eight thirty that evening, when debate of the question of the reserves appeared to have reached an end, Prat Gay tried to step up to the plate.

"We have some questions about the rest of your administration," he said.

"I'm all right with that," I said, "but if that's what you want to do, you're going to have to call a lot of officials to testify."

My intention was for other public servants who had been technically involved to pass before the committee, in the same way that Moiseff and syndic Hugo Álvarez from the administration's camp had been called to testify. I was in agreement, on the other hand, with their having called María del Carmen Urquiza, whose report at the end of 2009 had been impeccable.

Clearly, however, the prevailing idea was that this should be an "express process," and, for that reason, nobody else was called. The meeting ended at about nine, and we agreed to meet again the next day.

January 28

While during the first day we had concentrated exclusively on Decree 2010, when we met the next day at eleven o'clock in the morning, we talked about other issues related to my administration. Prat Gay was questioning me about an advance that we had granted the Treasury on October 21, 2008, affirming that by making this transfer we had exceeded the monetary base limit. He was bent on showing that, during my term, we had given the administration more money than was proper. But I used audited figures to show him that this wasn't true. Moreover, I pointed out that, after intense discussions with the Economy Ministry in 2009, the Treasury had obtained ARS 1.9 billion, which was under the limit established by law.

Later, we talked for a long time about the price indices that the Central Bank uses. I explained that we had quit using the CPI, making use instead of the indices for implicit prices, construction and raw materials. The discussion was between Prat Gay and me. I got the feeling that Cobos and Marconato were getting bored.

Then we analyzed the solvency of the Central Bank balance sheet, the relationship between its net assets and distribution of earnings. I showed that we'd had an absolutely conservative and anticyclical policy, especially in the first years, when the Bank capitalized itself strongly, and in the last two, when we distributed more than what had been capitalized due to the world financial crisis, as I explained earlier.

The general climate was cordial, except when they asked me questions about the Central Bank's role in fighting inflation.

"There are two instruments that the Central Bank can use," I explained. "Interest rate and exchange rate. If one thinks that more could have been done about inflation, then that would mean that the exchange rate should have been held back. Look, Alfonso," I said, "how, in an inflation report from October of 2003, you, as Central Bank president, said that with the exchange rate alone it wasn't enough, that there had to be a convergence with the rest of the policies."

Although it wasn't my intention, I had touched Prat Gay's pride.

"It's not my administration we're evaluating, but yours," he said dryly.

After my presentation, I realized that I felt more at ease and that it was time to step aside. I had, after all, taken all of the institutional steps that corresponded to a central bank president.

"Gentlemen," I said, "I thank you for your time, but my cycle at the Central Bank has ended. Under these conditions, I no longer have the will to go on."

It was half past one in the afternoon, and it was all over.

January 29

I prepared the text of my resignation. The political tug o' war centered on the figure of Cobos, who was receiving pressure from several different sectors. It made no sense to wait until the committee handed down its decision, since the police kept me from returning to the Bank. I had met my other goals: first, prompting congressional intervention; second, making it clear that, during my administration, the reserves were managed strictly within the framework of the law; and third, demonstrating that the reserves were safe, thanks to the time that I was able to return to the Bank on the strength of my reinstatement by the court and thanks also to three legal actions headed up by Congressman Pinedo, Senator Morales, and Congresswoman Caamaño.

I sent a copy of the text to each of the three members of the congressional committee. Among other concepts, I highlighted the following:

"Having been called before the Joint Congressional Committee and with the judicial suspension of the application of Decree 2010/2009 in place, and in the understanding that, for the time being, neither the reserves of the Argentine people nor the autarky of the Central Bank are at risk, and in a desire not to constitute a reason for further disturbance of the institutional order that should reign in the Republic, it is my understanding that the most favorable decision for the general interest is that I present my resignation from the post in which I have performed with the utmost responsibility for nearly six years.

"This resignation does not imply surrender in the face of illegal conduct. On the contrary, I have demonstrated myself to be capable of facing up to pressure and complying with the mission assigned to me by the Congress of the Nation, preserving the autarky of the institution, the value of currency and the savings of the Argentine people.

"Today, it is up to the National Congress to decide, by constitutional mandate, regarding the future of the Central Bank, of its reserves and of the policies that will be carried out from now on. I leave this post with which I have been honored, with the complete satisfaction of knowing that I have contributed to the institutional life of our Republic."

* * *

By that afternoon, the media had begun to talk about my possible resignation. I thus called a press conference at the Marriott Plaza Hotel for eight that evening. I wanted everyone to be able to ask questions openly and without restrictions.

I knew that these would be my last words as president of the Central Bank and that I should find the perfect balance between criticizing the administration for its behavior in the case and bringing peace of mind to the people in terms of the exchange rate and the safety of their deposits. It had been a fight to the finish to protect the reserves from discretional political use.

"The administration wanted to ride roughshod over everything in order to make use of the reserves, which are the backing for the savings of every Argentine," I said. "It had already attempted to do so on several occasions—the purchasing of YPF, a change in the Central Bank charter, and the placement of a compulsory bond in the financial system."

I said this in order to demonstrate that my conduct had always been the same. It was the administration that had decided to break with a relationship of professional respect and trample over the Central Bank Law.

Later, I explained in figures the danger signified by using reserves to finance the deficit: with full use of the resources of the Bicentennial Fund, it would have been necessary to issue ARS 80 billion in currency, thus generating a high risk of inflation.

I also sought to underscore the support received from common, everyday people and from several other central bank presidents, ranging from Bernanke to Trichet, and including several of my peers from the Americas, Europe, and Asia.

A few minutes earlier, I e-mailed a letter containing my resignation to the President who was in the Province of Santa Cruz. I formalized this the following Monday by presenting a copy of the letter at Government House. In it, I expressed the following:

"I hereby comply with the duty of writing to you to present my resignation from the post of President of the Central Bank of the Argentine Republic, for which I was designated by means of Decree 1468/04, with the agreement of the Senate and in keeping with Article 7 of the Constitution.

"Later, your decision as President of the Nation to dismiss me from that post by means of DNU 18/2010, was refuted in a Federal administrative court, where I maintained that the requirement established in Art. 9 of the Charter prescribing that the causes for my removal require the prior counsel of a Joint Congressional Committee, had not been met, and that no cause existed for my removal.

"This was recognized both in a lower court decision and in that of the Administrative Court of Appeals and I must hereby state that a certain part of this last Tribunal did validate my removal.

"One day prior to the handing down of the appellate court's decision, Madam President changed her opinion and sent a note headed Executive Branch No. 421 and dated January 21, 2010, to the President of the Honorable National Senate, calling for the convening of a Joint Congressional Committee for Tuesday the 26th at ten o'clock in the morning, in compliance with Art. 9 of the Central Bank Charter.

"This change of opinion on the part of Madam President, although without expressly repealing Decree 18/2010, implies, at least, a tacit willingness to make this right (as suggested in the Appeals Court decision), or to leave it without effect.

"Nevertheless, nothing of the sort happened, and moreover, instructions were imparted by which the undersigned was kept from entering the institution, and threatened with the use of public force, despite the lack of a court order from a competent judge.

"Faced with this new situation to which Madam President had given rise, I presented myself before the Joint Congressional Committee for the purpose of clarifying the lack of any cause for my removal from office and the fact that the Executive Branch had failed to repeal the DNU that provided for same.

"In no part of the note that I sent did I state that I was setting conditions for my appearance in meetings before the Joint Congressional Committee which I was asked to attend, and, as announced, I indeed attended two such meetings held on the 27th and 28th of this month.

"As for the non existence of causes by which attempts were made to execute my removal, I herewith attach copies of: 1) the lower court decision by Judge Sarmiento dated January 8, 2010; 2) the January 22 decision of the Court of Appeals, and 3) a note presented to the Joint Committee of the Honorable National Congress, convened by Madam President.

"Within this scenario, having complied with the summons from the Joint Congressional Committee, and with all of the elements having been gathered with which to issue a decision regarding Decree 2010/2009, it is my consideration that, for the time being, neither the reserves of the Argentine people nor the independence of criteria of the Central Bank are endangered. Regardless of this, I understand that the most favorable decision to the general interest is for me to present my resignation from the post in which I performed by job with complete responsibility for nearly six years. From this point on, there can be no doubt that it is the Congress of the Nation to which, by constitutional mandate, the decision corresponds, as to the future of the Central Bank, its reserves and the policies that must be implemented.

"I leave my post with the full satisfaction of knowing that I have contributed to ensuring that this reality is present in the institutional life of our country.

"I am satisfied that in the period from 2004 to 2010, the Central Bank overcame the most important financial crisis of recent decades, providing monetary and financial stability and exchange predictability to all Argentines.

"Finally, I repeat that the decision to resign as President of the Central Bank of the Argentine Republic comes after meeting the objective of safeguarding compliance with Articles 3 and 9 of the Bank's Charter, defending the institution's autarky and the republican values of Rule of Law."

* * *

I could ask for no more. I had reached the end of the line and couldn't have cared less about the chicanery of Aníbal Fernández, who, on presidential orders, rushed desperately to several television channels to state that I couldn't quit, that the government was firing me.

It was the last of a long chain of absurdities that the administration mounted as of December 14, 2009, the same administration that, a week before, hadn't let me enter my office and that affirmed that I was already the ex-president of the Central Bank.

Around ten o'clock that night, I returned home, feeling relieved. I had left my post by my own means and with my own convictions intact, having complied with the objectives that I set out for myself on January 6.

* * *

A few days later the attitude of Julio C. Cobos was demonstrated to have been less than serious and totally lacking in rigor when it came to evaluating the facts. A committee that was formed to judge my decision to safeguard Central Bank reserves moved on the sole strength of political issues and not of genuine interest in reaching the truth in the matter arising from Decree 2010. It did not lead to responsible analysis of foreign reserve use and its consequences, or of the role of the Central Bank and its independence from the Executive Branch.

Unfortunately, that committee was null and void, since it always acted as a council after the fact, rather than as a source of preliminary counsel, as demanded by the Central Bank charter. My removal was never repealed, and administration spokespersons publicly stated that my resignation had not been accepted. Under such circumstances, just what kind of council had this been?

Julio Cobos turned his back on the people and took part in the act of institutional abuse perpetrated by the administration itself. His interest was political, with his only thought being his image as a candidate in 2011. He gave legality scant importance.

* * *

Immediately and prematurely, Miguel Pesce assumed the presidency of the Central Bank and planned his interim status until September, when a new Bank president was to be chosen. The President designated Mercedes Marcó del Pont to take over as head of the institution. A new decree under a new name was dictated to transfer funds from the Central Bank to the Treasury. The courts once again locked the transfer. The opposition in the Senate rejected the appointment of Marcó del Pont at committee level, but was unable to achieve a quorum in the full Senate. The administration began to make use of funds to pay multilateral agencies. A court of appeals permitted the government to make use of all of the reserves. The opposition stated that it would not appeal the decision, but would fight this from within Congress. March ended with some major definitions, and April began with some important questions:

Would the administration blatantly use all of the reserves, even knowing the inflation risks that this involved? Would the new Central Bank rubber-stamp everything the administration ordered it to do, without regard for the preservation of what the law requires of it, which is to preserve the stability of domestic currency, or, in other words, the value of the Argentine people's labor?

Would the opposition be able to escape falling into the administration's constant power games, in which it sets out the issues, will listen to no alternatives, and, if backed into a corner, redoubles all of its bets?

Under these conditions, how will Argentina reach the end of 2011, when the administration is slated to change?

Chapter 12

My Balance Sheet

Creating an economic policy—or in my case, a monetary policy—is a complex exercise. You have to consider countless technical variables and just as many involving human behavior, as well. This last has its peculiarities in Argentina, not only because of our history, but also because of the traits of our sociology and social psychology.

I met the main goal of my administration: that of defending the reserves, so as to protect the savings and pocketbooks of the Argentine people, by establishing sound structures that, for the first time in decades, permitted the normalization of monetary, financial, and exchange variables. Above all, it was an administration that set limits on the use of reserves, on exchange rate setting, and on the financing of the fiscal deficit—in other words, financing without inflationary currency printing. Toward the end of this administration, we set a precedent that will be in effect for decades: No President of the Republic will again be able to carry off the Central Bank reserves without triggering a corresponding debate in Congress.

I would have liked, of course, to have achieved more high-profile results. But it's not the same to outline an economic analysis within an academic environment as it is to be an official of the Central Bank. To put this thought more graphically, no matter how impeccable a surgeon's credentials may be, *when he walks into the operating theater, he must operate without a manual.*

Something similar happens in public service. Decisions are made beyond the confines of the university blackboard or the consultants' think tank. Because of all of this, I set a rule of thumb for myself with regard to economic policy: At least 70 percent of the ideas and concepts that a person studies and develops within the professional field should be achieved.

When it comes to pointing out errors, I think my worst one was to have trusted in the strength of the results of my administration alone. Let me explain: To my mind, managing the Central Bank is a technical task that should be judged in that light. Never, then, did I feel that it was necessary to engage in political networking and create personal ties in the political world beyond the specific queries that I might get from this or that congresswoman or senator from the government or opposition camp. When there are no clashes, this facet of the job seems irrelevant. But when there is friction, it becomes indispensably important to have political friendships in order to face the kind of battle I had to face.

Our administration can be characterized as "gradualist" in terms of using the instruments at its disposal. It can be defined as the most orthodox of the heterodox spectrum, but at the same time, as the most heterodox of orthodox thoughts. Although this may seem like a play on words, Argentine reality demands, to my mind, a kind of gradualistic behavior, which generates criticism at both ends of the ideological spectrum.

Teaching the lessons of inflation, meanwhile, has been insufficient. This has meant that it has been impossible to overcome the experience of monetary disorder seen in recent decades. Money, like any other product, has a price, which is determined by the amount of it that people have in their pockets. This means that you have to be able to see both sides of the coin at once. In other words, you have to offer the amount of money for which there is demand. To give an example, if there were no demand for the dollar in the world—and there is, since it is used as a reserve value everywhere—the Federal Reserve of the United States would not have been able, in the last couple of years, to increase several times over the amount of U.S. currency in circulation without creating inflation.

Under my mandate, we committed ourselves to ensuring that the supply of pesos did not exceed demand, and we met this goal systematically quarter after quarter. In our reports and public presentations, we explained that in our country inflation is the result of a variety of causes. The most important of these causes are fiscal, wage-related, and revenue-related, as well as having to do with scant competition and backsliding in some regulated prices, like energy-related rates, among others. In order to properly attack the inflationary problem, then, it is necessary to work with all of these factors at the same time, in accordance with a coordinated plan with the convergence of these variables. To think that the Central Bank can control price increases making use of only two instruments—the interest rate and the foreign exchange rate—is to be ignorant of the complexity of this problem in Argentina.

* * *

When it comes to my tenure balance sheet, from 2004 to 2010, our most important achievement is the creation of a solid cornerstone that is still upholding the Argentine economy. During this period, the Central Bank consolidated three public goods that had been absent in Argentina's economic history up to that point: exchange rate predictability, monetary stability, and financial stability, placed at the disposal of all the people. Indeed, over the course of these years, we broke a losing streak in the country's history, since in the thirty previous years, Argentina went through a monetary and foreign exchange crisis every seven years.

In 2009, practically everyone was predicting problems with the dollar/peso rate and with the public's deposits in the banks. If this predicted crisis didn't come, it was due to the policies that, with genuine patience, the Central Bank implemented over the last five years. In fact, the country's monetary and financial system has shown itself to be very sound, in the face of the worst international crisis in the last eighty years. People's savings and credit continued to grow, while fluctuations in the interest and exchange rates were gentle, thus dissipating the "phantoms" of the past. The "acid test" passed once and again by the Central Bank also made it possible in 2009 for the capital flight trend to be reversed.

In this way and with results, our policies have demonstrated their capacity to generate stability in the variables that the monetary authorities control. The savings of Argentina's citizenry were never at risk in this time and no banking institution required the assistance of the Central Bank, while in other countries, the financial crisis left victims among depositors in its wake and sparked bank closures or mergers.

This result is the product of the silent and effective work of the team of professionals that accompanied me throughout these years. The regulations designed between 2004 and 2009 provided mechanisms for injecting liquidity, so as to keep the terrain irrigated in case of a foreign capital drought, and set high solvency standards for banking. Specifically, our persistent policies permitted citizens to have a change of expectations in the face of international turbulence. The Central Bank made it clear at all times that it would be the lender of last resort, providing liquidity in both pesos and dollars—broadly but not free of charge—multiplying the channels for injection, so as to prevent a break in the payment chain and as a means of preserving credit in the face of the adverse effects of the world crisis.

Obviously, at the height of the crisis, deposits and credit grew at a more moderate rate, but by the third quarter of 2009, both variables had regained a swifter rate of expansion. Certificates of deposit, one of the barometers for reading the mood of depositors, today are showing noteworthy growth. The interest and exchange rates (two key "mood" indicators) responded well to the proven sureness of the course the Central Bank set during the storm. In 2009, interest rates stabilized at substantially lower levels than for the previous year, and as financial conditions began to return to normal, the Central Bank continued with its countercyclical policy, with swift reductions in the prime interest rate. This led to a gradual reduction in the cost of money on the short-term market. All of this has contributed to a more dynamic channeling of savings toward credit for businesses and individuals.

Management of the foreign exchange rate produced something unprecedented in recent decades: the peso maintained a completely natural movement despite the shock suffered in the world economy, showing no sign of trauma and without producing jitters or runs. The dollar operated on an even keel, continuing on its long-term trend and eluding any unnecessary volatility that might have undermined savings and investment decisions.

* * *

The system implemented has passed several tests of unprecedented tension. The groundwork has been laid for a strengthening of the link between savings and investment, through credit, so as to sustainably uphold Argentina's economic growth. Thanks to the policies implemented, the banks, for their part, have concluded their path to normalization in the case of both assets and liabilities, recomposing their levels of liquidity and solvency. In this way, loans to the private sector amply outdistance credit given to the government. This exemplifies a system focused on attending the needs of families and businesses.

Furthermore, a fundamental requirement of a monetary policy is that it be accountable for the measures adopted, demonstrating a reasonable degree of transparency in its everyday activities. This calls for clear communication not only of objectives or goals to be reached (as set down in the Annual Monetary Policy Review presented before the Senate), but also of how they will be achieved (a definition of the instruments to be employed), the rationale behind the measures (based on an analysis of the current and future situation of the domestic and international economies), and the reasons behind—and measures to correct— deviations from originally planned goals. Along these lines, we met these communications goals by means of a vast number of publications including: the Monetary Program (a report presented yearly to Congress), Monetary Program quarterly review, Inflation Report (quarterly), Report on Banking (monthly), Financial Stability Bulletin (bimonthly), the report on Private Foreign Debt, Exchange Market, and Direct Investment by Resident Firms (annual), as well as numerous research papers.

Also included here must be activities oriented toward the reinsertion of the Central Bank into the international community, where it recovered a place of relevance among emerging economies. The Bank's active participation in the Group of Twenty and the Bank of International Settlements in Basel permitted its participation with voice and vote, into the Financial Stability Forum and the Basel Committee on Banking Supervision, which are at the center of the current architectural reform of the international financial system. There, our Central Bank has contributed to the development of new measures to bolster the stability of this international system, based on past experience and present results. Argentina was elected to preside over the Consultative Council for the Americas, which carries the interests of the region to the Swiss-based institution's board of directors. Also along these lines, the Bank has held daylong meetings and longer seminars of international prestige, like its annual Monetary and Banking Meetings, which have come to be held as one of the major international forums among academicians and central bankers. Our Economic Research Division has allowed it to position itself as one of the most important macroeconomic and monetary research centers in the entire region.

* * *

Our communications policy, which promotes transparency and openness to the community has not been achieved merely at a technical level. The Central Bank is an institution of and for all Argentines. For this reason, it has carried out actions oriented toward the public at large, through interaction with the community in the form of scholarship programs, economic research prizes, and promotion of the arts.

Criterion of Independence Applied from 2004 to 2009

It would be naive to pretend that the decisions adopted during this period have been totally divorced from political pressures. But in effect, throughout this entire term, the exchange rate would have been different (higher and with the subsequent inflationary effect that this would spawn), the interest rate would have been inconsistently lower (with no comprehension of its effects on financial stability or its role as an intermediary between savings and investment), and the level of international reserves would have been lower (had the ingenuous proposals for the use of these funds been heeded), if the Central Bank had not maintained its decision-making independence or its technical criteria with regard to these different variables. Had the parameters of the political cycle been obeyed, those who predicted yet another disruptive cycle for the end of this decade would have been proven right.

Moreover, *the Central Bank has also aborted several non-conducive initiatives that came to it from the political power*: in April 2006, the Executive Branch weighed the possibility of using foreign reserves to buy part of the share package of the oil company REPSOL (YPF); in February 2007, a request was put into the Central Bank for allocation of reserves to finance part of the National Infrastructure Plan; in January 2009, the Executive Branch asked us to evaluate the granting of rediscounts oriented toward promoting new car sales.

Nor did the public sector spare any generation of tensions in seeking to cover its mounting financing needs through attempts to expand pre-existing limits directly via the Central Bank or indirectly via the private financial system. In spite of such pressure plays, throughout these five years, Central Bank financing of the Treasury never strayed from the boundaries established in the Bank's charter. Furthermore, regulations governing the banking sector were made consistently stricter with regard to financing the government, so as to free up resources for private sector credit. The Central Bank also discouraged any placement of "non-voluntary" debt among players in the financial system, making specific mention of the problems that similar measures had brought in the past.

Prudence was also applied in the distribution of Central Bank earnings. Unlike our regional peers (Brazil, to cite just one example, transfers the whole of its operative and financial profits to the government), the Argentine Central Bank applied an anti cyclical criterion to its earnings distribution policy. During the favorable phase of the international cycle, between 2005 and 2007, it transferred only 25 percent of its earnings to the Treasury (capitalizing the rest and constituting a special reserve with the remaining 75 percent). This kind of savings allowed the Bank to invert this ratio during the contractive stage in the world economy (2008–2009), when it distributed 75 percent and capitalized 25 percent.

This practically exercised instrumental independence doesn't respond to any dogmatic or ideological preconception, but to the basic tenets of public administration, which transcend any government and include:

- **Control through Opposition** to the financing of spending: Currency printing cannot be in the same hands that execute public spending (the Executive Branch), so as to ensure that no one falls into the illusion of thinking that he or she has a hand on the crank of the "joy machine," or that wealth can be created simply by turning that crank to print money. Any Argentine over the age of forty knows full well the inflationary effects of this practice, which has wrought such damage on the equitable development of our country.

- **Temporal Inconsistency** (or shortsightedness): Since the pernicious effects of reckless monetary issue are not immediate, but mediate—they appear somewhere between four and eight quarters down the road—a governing authority might, at any given time, increase spending (probably with electoral intentions) and finance that spending by printing more money at a rate beyond all prudence, thus bequeathing the inflationary problems to his or her successor.

This does not signify confusing autonomy with "autism" (a Central Bank that withdraws into itself). What is necessary is coordination and convergence of the monetary, financial, and exchange policies with the rest of the branches of economic policy-making, and especially with the fiscal policy. This is necessary in order to make policies that are sustainable over time. Otherwise, if there is no coordination, each policy decided on an isolated basis and without a joint vision could turn into a source of instability and into a schizophrenic message for society.

But coordination is not to be confused with subordination either. Fiscal policy cannot take an autonomous path, demanding that all other variables, such as the exchange rate or inflation, passively adapt to its financing needs. The economy must be understood as a system of interdependent variables, in which the action deployed on a single front may be inconsistent with the objectives of the whole.

The level of public spending has a direct impact on the interest rate, the exchange rate, the availability of credit to the private sector, the competitiveness of the productive sector, on the tax pressure, and on financial and foreign exchange stability. Pretending that each variable can run its own course is not only illusory, but also inconsistent, and when some variable is knocked out of whack, it always sparks tensions—which are not always controllable—on the rest of the fronts.

In the end, no sound monetary policy is possible if it is accompanied by an inconsistent fiscal policy. In any case, the credibility of the monetary policy—a *sine qua non* condition for the success of its anti-inflationary mission and for its providing a "nominal anchor" for the public's expectations—is tied to the development of public accounts, as witnessed by the historical correlation between inflation and budgetary financing experienced in Argentina over the course of recent decades.

* * *

The Heritage and Future Challenges

It was only possible to build the current monetary and exchange rate system—which, for the first time in decades, has permitted Argentines a guarantee of tranquility—under the umbrella of independent criteria and with a strictly technical focus.

The soundness of the system was put to the test between 2007 and 2009, when it kept Argentina from collapsing into financial instability and into an abrupt change to a system of devaluations and confiscation of savings.

This good performance was no coincidence. The risk management approach adopted by the Central Bank at the end of 2004, which consisted of designing and deploying alternative strategies with which to face changing scenarios, allowed it to build up anti-cyclical funds or "shock absorbers" with which to mitigate any domestic or foreign impact that might affect financial stability. The most noteworthy facets of this framework include:

1. First the accumulation of reserves with which to protect the savings of the people, which permitted the generation of an anticyclical policy, consisting of putting money away in the times of bonanza, so as to be able to better manage the lean times that might come later. In a world in which there is a certain degree of anarchy in the international financial structure, where the International Monetary Fund is developing new strategies, and where global imbalances and insufficient financial regulation presaged a major crisis (in which excess U.S. consumption was being financed with the savings of Asia and the

Middle East, with no role being left to automatic stabilizers like the exchange rate), the accumulation of reserves, as practiced by the entire spectrum of emerging economies, has proven to be an effective policy in the face of global challenges.

Like any other insurance, its benefits are abstract and its cost concrete during the period of accumulation (just as with an insurance premium). But this equation is inverted when a misfortune takes place: It was the level of reserves, and not the instrument, which allowed the country to face the international crisis. And in confrontation with the political branch of government, which sought constantly to raise the exchange rate, without bothering to evaluate the inflationary consequences that this could bring, the Central Bank placed US$8 billion on the table during the most critical stage of the capital flight process, recorded between mid-2007 and mid-2009. In effect, the Central Bank's attitude and the volume of foreign reserves acted as a main dissuasive element in sweeping aside the "ghosts of the past" and preventing the disruptive effects on the local economy of the worst international crisis in the post-World War II era.

2. As a complement to this previous consideration, another cornerstone of this strategy was application of a managed floating exchange rate.

Perhaps this was not so much a political decision as it was a restriction imposed by reality: The aversion demonstrated by the average Argentine to exchange rate volatility, following decades of instability and an extremely erratic utilization of the exchange rate tool, greatly narrows the monetary authority's available margin of action for using this instrument.

Without offering free insurance to investors and with the conviction of not adapting the exchange rate policy to temporary market forces, the managed floating successfully attenuated cyclical movements in the exchange rate, but without seeking to *sail against the wind* of genuine factors, such as the price levels for our export goods, the exchange parity with the currencies of our trading partners or the productivity of our economy.

Different econometric models show that administrating fluctuations in the exchange rate provides for better results, not only in terms of inflation but also of GDP volatility. On this point, it is important not to fall into simplistic comparisons with the strategies applied in other countries. Our neighbors didn't have a rigid monetary policy in place for ten years like our Convertibility System, nor did they suffer a crisis of the same intensity and magnitude, which simultaneously included an institutional breakdown, a major devaluation, the destruction of the financial system and cessation of payments on the public debt.

Similarly, historical studies of the exchange rate generated by the Central Bank allowed me to provide the theoretical consistency to the development of this strategy. In this way we could be sure to always be close to a point of equilibrium, far from the risks of unemployment associated with too low of an exchange rate, and far too from the risks of persistent inflation that follow an exchange rate that is set too high.

3. Third, the anticyclical norms applied, which not only guaranteed the savings of deposited in the financial system, but also provided the system with liquidity and solvency, as well as eradicating the "deadly sins" that had deepened the 2001–2002 domestic crisis, such as banking's high exposure to the public sector and the currency

mismatch between assets (loans) and liabilities (deposits), which ended up prompting asymmetrical "pesofication" and the subsequent freeze on deposits (*corralito*).

Here we need to take into account the normalization carried out in the financial system's balance sheet: In terms of assets, the standards applied brought a reduction in public sector exposure - which went from representing 40 percent in the banks' portfolios to a current level of 12 percent, thus clearing the way for increased assistance to the private sector. With regard to liabilities, Argentina witnessed an action that is unprecedented in its history - namely, the restitution of all moneys (more than US$20 billion) loaned by the Central Bank during the crisis, in order to mitigate illiquidity, and the return of deposits as the main source of credit funding.

Similarly, prudential regulation also made it possible to avoid the kind of "shortcuts" that encourage the formation of bubbles or the explosive growth of credit and consumption. Even at the cost of shaving a point off of growth or of sacrificing a more dynamic credit performance, the Central Bank was strict about not implementing mechanisms that could cause currency mismatch - or in other words, the results of lending in foreign currency, while deposits are being made in local currency, which had previously prompted the asymmetrical "pesofication" that was a factor in sparking the 2002 economic crisis in Argentina.

Finally, it should be borne in mind that, between 2004 and 2008, the economy went through a period of transition from crisis to normality, in order to achieve monetary and exchange rate credibility following repeated meltdowns throughout Argentina's history. This process had to make allowances for relative price adjustments left pending, following the disorderly currency devaluation of 2002. These adjustments manifested themselves progressively throughout the entire period. Furthermore, the typical after-effects of a crisis like that of 2002, which left behind a very reduced financial system (private sector credit amounted to less than 10 percent of total national production, or in other words, 90 percent of the economy lay outside of the Central Bank's sphere of influence), clearly limited the use and availability of conventional monetary policy instruments, such as the interest rate. What this meant was that any highly aggressive interest rate increase implemented as an anti-inflation tool would have destroyed the very same financial intermediation channel that we were seeking to recreate. Gradually but persistently, though interest rates grew without interruption throughout the positive phase of the cycle, when it was necessary to defend the demand for domestic currency and ensure stability, during four episodes of tension experienced between 2007 and 2009.

Consequently, the Central Bank's policy consisted of guaranteeing equilibrium on the money market, by means of a mechanism that systematically placed a ceiling on the amounts in circulation, keeping it under the variation in domestic production (seeking not to underscore inflation pressures), and that became more and more sophisticated through application of a variety of technical measures.

Looking Ahead toward 2015

The great legacy that our current monetary system bequeaths to society is a solider starting point for the next five years. The internal and external conditioning factors that were in place at the beginning of my term have been removed, providing the incoming authority with a greater degree of freedom.

In the first place, whoever directs the monetary authority in the years to come will enjoy a degree of institutionalism that is more deeply rooted in the political community and civil society, as a result of the comprehension spawned of the importance of its independence from the powers that be.

Second, in a country that has been traditionally vulnerable to foreign crises, for Argentina to have come through the world's worst financial crisis of the postwar period unscathed is no small feat, in terms of the margin of management freedom that the next administration will have. This is true despite the fact that the crisis sparked capital flight of almost US$45 billion (nearly 8 percent of the GDP) between mid-2007 and mid-2009, but did so without prompting the confiscation of deposits and without causing the purchasing power of people's savings to melt away through sharp devaluations in local currency.

Conventional monetary policy tools like the exchange rate and the interest rate will be more available for use by the monetary authority. The fact that the nominal exchange rate has been able to move significantly but in orderly fashion over the course of 2008 and 2009, without panic and without spiraling of any kind, may well have contributed to the public's understanding that anti-seismic construction is not characterized by its rigidity, but indeed by the flexibility of its elements, so as to permit it to absorb tremors without any dramatic impact on the level of economic activity. And this is a truly important factor in preserving the job level.

It is an eloquent fact that, even at the height of the crisis, the exchange rates on the futures market for one-year transactions were not over 15 percent or 20 percent higher than the spot price. Five years ago, this would have seemed like a miracle. In other words, today Argentina is a normal country at least in monetary and where apocalyptic predictions are simply implausible.

Nor is it any coincidence that in the last stage of the international crisis, even with capital flight in the first half of this year, it wasn't necessary to raise the rate in order to preserve deposits and financial matters stability. The market too has understood that a Central Bank exists today that is capable of providing sufficient guarantees as to act as a lender of last resort.

* * *

The next administration will inherit a system with a strong backbone, with non-performing indices riding at historical lows, a system immune to external shocks, one that is reinforced against credit, currency or market risks. It will intermediate between savings and investment (with the public's deposits having made a comeback as the main source of funding and with private sector loans having become the main target of application for these funds). It will have sufficient liquidity to face any lack of confidence on the part of depositors, a level of liquidity that has withstood critical episodes without requiring financial assistance on the part of the Central Bank (indeed, for the first time in history, over the last five years, the Bank recovered all of the assistance that it had lent to banking in 2002). And it will be "free of deadly sins" because, at present, there is no currency mismatch in the balance sheets of the banks, of companies or of individuals. Nor does the solvency of the financial system now depend on fiscal performance.

It is noteworthy that, despite institutional uncertainties, the barometric readings that measure the mood of depositors and investors, such as the development of fixed-term deposits (CDs) or the peso-dollar exchange rate, have performed with complete normality, thus revealing the public's confidence in the soundness of the system constructed.

No less important is the margin of action that a good level of international reserves provides, serving to dissuade any speculative attacks that might affect the value of the peso. Perhaps the world will someday advance toward new and more effective systems of ensuring liquidity, managed by supranational agencies. But in the meantime, faced with a lack of certainty regarding what the new international financial architecture will look like, the accumulation of reserves remains the most effective form of "self-insurance" available against the unpredictability of external fluctuations.

Pending Challenges

Having overcome the myth of "a crisis every seven years" that characterized the period from 1975 through 2002, the main challenge facing Argentina in this next stage is that of taking advantage of the institutional platform and the greater margins of action afforded by classical monetary policy, in order to overcome Argentina's main weakness of the last forty years, by providing the local community with a domestic currency that serves as a refuge for savings (by preserving its purchasing power), and as a unit of account for long-term credit.

This is not a technical challenge, but a political and social one: There will be no eradication of poverty without growth, no growth without credit, and no credit without low inflation and a local currency suitable for long-term contracts.

The central banker must now show expertise in *steering the ship through normal times,* with two concrete and interrelated objectives: achieving a strong credit market and converging upon an international (single-digit) inflation rate.

Self-financing by businesses and homes alike was important in the recovery and growth process experienced between 2003 and 2008. But now, this would be insufficient to sustain the quantity and quality of savings and investment needed in order to keep growing. More credit, meanwhile, can be derived only from the broadening of savings and investment horizons. And it is for this reason that low inflation is an indispensable requirement.

It would be a grave error, nevertheless, to think that the expansion of credit can be achieved through mere goodwill. Credit will not magically expand through rediscounts given to banks or by means of issuing currency to finance public spending. On the contrary, Argentina's experience has clearly demonstrated that every time there has been indiscriminate monetary printing, the demand for money has dropped, credit has declined and inflation has heated up. It is no mere coincidence that the period from 2003 through 2009 was the one of greatest growth of credit in real terms, in the last fifty years. This was only possible by means of the implementation of a policy of controlled issuance, limited strictly to the economy's true need for monetization.

Applying fictitious monetary stimuli to the demand for credit is counterproductive, with these ending up being channeled into the purchase of goods or foreign currency—in other words, they translate into inflation or exchange pressures—in the absence of genuine demand for credit. The supply of currency does not, in itself, create its own demand.

Taking the hardest road—but also the only sustainable one—of perfecting the role of domestic currency as a unit of account for transactions and contracts will be the only way to achieve the channeling our savings toward productive credit. The extension of these (deposit or loan) contracts will be directly proportional to the capacity of local currency to act as a reserve value, which means consolidating low, single-digit inflation.

It is also necessary to take advantage of the margin of action gained in terms of conventional monetary policy instruments. Just as the monetary program gradually gravitated toward a broader range of monetary aggregates (from the monetary base to private means of payment) as the system gained credibility, and just as other central banks in the region have gradually done, over the next five-year period, the interest rate will gain a more ample space in which to be used as mechanism for arbitration between savings and consumption. This instrument can coexist perfectly well with a managed floating policy, as demonstrated by the experiences of countries that have been successful in maintaining reduced inflation guidelines and low short-term exchange rate volatility.

Finally, the axiom that applies to our situation over these five years still stands: No anti-inflation policy can be successful without a consistent fiscal policy or without strong coordination—not subordination—with the rest of the economic policies. Convergent policies require that the Economy Ministry, Central Bank, and Labor Ministry, respectively, aim at maintaining the intertemporal solvency of the public sector, monetary and financial stability, and consistent wage guidelines.

In short, the bases have been established to make growth with price stability a tangible reality, in the immediate future, for all Argentines, and this is the only true path to sustainable development with social inclusion.

Chapter 13

A Central Bank Committed to the Society

At the start of its seventy-fifth anniversary year, I left a Central Bank that was sounder than I had found it in 2004.

Without a doubt, our greatest contributions had to do with laying the groundwork on which to build a monetary and financial policy for the decades to come. But we also created a more human profile for the institution.

To this end, as of the beginning of 2005, we introduced a plan that encompassed institutional actions oriented toward reflecting an integrated, unique, committed, transparent, flexible, and dynamic organization, so as to achieve an optimum identity.

The strategic intention of this policy was to formulate a cross-section that would permit us to have a direct link with the country's citizens. We sought to bolster processes aimed at building relations with our historical audience—the economic and financial community, our employees, and the community at large. To do this, we worked in two simultaneous stages involving actions to redefine the identity of the Central Bank through an Institutional Identity Program, as well as institutional actions through a Bank-sponsored Education Program and a Cultural Program.

The social responsibility that the Central Bank exercised today, seventy-five years after its creation, was assumed with a clear long-term commitment, aimed at assuring that the actions undertaken continued over time, through open and direct dialog with the community, founded on two basic courses of action: the promotion of education and culture. In any case, our Central Bank has joined the evolution of other monetary authorities elsewhere in the world, one of the most relevant traits of which is the abandoning of a traditionally reserved profile and the opening of the institution to the community.

A key program was one that promoted economic and financial literacy (PAEF). It is oriented toward youngsters in the latter years of primary and high school education. The prime objective is to provide them with comprehension of economic and financial concepts as they apply to everyday life. This program makes use of an active teaching and learning concept that changes the students' cognitive structures. It is anchored in the school curriculum within the fields of Ethics and Citizenship, Social Sciences, Mathematics, and Language. It is also committed to the transversal nature of such concepts as accountability, respect and solidarity, which underlie the economic decisions that citizens must make.

In my five years at the Bank, this was one of the activities that I found most satisfying. This is true to such an extent that every Wednesday morning, I made room in my schedule to personally conduct the classes that members of our team gave in schools. This direct contact with students allowed me to keep in good shape to be able to answer any type of question that was thrown at me.

I explained to them that the Central Bank, which was founded in 1935, is an institution that has the power to issue money and that governs the domestic financial system. To comply with its mission, it must formulate and execute monetary and financial policy.

The attributes that are instrumental in its mission include regulation of the amount of money in circulation and the supply of credit in the economy, and the dictating of monetary, financial and foreign exchange regulations in accordance with current legislation.

The Central Bank's functions include making sure that the financial market operates properly and applying the Financial Institutions Law and all other relevant legislation.

To achieve its monetary stability objectives, the Bank possesses international reserves, which are an authentic guarantee in generating credibility among the nation's citizens.

Between 2008 and 2009 alone, more than fifty thousand students and 630 primary and secondary schools took part in a program called "The Central Bank Goes to School," in the City of Buenos Aires, the Greater Buenos Aires Area, and other points around the country, including Santa Fe, Misiones, Chaco, Corrientes, Formosa, Córdoba, and Entre Ríos. Emphasis was placed on promoting exploration, direct experimentation with reality, problem-solving, and the practical application of knowledge.

In 2007, the Central Bank instituted the Central Bank National Prize for Painting, with the aim of preserving and encouraging our artists. This annual cultural event was part of a trend toward greater openness of the institution to the community and toward creating venues in which the Bank could present itself as a capable, highly transparent, and relevant medium for the acquisition of domestic works of art. This program also allowed the bank to create a broader sense of federalism though its actions, by reaching new publics, beyond strictly technical groups: in particular, young artists, relevant institutions and museums, provincial culture secretariats, and journalists specializing in the world of culture.

The prize received broad national coverage by means of a traveling exhibition that acted as an intercultural bridge between the artists and society. The goal was to place cultural centers in the limelight, while underscoring the value of artists from different generations, schools, and trends.

This was pointed out by renowned art critic Alicia de Arteaga in a column she wrote for the mass circulation daily *La Nación*, entitled "The Other Martín Redrado," published in February 2010. "The outgoing Central Bank president laid the groundwork for Argentina's most important painting prize," she wrote.

In 2007, 2008, and 2009, the traveling exhibitions made their way to a number of different artistic venues: the National Museum of Fine Art of Neuquén, Casa Beban in Ushuaia, the Municipal Museum of Art of Mendoza, Palacio Ferreyra in Córdoba, the Contemporary Art Museum of Salta, Villa Victoria in Mar del Plata, the Puerto Madryn Railway Station, the Galisteo de Rodríguez Central Bank National Prize exhibit in Santa Fe, and the Dr. Urbano Poggi Municipal Fine Arts Museum of Rafaela.

In November 2009, the Central Bank co-organized the First National Meeting of Cultural Heritage and Public Agencies. Since 2005, the Bank has also, jointly with the Internal Labor Commission, organized a plastic arts exhibition called Art in the Central Bank. Participants include both active and retired staff members.

In September 2009, the PAEF was awarded an Honorable Mention certificate by UNESCO and the Inter American Development Bank for being one of the best practices in the field of policies and programs oriented toward youth in Latin America and the Caribbean. The PAEF was selected from among six hundred practices in thirty countries throughout the region.

Additionally, the Bank has established other strategic alliances with the Education Ministry. The Central Bank agreed to work on a reciprocal basis to incorporate economic and financial literacy contents into the media made available to it. Work was carried out as part of the provision of training courses for teachers, in a program planned and executed by that ministry.

The list of actions taken in this effort to open the Central Bank up to the community could go on for many more pages. But let what we've mentioned here suffice to provide an understanding of how we not only sought but actually managed to break through the gigantic wall that tends to separate central banks from their societies, beyond the comings and goings of politics and economics.

Chapter 14

Argentina Needs a Sound Plan and a Reliable Team

I am thoroughly convinced that Argentina is in the presence of a historical opportunity arising from the world's geopolitical evolution. The 2008–2009 crisis will mark a turning point in the history of Mankind. An era is taking shape in which the emerging countries have increasing weight and decision-making capacity. The world is currently bearing witness to the rise of regional powers that will mark a greater dispersion of political, economic, financial, and monetary power. Within this context, our country is positioned—for the first time in a very long time—in the vicinity to which the world is attracted. Those of us who have some degree of public responsibility are obliged to work to ensure that this new stage doesn't pass us by.

The experience gathered in the Central Bank has permitted my team and me to make a deep study of the shortcomings and challenges that our economy is facing. From these analyses emerges the need to generate a benchmark model that expresses the differential attributes of our society, the means to develop them and the distribution of social responsibilities necessary to achieve them. The citizens of this country must be made to feel that this model belongs to them, so that they will be willing to mobilize all of their energy, on a full and sustained basis, in support of this common national project.

The changes necessary are generated by concrete individuals, organized in the form of institutions: scientists, businesspeople, employees, artists, intellectuals, professionals, and politicians, driven by the desire for progress, stimulate creativity and effort, thus generating the enthusiasm necessary to reach these goals.

We need to collectively assume the fact that when the individual's desire for progress is discouraged, productive investment is undermined, the rate of growth decreases, and the wealth-generating system loses its incentives. As a consequence, investors can choose the place in which they will develop their projects, deciding, say, to operate in Chile or Uruguay and not in Argentina, or to invest in China and not in Africa.

As demonstrated in the preceding chapters, our economy successfully survived the severe test imposed by the global financial crisis. The policy system implemented proved capable, in the last two years, of overcoming successive episodes of tension (a total of four) on domestic financial markets. So it was that, for the first time in more than a quarter of a century, the occurrence of a severe shock—of the kind that locally takes place with fateful and astonishing "regularity" approximately every seven years—did not end up in the replacement of the set of policies in effect. This was a fact of extraordinary value, considering that the country's citizens had adapted in the past to living within a very uncertain climate, in which one of the fundamental factors characterizing this volatility was, precisely, the high frequency of major policy changes.

Once a test like this has been passed, however, one must face important policy challenges in order to regain the pace of sustained growth and development. For one thing, it is crucial to normalize relations with the international financial community and to return to the voluntary credit markets. It is neither feasible nor desirable for an emerging economy to try to cover all of its financing needs with budgetary results—in other words, to attempt to cover principal and interest with the fiscal surplus—since this implies sacrificing already scant resources that should be used for higher priority needs.

Similarly, it is necessary to supplement these initiatives with actions that provide clear signals of a will to open up a longer-term horizon. It is of indispensable importance to set up a "system of markers" to provide parameters for our citizenry's economic expectations. The need to generate an investment perspective capable of permitting the generation of an overall anti-inflation-ary orientation, so as to avoid major economic, social, and politi-cal costs, is the job of the political authorities.

If no corrective measures are taken, the nonexistence of idle capacity in the main productive sectors will be accompanied by another new leap in the inflation rate, which could end up jump-ing to a step systematically higher than the previous one. Price hikes have already begun to show traits of growing persistence. The risk is that this might imbue the inflationary process with a certain inertia and make its future eradication much more costly, in terms of economic activity and jobs. That's why it is of crucial importance to act preventively and to avoid adapting more per-manently to this process of continuous high inflation.

* * *

It is highly probable that an improvement in the international environment and the outlook for a good agricultural harvest will, for the time being, translate into an appreciable economic reacti-vation in 2010. Be that as it may, if the problem of rising domestic costs is not solved, it is also highly probable that this growth will end up not being sustainable, and that it will be characterized by a low investment ratio and high levels of distributive rivalry. It is not unthinkable, then, that once the expansive effect predicted for these cyclical factors runs its course, aggregate performance might lose its momentum, with the economy at the beginning of 2011 tending to look lackluster in the face of high and persistent inflation.

Meanwhile, betting on a simple repeat performance of the set of policies and the macroeconomic dynamic that were in effect in the period from 2003 to 2007 has little chance for success today. That period of very high growth enjoyed several exceptional traits and it would be unrealistic to think that, under current conditions this could happen once again. In the first place, the recovery of economic activity was driven, to a large extent, by continuous and sustained improvements in the prices for our export products abroad. Secondly, the intensity of the recovery came as a result of a very particular set of cyclical internal conditions: a special configuration of relative prices backed by a higher exchange rate and the existence of enormous excess capacity in productive resources, which made it feasible to finance the recovery and later expansion of capacity almost exclusively based on extraordinary company earnings. None of these conditions will be reproduced in the next period.

Under these circumstances, two courses of action should follow. The first one: In order to attain sustained growth, there must be continuous expansion of capacity to accompany production growth and this necessarily requires a sustained investment effort as well as continuous increases in productivity. The second one: Since companies will not necessarily now enjoy extraordinary benefits, the investment effort will have to be financed using external funding, and not merely from withholdings on profits.

These two questions are inextricably linked with provision of a set of compatible economic variables and longer terms than those currently in effect. Within a context of high costs, citizens will display microeconomic behavior that is adaptable and of a high level of "preference for flexibility." In particular, the relevant temporal horizon for decision making becomes highly compressed, because the risk of erroneous decision making increases. Under such circumstances, reluctance to commit resources for long periods of time translates into a scarcely dynamic investment and innovation scenario. Furthermore, because of the high risk involved, people become reticent about getting involved in "long-term" contracts, the result of which is a reduction in the level of financial intermediation and, in extreme cases, the complete disappearance of major segments of the credit market. An environment of these characteristics causes growing erosion of all nominal domestic references that might be useful in the formulation of plans and commitments. Without investment and with a dilapidated financial system, it becomes difficult to return to a rhythm of sustained growth without any available shortcuts or alternatives for achieving a reduction in the pace of price increases.

* * *

The central axis of any new economic plan should be the coordination and convergence of the fiscal, wage, and income policy with the monetary and exchange policy. In order to achieve this, all variables determined by the different government agencies should grow at levels that are compatible among themselves, so as to generate, in this way, a broader horizon for economic decision making.

The necessary condition for such a program is that its execution be in the hands of a solid technical team, whose members display proven capabilities in terms of cohesion, professional expertise, integrity, and experience in management and teamwork, so as to be fit to effectively comply with the multiple and complex functions involved in economic policy and administration.

In order for the program proposed to produce the indicated results, the first requirement is to bring about a reversal of the generalized skepticism that exists, so as to permit local and foreign economic players alike to verify the fact that, when they make significant and sustainable short, medium, and long-term investments, the only risks they must assume are those involved specifically in their projects themselves.

The core of this program should be upheld through the creation, by law, of a Council that would report to the Economy, Presidency and that would be made up of the office of the Cabinet Chief, the Labor, Industry, and Agriculture ministries, and the Central Bank, so as to foster the institutional coordination of the different branches of macroeconomic policy. The objective of this formal body would be to establish a range for the growth and inflation rates on a biannual basis and to articulate nominal goals for the different areas of government: development of public spending, tax pressure, wage guidelines, and monetary aggregates, with all of these being compatible among themselves. This council should present and discuss its objectives in both houses of Congress annually and should explain any deviation from these goals that might occur, as well as providing corrective measures for such deviations.

As a complementary measure, the managed floating exchange rate system should be further perfected, so as to avoid pronounced fluctuations or potential bubbles, although while helping citizens to take increasing exchange risk in stride. Logically enough, there is a subsidiary role to be played by capital control measures. That is to say, at any rate, that the structural surplus and the formation of a counter cyclical fiscal fund should be introduced as a fiscal rule.

What should be clearly established is the will of the economic authorities to gradually create a single-digit inflation environment, so as to provide all contracts with a credible reference point. This would help the country's citizens in their decision-making, which would undoubtedly benefit both investment and growth. If credibility and effectiveness are to be achieved, this objective must necessarily by accompanied, in a consistent, coordinated, and coherent manner, by the macroeconomic policy as a whole. This is clearly the logic behind this approach.

A program and a team of these characteristics must be accompanied by a series of pro-investment and pro-employment measures to complete the change of expectations generated by the macroeconomic coordination plan. My team and I are working on formulating specific legislative changes to make these principles operational. Of particular importance is the reversal of a framework of distortive subsidies currently in place in the transport, energy and agricultural sectors, because they cost the country ARS 40 billion (currently equivalent to US$10 billion) per year. In place of these programs, the government should be giving direct attention to the population that is living under the poverty line. In other words, instead of subsidizing companies, the government should be lending support directly to the citizens that need it.

* * *

No program that proposes significant, persistent, and sustainable growth of the domestic economy can limit itself to merely attending domestic demand.

We cannot fail to recognize our competitive capabilities in such wide-ranging sectors as steel, cultural enterprises, biotechnology, tourism, farm machinery, the nuclear industry, the automotive industry (at least regionally and for certain auto parts), aluminum, mining, forestry, bio-fuels, textile design and manufacturing, and leather, to mention just a few examples.

But without disregarding the importance of these sectors or those representing other goods and services, special attention should be given to the food industry, due to the expectations for worldwide demand and our possibilities for being a major player on an international scale.

In recent decades, there has been a powerfully expansive and diversified leap in international demand for these products. This increase is explained in part by population growth: In developing countries, the overall population is expected to go from its current level of 5.5 billion to around 11 billion by 2050, while in the more highly developed countries, it is expected to rise from a current 1.4 billion inhabitants to about 2.3 billion by 2050.

Moreover, for the first time in history, the urban population is greater than the rural population. This trend is expected to grow, to such an extent that, by 2030, some 5 billion people will be living in cities while only 3.5 billion will be living in rural areas. And while today the number of mega-cities in the world totals 18, by 2050, the total could rise to 400.

To these figures must be added the growth of the average level of per capita income witnessed in the countries where around half of the world's population lives, and which translates into an increase in the diversity and quality requirements for global food demand.

On the world food scene, Argentina has already reached a significant level of competitiveness in the initial stage of the productive process, where, today, it is a major world player. But the country remains far from this status in the processed food sector, where the greatest value can be obtained.

It must be borne in mind that in the last year, of Argentina's total agro-industrial exports, 40.6 percent corresponded to raw materials (grain and oilseeds), 41.5 percent to pre-elaborated primary goods (fish, pellets, ovine-based products, milk, flours, fodder and balanced feed, forestry products, textile fibers, leather and skins, sugar, edible oils, etc.), while only 17.9 percent corresponded to actual foods and other finished products (cheeses, chicken, giblets and offal, shellfish, juices, transformed and fresh fruits and vegetables, stimulant crops, Hilton quota meat cuts, processed meats, fresh meats, among others).

Therefore, our food industry is growing in the primary and pre-elaborated primary segments, but it is not, as yet, an active world player in the sale of products and trademarks, which is precisely where the capacity to grow sustainably is generated. This field is still dependent on multinational suppliers and a handful of local ones. Its strengths (processing technology) can be copied. It has little market penetration, scant brand building, and a negligible relationship with consumers. Nevertheless, there are some positive experiences to mark the way, such as the wine industry, in which Argentina is an important player, with solid marketing and strategic planning for the Malbec type.

At this point it is worthwhile pausing to clear up the mistaken supposition that farming adds no value to the mix because it produces wheat, corn, or soybeans, which are considered to be primary goods because they are basic and natural (like those produced by the Mayans in the pre-Columbian era). But this is a prejudice born of considering that value only resides in the product itself and not in the process by which it was produced. It may be true that a kernel of corn today is almost identical to one from the past. But what has changed are the know-how and procedures utilized to produce those two kernels. The Mayans produced 50 kilos (about 110 pounds) of corn per hectare (two and a half acres). Today, production runs 10,000 kilos (around 11 short tons) per acre or even more.

This transformation has been made possible by applied genetics and new machinery and processes that make increased productivity possible, despite the deterioration of the soil's natural fertility due to long years of exploitation. This serves as proof that there is essential added value in the process and in the know-how applied to that process.

Just as the sale of a medication, a car, or a book is how a pharmaceutical firm, an auto manufacturer, or a publishing company captures the value of its work and investment, crop sales are how a farming operation captures the value of its business. And just as innovation has transformed agriculture in Argentina, so too must industry transform itself in order to create an innovative chain and thus capture greater value for its products.

An example of the world market trend is provided by China. Over the last thirty years, its population has gone from consuming seven kilos of meat a year per inhabitant to consuming fifty kilos a year. This process will very likely broaden with increased consumption of meat-based protein throughout Asia and Africa as average per capita income increases in these areas of the world.

In order to produce these meats, at least for now, the basic, most competitive and irreplaceable raw material is soy flour. In just twenty years, Argentina has gone from being the supplier of 13 percent of this export on the world market to providing 33 percent of the total supply on the global market. This specific trend forms part of a more general process by which, in the first decade of this century, the volume of Argentine agricultural raw material and manufactured product exports grew by more than 50 percent.

Today, more than half of the world population has no access to industrialized food products. This means that the market for processed foods is still quite small and has great growth potential. It is also worth noting that in the field of industrialized foods, there is no significant concentration of supply, taking into account the fact that the world's twenty largest food companies concentrate only 9 percent of the global market.

Considering our capacity for supplying food to the world, and considering that the country possesses basic resources of both physical and human capital, Argentina should be constructing value-added chains endowed with the full range of productivity to produce food items of adequate quantity, quality, diversity, and price, in order to sell them to a good part of the billions of consumers in existence worldwide.

Based on an economic program that contemplates the facets mentioned above, Argentina should integrate itself into the world, giving priority to a self-image based on the following attributes:

1. **Our Territory:** We possess an abundance of soil, water, minerals, and other natural resources that are desired throughout the world.
2. **Our People:** In this current stage of development, the most decisive and evermore important productive factor is human capital. Development of the creative capacity of Argentina's people through adequate training, so as to achieve high-quality skilled labor, is of essential importance.
3. **A Strategic Political Consensus for a Domestic Model:** Things went well for Argentina back when a broad-based consensus regarding what should be included in the economic and international trade cycle was held over and above political, economic, social, and cultural differences and when the country was selling the greatest quantity

of tradable goods possible—at the best prices possible—
on the foreign markets that demanded them. And in
this way, the country effectively obtained the resources
it needed, the domestic distribution and utilization of
which were, indeed, at the center of intense debate. This
happened between 1880 and 1930 in Argentina. It also
occurred between 1947 and 1960. Back then, within an
international cycle characterized by market protection,
there was agreement on the deployment of an import-
substitution industrialization model, in which here, as in
the rest of the world, the government played a very active
role in its dynamics. The basic consensuses achieved with
regard to the strategic guidelines for a shared national
model set the stage for widespread confidence in Argentina's possibilities for development that characterized
both of these periods in the nation's history.

4. **Quality of Government**: Those who exercised our country's government in its most successful eras were the
very expression of solid institutions, whose members
and leaders shared a general conception of society and
politics that served to sustain a free and voluntary discipline, and that imbued them with an effective capacity
to exercise power whenever it was their turn to assume a
position of governance. The services that the government
provided were satisfactory in both quantity and quality, in
part because of the existence of qualified technical teams,
which, in the different areas and at the different levels of
the government, formed part of an efficient bureaucracy
of public servants—in the Weberian sense of the concept.
In the present day, we must admit that one of the factors that affect the quality of the democratic system is the

deterioration of institutions, as well as insufficiencies, in both the quality and quantity of services provided by the State. This is due, in part, to the fact that an adequate network of professionals to man the bureaucratic structure, performing with an effective spirit of public service, backed by sound stability, and subject to management control systems, has not been achieved.

* * *

I trust that, by now, readers will have understood that sound economic policies are based on common sense and on knowledge of the history of the country in question. With this baggage in tow, we must now face the coming stage in Argentina focusing on our sustainable growth over the course of time, combined with social inclusion.

These are the main lines along which my team and I are working, so that we may continue to make professional contributions to our country. I would never be able to forgive myself if, after the decades to come, and with the unique experience of having lived through everything related in these pages, I should have failed to contribute to the change that Argentina sorely needs.

About the Author

Author photo © Alejandra Lopez

International policy maker Martín Redrado is a Harvard-educated, Wall Street-seasoned economist whose determination and willingness to stand up against authority led his country out of the 2008-2009 world financial disaster. The former president of the Central Bank of Argentina, Redrado is credited with recognizing government corruption and fighting for Argentina's economic survival. He created Fundación Capital, an economic think tank in Latin America, and he is author of four books: *How to Survive Globalization, Exports for Growth, Time of Challenges,* and *No Reserve.*

About the Translator

 Born and reared in rural Ohio, Dan Newland has lived and worked in Argentina since 1973, where he worked for thirteen years at the *Buenos Aires Herald*, a daily renowned for its valiant human rights campaign during Argentina's bloody era of military rule. Newland's editorial comments contributed to that effort. He reached the post of managing editor before leaving the *Herald* to begin his current, life long career as an independent writer, translator, and editor. His translations include *Hispanic New York - A Sourcebook*, edited by Claudio Iván Remeseira; *Patagonia - Land of Giants*, by Daniel Rivademar and Alejandro Winograd; *Sustainability 2.0* by Ernesto van Peborgh and the Odiseo Team; and *La paz, esa ilusión*, by Uruguayan media executive and writer Roberto Vivo, which is soon to be published in English as *God Beyond Our Grasp, Peace Within Our Reach*.